NEGOTIATING
COMPETITIVENESS

NEGOTIATING COMPETITIVENESS

employment relations and organizational
innovation in germany and the united states

KIRSTEN S. WEVER

HARVARD BUSINESS SCHOOL PRESS
BOSTON, MASSACHUSETTS

Library of Congress Cataloging-in-Publication Data

Wever, Kirsten S.
    Negotiating competitiveness : employment relations and
organizational innovation in Germany and the United States / Kirsten
S. Wever.
        p.   cm.
    Includes bibliographical references and index.
    ISBN 0-87584-554-1
    1. Industrial relations—Germany.   2. Industrial relations—United
States.   3. Collective bargaining—Germany.   4. Collective
bargaining—United States.   5. Trade-unions—Germany.   6. Trade-
unions—United States.   7. Corporate reorganizations—Germany.
8. Corporate reorganizations—United States.   9. Competition,
International.   I. Title.
HD8451.W45   1995
331'.0943—dc20
                                                        94-39672
                                                        CIP

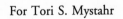
For Tori S. Mystahr

contents

preface

This book examines the relationship between employment relations and competitiveness in two of the most powerful advanced industrial countries—Germany and the United States. As firms, industries, and governments adjust to changing environmental circumstances, there has been increasing talk about the importance of tapping *human* resources more concertedly and effectively. The way this is done differs strikingly across the industrial countries, and in this regard the contrast between Germany and the United States is particularly stark. This book examines those differences, what impact they have on society and economy, and whether they are inevitable or possibly amenable to adjustment.

Uncovering, analyzing, and assessing those differences has been an extraordinarily rewarding undertaking, but it has also been very challenging. It has been rewarding because it has allowed me to interweave my personal background with my professional interests. Having been born in Germany and having spent a good portion of my childhood and teenage years there, I had the advantage of speaking the language and understanding the culture. This both intensified my curiosity about the comparison between the United States and Germany and, I hope, lent depth to that endeavor. But the project was also frustrating at times, as I struggled to come to terms with the very different ways in which Germans and Americans think about the relationship between economic efficiency and economic democracy. Put crudely, Americans see "labor issues" as matters of economics, while Germans understand them in social and political terms. On the face of it, these contrasting conceptualizations make sense as reflections of how labor looks and acts in the two countries. But to capture the full meaning of the comparison, it is necessary to take the next, epistemological, step: to try to understand the relationships between, on the one hand, the nature of our knowledge and thinking about the issues in question and, on the other, those issues themselves.

American unions engage in primarily enterprise-level collective bargaining about economic issues. They do not generally develop industrywide or national strategies about enduring political issues such as work-time reduction (which has been at the center of the German labor movement's strategy over the past decade). When

American unions do come together to engage in politics, they tend to do so around particular issues or candidates, and they forge alliances that do not always survive. The United States has no labor party. "Labor" is not as obviously "political" in the United States as it is, say, in Sweden or the United Kingdom or Germany.

Conversely, German scholars and practitioners are often surprised that anyone would seek to understand the *economic* ramifications of a fundamentally *social* phenomenon. Most German scholars, particularly the industrial sociologists and researchers focusing on the union movement, understand worker representation as a political phenomenon, based on the broad social consensus that advanced capitalism requires some measure of economic democracy. German public opinion—and, indeed, employer opinion—views the system of worker representation as a cornerstone of Germany's impressive postwar economic performance (see chapters 2 and 5). That is, Germans intuitively seem to believe in significant organizational, and ultimately therefore microeconomic, benefits of worker representation. This has not been the case in the United States.

I proceed on the premise, clarified by the comparison of the two countries, that the fact that American "labor" looks and acts relatively "economic" is a *political* phenomenon. Likewise, the social conception of unions and employment relations in Germany too is a reflection of politics. Moreover, in both countries the way that labor is thought about is changing as the employment relationship manifestly plays an increasingly important role in shaping the processes and outcomes of firm-level as well as national industrial change and adjustment.

This premise has two significant implications. First, it suggests the need to apply analytical frameworks that were established to capture one kind of reality in an entirely different kind of reality (which is, in essence, at the core of all comparative work). In other words, it calls for an analysis of German socioeconomic reality through American lenses, and vice versa. Second, and following from the above, it requires a self-consciously interdisciplinary approach. This seems to me the best way to make sense of employment relations and how we think about them, both of which vary across and within countries and over time.

In pursuing this course, I have focused on the link between what happens in organizations (microeconomic and organizational phenomena) and what happens in the environment in which they operate (political, institutional, meso- and macroeconomic, and social phenomena). Put simply, (1) many of the chief weaknesses of the German approach to the relationship between employment relations and competitiveness reside at the level of the individual firm; (2) the primary weaknesses of the American conception of this relationship are located "above" the firm level in the meso- and macrolevel environments in which organizations do business; and (3) the weaknesses of each case are paralleled by some of the most enduring and impressive strengths of the other.

In illuminating the political economic structures and processes that influence employment relations in both countries, I necessarily draw attention to the shifting boundaries between various academic disciplines and approaches, which also reflect profound and apparently continuous disjunctures in the processes of industrial change and adjustment. These boundaries were established to accommodate very different international, national, and local political economic dynamics, and they must continue to accommodate a changing real world. The ultimate measure of the quality of scholarship is the extent to which theories and methods can be adapted to such external changes. If this book makes a contribution, I hope it is in building bridges between political science, management science, industrial sociology, and industrial relations. If I have succeeded in this, I hope to have furthered the valuable mutual leaning that forms the basis of good comparative work.

acknowledgments

In 1986 my former teacher, Michael Piore, urged me to get out into the labor movement for a time before launching on a more traditional academic career path. Mike's advice ultimately led me to a position at the national offices of the American Federation of Labor and Congress of Industrial Organizations (AFL-CIO) in Washington, D.C., where I gained firsthand familiarity with the profound problems and challenges facing American labor in the late twentieth century. As part of my work at the AFL-CIO, I talked with economic historian Sanford Jacoby about these problems. It was Sandy who first suggested that I draw on my German background, to develop the comparison with the United States, and to think systematically about how the American labor movement might learn from the German experience. This conversation with Sandy inspired me in 1989 to "retool"—to return to Germany as a comparativist academic researcher. That decision ushered in the most rewarding period of my life, both personally and professionally.

My first field work in Germany, from the fall of 1989 through the summer of 1990 (what a time!), was financed by a fellowship from the German Marshall Fund of the United States (grant 3-53617). I am particularly grateful to Peter Weitz of the GMF for his early encouragement and insightful suggestions about how to approach this project. Several subsequent research trips between 1992 and 1994 were funded by the Hans-Böckler-Stiftung in Düsseldorf. The interest and guidance of Gerhard Leminsky, then at the Stiftung, were invaluable.

While in Germany I was a visiting scholar at the Wirtschafts- und Sozialwissenschaftsinstitut (WSI) in Düsseldorf, the union confederation's research arm, and then at the Institut Arbeit und Technik (IAT) of the state of North Rhine Westphalia in Gelsenkirchen. Two friends from graduate school, Kathleen Thelen and Gary Herrigel, put me in touch with many helpful German colleagues. I was especially helped by the friendship and insights of Gerhard Bosch, Gudrun Trautwein-Kalms, Matthias Knuth, Wiebke Buchholz-Will, Ulrike Wendeling-Schröder, and Ursula Becker-Töpfer. Much of my work took place while I was based as a visitor, thanks to David Soskice, at the Wissenschaftszentrum Berlin (WZB). Thanks are due to Eileen Applebaum and the Economic Policy Institute in Washington, D.C. for their financial support and interest. Also helpful in various phases of the research were Helmut Drücke and Ulrich Jürgens of the WZB, Michael Fichter and Traute Meyer of the Freie Universität in Berlin, Norbert Kluge of the Hans-Böckler-Stiftung, Ulrich Jordan at 3M Deutschland, and Wolfgang Pege of the Institut der deutschen Wirtschaft in Cologne.

In particular I want to express my deep gratitude to Matthias Knuth at the IAT and to Witich Roßmann at the IG Metall in Cologne. Both Matthias and Witich pointed me in the right direction, introduced me to the right people, took me to the right restaurants, and generally made my field work immensely rich and enjoyable. Both have become valued friends as well as inspiring colleagues.

The process of writing this book was for the most part great fun and very rewarding, due in large measure to my connections with people in my intellectual community. Dietmar Harhoff, Christopher S. Allen, Peter Brecke, Robert McKersie, Richard Locke, and Kathleen Thelen all read and thoughtfully commented on parts of the manuscript. Thomas Kochan and Lowell Turner read the entire manuscript in several early and later incarnations and offered extremely useful and detailed thoughts.

Three people have played seminal roles in my life while I worked on this project. Tom Kochan has been a wonderful mentor, friend, critic, and colleague. He has supported me in many ways at every turn for over ten years, and has helped me make the difficult transitions (still in progress) back and forth between the worlds of political science, industrial relations, academia, and practice. Lowell Turner provided huge quantities of high-quality humor, insight, information, and warmth. He also offers irrefutable proof that it is both possible and immensely rewarding to change careers in mid-stream, to work at the shifting boundaries of several different academic fields, and to do so with grace and power. Patricia Prior has done more than anyone else to help me to put my work in perspective and to develop and take the best possible advantage of the many kinds of resources on which I have drawn in this process. My relationships with Tom, Lowell, and Patsy continue to mean more to me than they can know.

NEGOTIATING
COMPETITIVENESS

chapter one

Negotiation Versus Unilateralism in Employment Relations

how labor, business, and government act and interact and what it means for competitiveness

In the 1970s, among advanced industrial countries, the German model of organizing the political economy was widely acclaimed to be the most successful model and the one most worth emulating. In the 1980s, the Japanese model came into vogue, particularly in the United States. In the 1990s, the American economy reasserted its resilience in international markets, and Germany and Japan touted American management as the most attractive model of best management practice, including in their praise U.S. human resource (HR) and industrial relations (IR) practices.[1] Can all of these claims be true? In this book, I examine the enduring strengths and weaknesses of the German and American employment relations (ER) systems and how they fit into their broader political economic contexts. My focus is on the relationship between employment relations and industrial adjustment, that is, on how employment relations influence the ability of companies and industries to adapt to changing international circumstances.

Most Germans and Americans do not understand each others' economies because the respective strengths and weaknesses of these economies are so very different. In fact, I will argue that the strengths of the German economy represent the shortcomings of the American economy and vice versa. The chief strengths of the U.S. economy reside at the level of the organization, while the chief strengths of the German economy have to do with the ties that connect organizations and institutions from the level of the individual firm to the level of the national economy. Much of Germany's competitive strength is derived from a set of integrated and widely accepted institutions in which the many stakeholders in the economy

1

come together to negotiate how organizations will respond to external pressures. While the economy as a whole is extremely stable, these institutions have made it difficult for workers and managers at the point of production and service delivery to develop locally appropriate innovations to meet the daily challenges they encounter. Americans, on the other hand, excel at developing innovative solutions to immediate local problems. Still, while individual companies and industries in the United States have been able to capitalize on these innovative talents, the U.S. economy as a whole is characterized by large pockets of striking weakness, many of which can be traced to the lack of coordinating institutions that facilitate negotiated adjustment.[a] Thus, the American institutions and practices that parallel those in Germany hamper the competitive strength of the economy as a whole but bolster organizational innovation.

What happens in the German social market economy, which is characterized by wide-scale business acceptance of regulation, private sector coordination, and extensive mechanisms for worker democracy, cannot be explained by an efficiency-oriented free market model of how the world works. Likewise, the coordinated German social market framework is of limited use in helping Americans to understand the flexible, innovative successes of U.S. industry. Such mutual misunderstanding is likely to become increasingly costly to both countries. All advanced industrial countries have come under mounting pressures to adapt to a rapidly changing and increasingly competitive international economy. Given these pressures, governments, institutions, and organizations should place a higher premium than ever before on learning from the experiences of others. To this end, I will examine the assumptions and motivations underlying German and American labor-management relations at the enterprise level and employment relations in general and place them in a com-

---

[a]The fundamental differences between the two countries are reflected in many aspects of their social, political, and economic lives. For example, while the United States offers the best possible education in most, if not all, fields, the overall level of education among Germans is much higher than the level among Americans. To take another example, the U.S. economy boasts the most internationally competitive firms in the world in many of the high technology industries. At the same time, however, the rate of company failures overall in the United States is considerably higher than it is in Germany.

parative frame of reference, translating events and dynamics in each country into terms that make sense in the other.

This comparative undertaking is important for Americans because the competitiveness of the U.S. economy is hampered by distant and often suspicious relations between business, labor, and government. These relations are not difficult to explain, given that enterprise-based collective bargaining and minute, detailed government regulation of labor relations entail significant costs to businesses in terms of money, time, and other resources. Because these costs do not appear to be balanced by any obvious benefits, it makes sense for business to pursue a unilateral strategy in which it attempts to avoid government regulation and employee representation mechanisms that interfere with managerial autonomy. However, there is nothing about regulation, private sector coordination, or collective worker representation per se that opposes business interests. On the contrary, the evidence considered here suggests that long-term American economic performance would benefit from *more,* not less, regular, open contact and cooperation among companies and between them and secure collective employee representatives, especially given today's international economic challenges. Overall, the German experience casts doubt on the widespread assumption that the freer the market, the more competitive the firms operating within it. The deep recession that characterized Germany in the years immediately following unification has ended. The German economy is poised to recover fully and to grow substantially as investments in the economy of the former East Germany begin to pay off and continuing European economic integration further strengthens the country.

Throughout this book, I will use the term "industrial adjustment" to refer to the process by which companies, collective representatives of workers (unions in the United States and unions as well as works councils in Germany), and other stakeholders (banks, government, industry and employer associations, for instance) change how they act and interact to accommodate external circumstances. Negotiation among the main actors involved characterizes German adjustment processes, while American adjustment in most cases (but not all) is more or less unilaterally shaped by business.

It is common to think of the German model as a set of institutions: industrywide, regional collective bargaining; a centralized universal banking system with close ties to capital; extensive ties among companies that join forces in encompassing industry and trade asso-

ciations and chambers of commerce; a national apprenticeship training system; and so on. What is most interesting in studying the
German and American political economies, however, is not the institutions or the lack of institutions in these economies but the dynamics that drive the processes of negotiation and mutual accommodation within them. German negotiated adjustment processes (arrived
at by consensus involving all major stakeholders) enhance overall social and economic outcomes and, over time, adjust and reinforce the
system itself.[2] American practitioners and researchers can learn from
Germany how *politics* (including the infrastructure of public and parapublic sector regulations) creates incentives for the parties involved
to bargain over the processes of organizational change and industrial
adjustment.

If Americans have something to learn from Germany, Germans
too can learn from the U.S. experience. The 1990s have presented
Germany with a raft of formidable political and economic challenges,
including the social, political, and economic costs of unification between West and East Germany. Unemployment in the former East
Germany will doubtlessly remain high through the turn of the century; Bonn has been unusually impotent in dealing with the ugly
reemergence of antiforeigner violence and the social strains it has
revealed; business leaders complain that the pressures of the single
European market are making it harder and harder to sustain the
country's high wages and social benefits;[b] labor-management clashes
in and over the former East Germany have been particularly dramatic; and gross domestic product declined significantly in the early
1990s. Meanwhile, Japanese and American companies are leagues
ahead in high technology industries.

As noted, during an interview, by the director of technology at
Henkel, a large, multinational cleaning products manufacturer, "We
Germans tend to do things the way we do things because that is the
way we have always done things." In contrast, Americans appear to
be particularly adept at discovering new ways of doing things. In a
variety of industries, employers and employees have redesigned the
labor-management relationship fundamentally, leading to higher
quality goods and services as well as better paying and more interest-

[b] In Germany, this issue is referred to as the problem of *Standort Deutschland*,
loosely translated as "Germany as an investment site." I return to this issue in
chapter 7.

ing jobs. In these cases, those involved display an impressive knack for decentralized, on-demand brainstorming, rule-breaking, and trial-and-error problem solving. Because of the lack of institutions and rules governing the interaction of managers and employees in the workplace, Americans can develop completely new ways of organizing employment relationships. At General Motors' Saturn Corporation, for instance, all management positions are co-occupied by representatives of the company and the union. This has led to a form of codetermination that goes well beyond anything the Germans have done. In Germany, deeply ingrained organizational structures and management strategies make this sort of informal innovation quite difficult. It would be difficult, for example, for labor and management in Germany to establish Saturn-style comanagement because the division of labor (between managers, between workers and their representatives, and between labor and management) is rooted in long-established structures and institutions that do not allow for such radical departures from the norm.

In the remainder of this chapter, I will survey the ER system in the United States, look at the key strengths and weaknesses of the German and American political economies, and discuss the key policy challenge for both Germany and the United States: how to take advantage of essentially foreign adjustment mechanisms.

Defining the Problem

U.S. Labor and Management in the Post-Fordist Era

It is not easy to make sense of the relationships among business, government, and labor in the United States since the late 1970s. On the one hand, there is ample evidence of the cooperative and participative employment relations that are often associated with high performance work systems, those methods of work and production organization that support a competitive strategy based on high labor-value-added, high quality, and high productivity. Hewlett-Packard, the Saturn Corporation of General Motors, and BellSouth Telecommunications are frequently cited examples. The idea behind these systems is to take the maximum possible advantage of human resources. By investing heavily in worker skills, creating a stable and lasting relationship between employees and employers, allowing workers to make decisions traditionally made by managers, and reducing the directive side while enhancing the participative aspects of the employment relationship, these companies derive their competitiveness from highly skilled, well-paid workers producing products and services that compete on the basis of differentiation and quality, rather than price. Indeed, it is not hard to find examples of employee participation in decision making and a relatively high level of trust and information exchange between employers and employees in both union and nonunion settings. Since the late 1970s, the management literature has hailed the folding of employee interests into corporate governance at companies deemed to be "excellent" and the employee-centered focus of those firms considered to be "strategically adaptive." Countless organizations have adapted the cooperative Japanese model.[3] In these organizations, the Americanized version of the Japanese model emerges in the form of team work, increased attention to the extent and nature of the skills of the workforce, promises of employment security whenever possible, and the development of elaborate "internal labor markets" that guide employees' careers within companies, among other things. Many of these innovative HR practices promise to be particularly competitive models of labor-management relations.[c]

On the other hand, a quick look at the overall climate of labor-management relations in the United States during the 1980s and into the 1990s might lead to the conclusion that unions and private sector organizations were playing a zero-sum game and that collective worker representation entails great costs to employers and society at large. The U.S. business community frequently argues that organized labor's interests, which are sharply distinguished from the interests of individual employees, conflict with those of employers.[4] Many managers—perhaps most—see unions as drags on profitability. Employers complain of rigid union work rules that prevent the flexible deployment of labor. They resent freezing wages and working conditions for the two- or three-year term of a collective bargaining contract. With the recession of the early 1980s, many employers began to demand substantial economic concessions from their unions.[5] Conflictual union-management relations in which economic downturns translate into layoffs or pay cuts, with high employee turnover and grievance levels, have become increasingly visible. Such relations

---

[c]Two of the best known examples of these practices are found at NUMMI and Saturn. NUMMI, New United Motors Manufacturing Inc., is a General Motors–Toyota joint venture involving the United Auto Workers. Saturn is a project of GM and the UAW.

combined with conflicts over the distribution of losses in economic slumps that underlie many bitter labor-management confrontations. During the 1980s, well-known protracted conflicts took place at Eastern Airlines, Greyhound Bus Lines, and Pittston Coal.[d]

Labor-management relations at nonunion companies, which employ perhaps the largest portion of the American workforce, can also be characterized by low levels of trust between labor and management. Janitors, hotel cleaning staff, restaurant workers, migrant farm workers, security guards, many clerical workers, cashiers, and food counter workers are part of this workforce. Their jobs, which are likely to be either temporary or part time, tend to be organized according to the principles of mass production and characterized by low wages and skills, poor working conditions, and "employment at will" (the employer's will).[e] These workers are thought to be relatively uncommitted to their work, as reflected in low levels of quality and productivity.[6]

The social and economic implications of the low-trust approach are significant. In the petrochemicals industry, for instance, vital questions concerning workers' health and safety remain unaddressed because of suspicion and mistrust among the companies, contractors, and unions involved. Moreover, the skills and competencies of much of the American workforce continue to decline in substantial part because of inadequate training for workers in the low-trust segments of the economy. Over the last decade it has become almost axiomatic that the lack of skills and competencies in these sectors threaten the competitiveness of the economy as a whole.[7]

Macroproblems, Microsolutions

Why do impressive examples of innovative HR practices coexist with cases of abysmal employee relations that benefit no one and obviously harm all concerned? Two facts of American political economic life are commonly cited as reasons for this coexistence, but there is also a third important dimension that needs to be discussed in detail.

---

[d] The tone of labor relations in that decade was set by President Reagan's firing of striking air traffic controllers in 1981.

[e] This juxtaposition of the adversarial and cooperative, or low trust *versus* high trust, approaches is highly stylized, and examples of both modes of behavior occur in most cases.

The United States is the only advanced industrial country that has no employment security guarantee for most workers.

First, as various observers have pointed out since the early 1980s, the disadvantages of a distanced, low-trust labor-management relationship have emerged only with the decline of the Fordist forms of mass production that underpinned the growth of the economy during much of the postwar period. (The term "Fordist" refers to the assembly line operation pioneered by Henry Ford.) The associated "Taylorist" organization of work, named after Frederick Taylor and based on a minute division of labor and narrow job classifications, was fairly well suited to a distanced labor-management relationship that required little or no joint labor-management problem solving.[8]

The growth and diffusion of new ways of organizing how work is done, however, has led to the need for new forms of labor-management relations. Although a more collaborative model of labor-management relations that supports the development and implementation of new work practices has emerged, many—perhaps most—companies find it difficult to pursue this model because of what economists would label a "public goods" problem. These new practices usually involve significant investments in the workers' skills, wages, and retention. A company that spends a lot of money on training its workers, however, has no guarantee that the workers will not be "poached" by a competitor who will take advantage of the skills investment without having to pay for it. The training the workers have received has become a public good in that it is available to any company that wants to hire away the trained workers. Consequently, a collaborative, high-wage/high-skill approach to employment relations tends to make sense only for companies that are economically secure enough to be able to finance costly investments with uncertain long-term payoffs or for companies that are in such deep economic trouble that they see no other way to improve productivity fast.[f] Research has found that about two-thirds of American companies have not adopted this approach at all, and the remaining one-third has implemented it only piecemeal.[9] Some companies, for example, may step up training for one group of workers (usually relatively skilled to begin with) but not for the bulk of the workforce. Other companies may offer "contingent pay" (pay dependent upon, for example, the company's financial performance) to increase incen-

---

[f]In the 1980s, after the rise of minimill competition from abroad, this type of experimentation occurred throughout the steel industry. It was also common in the airline industry after deregulation.

tives to raise productivity, but without meaningful mechanisms that would allow workers to influence the outcome. The reluctance of many companies to pursue a more collaborative approach, given the public goods problem, accounts for the existence of strikingly different types of labor-management relations throughout the U.S. economy and within industries and companies. It also helps to explain the relative isolation of even widely praised experiments in labor-management cooperation and employee participation.

Second, the diversity of ER models in the United States has a great deal to do with the unpopular nature of government intervention in employment relations in particular and the economy more generally. Governments in most advanced industrial countries attempt to standardize certain aspects of employment relations to level the private sector "playing field." Americans, however, tend to believe that political intervention in markets should foster individual rather than collective opportunity, should be extremely limited, and should not involve active labor or industrial policies.[10] This line of thinking assumes a more or less natural or inevitable separation between the public and private spheres, between politics and economics. Against this backdrop, regulation, to many Americans, has meant detailed government intrusion into and control of markets. There is a tendency to associate government intervention with extensive substantive rules about specific issues. This is the kind of regulation that governed the airline industry until the early 1980s and the banking sector. It is the kind of regulation American public opinion abhors.

In fact, U.S. labor law reflects some of the most intrusive aspects of this sort of regulation. The National Labor Relations Act of 1935 (amended substantially in 1947 and 1959), known as the Wagner Act, established a framework for labor-management relations in the United States. It lays out an elaborate and lengthy set of procedures for organizing union members and specifies how collective bargaining is to be conducted and what types of workers will be allowed to join unions. It also restricts bargaining by delimiting the kinds of demands the parties can make and by curtailing the sorts of extracollective bargaining relations they can engage in. For the first several decades following World War II, regulation of the unionized sector indirectly but profoundly influenced employment relations throughout the economy.[11] Important central features of the HR policies of most large nonunion firms (such as formal grievance procedures or cost-of-living wage increases) originated in the collective bargaining contracts of such heavily unionized sectors as the auto and steel industries. These features, which were innovative at the time, often reflected particularly efficient and effective policies and, therefore, were attractive even to companies in which there were no unions to demand them.

However, the type of labor-management relationship that the Wagner Act fosters is adversarial (as opposed to cooperative), sporadic (rather than continual), and zero sum (versus positive sum). Because this relationship often no longer benefits either labor or management, business and labor leaders as well as public policymakers have become increasingly dissatisfied with the act. Legislation developed in the 1960s and 1970s, including equal employment opportunity provisions, health and safety laws, and the codification of a variety of civil rights, typically supports individual rather than collective rights. This legislation does not encourage labor or management to develop a complement or substitute for the Wagner Act. Experimentation with alternative types of labor-management relations reflects a growing awareness of the inappropriate nature of this framework. Yet blanket suspicion of government regulation persists, and no new mechanisms have emerged. The problem is perceived at the microeconomic level as one that can be solved only by individual firms.

There is, however, another set of factors that strongly influences employment relations and thus corporate and labor adjustment strategies in the United States. The institutions that make up the political economy exert enormous pressures on companies and unions to pursue particular types of competitive strategies that have particular implications for how employees are hired, trained, paid, and utilized. In order to make sense of these structural variables, American academics, practitioners, and policymakers need to adjust how they think about the "competitiveness problem."

How Americans view this problem is reflected in the places they have looked for solutions to it. For the most part, U.S. employers have looked to Japan for lessons on how to improve economic performance. In turn, Japan has supplied American companies with many new ideas about the organization of work and production, including cooperative labor-management relations, lean production, and just-in-time (JIT) inventory systems.[12] While the vast cultural differences between the two societies explain some of the limitations of the Japanese model in an American setting, recent analyses have offered a more concrete explanation for these limitations. The explanation is consistent with several striking similarities between the German and Japanese political economies.[13] Although the cultural gap between Japan and the United States is probably no greater than the cultural gap between Japan and Germany, the contrast between the United States on one hand and Japan and Germany on the other is *sharper* in certain regards than that between Japan and Germany.

Compared to the United States, both Germany and Japan feature more cooperative labor relations than adversarial ones; both share a traditional focus on product quality and the work process rather than output; and both give training pride of place. In both countries, relations between the worlds of finance and business are relatively close and congenial, and government involvement in the private sector is accepted as a matter of course. Indeed, in both countries the distinction between the public sector (the social or political sphere) and the private sector (the economic domain) is considerably more blurred than it is in the United States. Finally, the economies of these two countries, which pose the greatest competitive threats to the United States in the international economy, represent considerable departures from the neoclassical free-market model.

The shared logic underlying the organization of the German and Japanese political economies is not cultural. It is the logic of institutional and organizational linkages. These linkages systematically incorporate certain interests of society at large and of employees in particular into corporate governance practices.[g] In both countries, *structures* (in Japan, organizational structures; in Germany, political economic structures) create incentives that support the sharing of information and knowledge and thus encourage the diffusion of organizational innovation.[14] In other words, the Japanese and German political economies make it easy for labor and management to disseminate improvements in work systems, methods of production organization, labor-management relations, and so on throughout companies, industries, and the economy. In both countries, these improvements hinge on the extensive and intensive education and training of the workforce as well as highly effective mechanisms for helping those who have finished school to make the transition to the private sector workforce.[15]

---

[g] Not all workers in either country benefit from union and/or works council representation. The formal incorporation of employee interests into management decision making holds mainly for core sectors in each country, such as the automobile, electronics, and chemicals industries.

Lacking a systematic method of coordinating various dimensions of employment relations (especially the development and maintenance of a national skills base), American firms can benefit from Japanese organizational innovations only up to a certain point. The next wave of innovation will require the creation of incentives for employees and employers to pursue innovative HR practices jointly. In this regard, American practitioners and policymakers would do well to turn their attention from the *micro*economic lessons of Japan to the broader *(macro)* political economic lessons of Germany. The key to discerning how the German case can illuminate theory and practice in the United States lies in a comparison of the linkages and channels that encourage (or discourage) regular and intensive communication and negotiation among major actors in the United States and Germany.[16] The comparison clarifies how the spread of competitive ER practices is contingent on these interconnections. What the German model can do is to inspire the development of American mechanisms for achieving similar results.

A New Conceptual Map

Toward Macrosolutions

Comparative work of this kind requires a new way of looking at employment relations. Think of employment relations as occurring at different levels—the individual workplace, the plant, the company, the industry (and/or region or state), and the economy as a whole. For the most part, the human resource management (HRM) literature is limited by its exclusive concern with events at and below the level of the organization, while traditional IR theory is about the processes and outcomes of collective bargaining, which also occur at the enterprise level. Certainly, some recent IR research has drawn attention to other important aspects of the labor-management relationship. In response to changes in how production is organized, important and widespread changes have taken place in how work is organized and thus in the nature of labor-management relations at the point of production. More and more, employers' strategic choices, such as decisions about the type and location of future investments, directly affect such basic employee interests as job security and the nature of skills.[17] The "strategic choice" perspective of this IR research traces these changes to the decline of Fordism and notes the emergence of a distinct, nonunion human resource management model of employment relations (the high-trust model discussed earlier). This model makes it easier for management to take advantage of the productivity benefits of new forms of work and production organization. For example, ongoing negotiations (as opposed to sporadic collective bargaining) are crucial for a rapid, flexible recombination of resources and redeployment of workers. If a product needs to be adjusted, employees and managers can agree on the necessary changes, reorganize how the product is made, and thus respond quickly to market demands. The chief strength of this IR model is that it focuses attention away from collective bargaining and on the workplace (office or shop floor) and strategic management decisions.

Some human resource management researchers have addressed the linkages between HR policies and broader corporate strategies.[18] But both the HR approach and the new IR approach have little to say about influences operating *above* the level of the enterprise. Both are typically American ways of thinking about the economy in that both assume it makes sense to explain how employers and employees relate in isolation from the broader political, social, and economic environments that influence how they behave.

This book will deal with the relationships among different levels of political-economic activity. I will frequently refer to structures, dynamics, and actions at the *micro*level of the organization or local community, the *meso*level of the industry, region, or state, and the *macro*level of the economy and society as a whole. Works councils, regional and industrywide bargaining, tripartite apprenticeship training forums, and so forth influence the strategies of the actors involved and the outcomes of their interactions. Politics and institutions shape the relationships between and among major social actors and the articulation of private and public sector organizations. Indeed, many recent comparative political economic analyses explicitly link microlevel labor-management relations to political, social, and economic developments at the local, regional, industry, and national levels.[19]

For example, the way in which employment relations are regulated in Germany encourages companies to join industrywide employer associations that engage in collective bargaining with industrial unions at the regional level. German law makes it difficult to initiate strikes or lockouts, thus creating incentives for the development of consensus through negotiations. The government can extend a collective bargaining contract throughout an entire sector to cover employers not even in the association. This takes the costs of collaboration with labor out of competition because all firms follow similar practices at similar costs. It also decreases the attractiveness of employer unilateralism. At the enterprise level, both labor and management also have incentives to bargain over the specifics of how agreements will be implemented and change effected. For instance, while the law does not require employers to involve employee representatives in new technology planning stages, many employers prefer to do so. This is because they want to keep the works council happy, to gain its acceptance of ongoing organizational changes, and to prevent its insistence on following the letter—rather than the spirit—of the law governing workplace-level labor-management relations. By encouraging labor and management to act together, ER structures (essentially, political artifacts) in Germany lead the actors to preserve and strengthen the national institutional landscape. This is one of the key strengths of the German political economy.[20]

Political economic analyses of employment relations usually focus on Western Europe. This is not altogether surprising since the United States has no extensive network of institutions to structure and moderate employment relations in general and American politics, lacking a labor party or a strong working-class movement, have shown comparatively little systematic labor influence.[21] Labor-management relations—in the United States, enterprise-based collective bargaining—would appear, then, to fall within the domain of economics. The fact remains, however, that U.S. labor-management relations are no less a reflection of political and historical circumstances than they are elsewhere. Indeed, the structure of the U.S. political economy strongly influences the nature of employment relations. To explain exactly how, we need a new understanding of regulation, one that incorporates the relationships between and among the actors and events at the enterprise, regional and/or industry, and national levels of analysis.[22]

The idea that institutions have mattered to Germany's development over the postwar period is hardly a new one.[23] What will be shown here, however, is that what is important is not which particular institutions have provided the backdrop for the German "economic miracle" but how they have encouraged the actors to negotiate the path leading to it. Many of the institutions have changed significantly over the postwar period, but the basic inclination toward the *negotiation* of adjustment issues has survived.

The Strengths of the German Model

The power of this argument hinges on the continued viability of the model for Germany, where a host of political and economic pressures have emerged recently, not all of which are related to unification. On the whole, the German economy began to show unmistakable signs of improvement on most dimensions of economic performance by the mid-1990s. GDP growth is widely expected to reach 3 percent in 1995. Unemployment in the western part of the country has consistently remained lower than the European Union average, at well under 10 percent. Wage costs have diminished since the late 1980s, and German labor productivity remains impressive by international standards.[24]

However, there are also signs that protracted economic problems will continue to play significant roles. The manufacturing sectors, which were the engine of Germany's postwar economic growth, are no longer in positions of unchallenged dominance in international markets. The incorporation of the East German economy raised imports sharply. Moreover, the worldwide recession of the early 1990s depressed production and exports in some leading industries. Machine tool orders, for instance, suffered a four-year low in early 1991 and have only marginally increased since then.[25]

Clearly, Germany is in a more economically vulnerable position than it has ever known in the postwar period. These developments have strengthened the argument sometimes made in the business press that international economic pressures alone have left companies everywhere with little choice but to loosen social restrictions on markets, pushing decision making—and therefore the locus of the action in labor-management relations—to the lowest possible level. In the United States, bargaining and pattern bargaining have given way to company-by-company bargaining in trucking, steel, airline, coal, auto, and other industries.[26] Many firms now encourage interplant competition for new investments or the chance to remain in operation. Even in Germany, centralized bargaining in some cases has been supplemented by plant-level bargaining. In 1992, German IBM took the unprecedented step of withdrawing some of its operations from the metalworking employer association. In 1994, the Hoechst chemical concern followed suit.

Increasing variation in enterprise-level employer strategies are said to stem from the need to meet the rapidly changing demands of hypercompetitive world markets and to lead to increasingly varied local industrial relations outcomes.[27] In Sweden, for example, the most highly centralized IR system in the world (and for decades an economic success story) is now characterized by increasing local diversity. Some analysts have pointed to this as an example of the inherent superiority of locally flexible forms of labor-management relations.

Broader European trends have also called into question the centralizing and coordinating role of meso- and macrolevel institutions. There has been a growth of so-called neovoluntarism among European multinational employers. This is a sort of cooperatist employer unilateralism, which can be seen in the establishment of works councils even in the absence of laws requiring them. Some observers believe increasing neovoluntarism may undermine the joint negotiation of a social dimension to the single European market.[28] In Germany, these pressures are compounded not only by the astronomical costs of integrating the former East German economy into that of the former West Germany but also by a sort of political paralysis that is reflected in national politicians' continued ambivalence about how to address domestic and international political problems.

Is the German model still viable? Are employers trying to get out from under precisely the institutions associated with negotiated adjustment? As the second part of this book will show, far from deploring their system, German employers value it highly. They perceive it to offer important competitive advantages in the face of the increasingly open single European market. Indeed, the strength of the model lies in the ability of the actors in the German political economy to make use of their ER system in different ways over time, and thus adapt to internal and external challenges. Therefore, centralized bargaining between employers and employee representatives remains resilient, and numerous connections and linkages between actors and activities at the micro-, meso- and macrolevels (lines of communication, forums for negotiation, methods of information exchange, and so on) continue to help employers adjust. In fact, some German employers have grown to appreciate the institutions regulating labor-management relations even more than they did before. With its centralized unions and decentralized works councils, the dual system of employee representation offers critical advantages. By extending collective bargaining agreements across entire industries and regions, it discourages employers from competing on the basis of labor costs. It allows companies to allocate many of those costs in ways that are tailored to local circumstances. It saves resources by requiring management carefully to justify decisions involving organizational changes, and it eases organizational change processes by involving works councils in the early planning stages, thus allowing them to garner employee acceptance of those changes.

This is not to say that German business embraces every aspect of the German model. Certainly bargaining with works councils over company- and workplace-specific issues has become increasingly important in recent years. There is no question that a more decentralized and flexible approach to managing in general is required if German companies are to meet competitive challenges. Indeed, many German managers recognize that they have a great deal to learn from American managerial techniques in this regard. The task facing German employers is to adapt some of the organizational lessons to be learned from the United States without sacrificing the strengths of the negotiated model.

Current challenges to the German political economy require precisely the sorts of collectively developed strategies that served the former West Germany so well during the postwar period. Effective competition in the single European market will depend in large measure on Germany's impressive skills base and cooperative form of labor-management relations. The integration of the former East Germany hinges on the continued, perhaps increasingly vigorous, cooperation of business, government, and labor from the level of the enterprise to the national economy. The attainment of national accords, such as the solidarity pact that distributes the economic burdens of unification across different actors and regions, is unthinkable in the absence of extensive formal and informal negotiations among labor, business, and state and federal governments. There is no evidence to suggest that employers are systematically trying to bypass organized labor in their efforts to revitalize the former East German economy, and there is plenty of evidence to the contrary. In some cases, unions and works councils in the former East Germany are playing an even more critical role in helping management develop productive enterprises and hospitable local and regional economies than they do in the west.[29]

Rather than a downward shift in activities, what is occurring is a restructuring of local, regional, and national strategies, alliances, and actions.[30] The task of rebuilding the eastern German economy, together with continuing international economic pressures, is fueling this realignment. In fact, the success of neovoluntarist (unilateral) employer strategies may actually depend on the existence of a pattern of communications linking individual firms with organizations and institutions at the micro-, meso- and macrolevels. The decentralized

and fragmented U.S. system of employment relations makes it difficult for labor and management to sustain or diffuse innovations in
labor-management relations, and the host of uncertainties facing
American labor and management make cooperative unilateral approaches to labor-management relations highly unlikely. Still, unilateral employer strategies for labor participation *can* be credible and
may benefit labor if they are accompanied by the channels of contact
that make negotiated adjustment possible and if they are embedded
in a context of stable and relatively trusting labor-management relations. If worker representatives, for example, know that their presence is accepted and valued by management, they are more likely to
put aside traditional controls on management than they are if they
are afraid that management will try to weaken or undermine them
at the first available opportunity.

In short, in Germany the pressures for neovoluntarist unilateral
employer strategies are counterbalanced by pressures on business, labor, and government to preserve and strengthen the negotiated ER
system. The success of either labor or management, which have become increasingly intertwined as a result of more than four decades
of negotiated adjustment, substantially hinges on the success of the
other. Their interests are joined, making some form of negotiated
adjustment the only feasible political, and economic, strategy to
pursue.

The Lessons of an American Model

The chief shortcomings of the German approach can be illustrated
by one of the most impressive strengths of what might be termed a
sort of American model. What has been striking about the American
economy over the past decade and what accounts for the fact that
many managers and workers have been able to implement extremely
effective changes in the organization of work, production, and the
labor-management relationship is a talent for innovative, adaptive
HR practices. To the extent that there is an American model, it is
really the *lack* of a typical way of doing things. This lack has permitted experimentation that makes the most of the unique set of locally
available resources, human and otherwise.[31]

Earlier I characterized as socially and economically problematic
the fact that the IR framework of the Wagner Act pertains in only a
minority of American workplaces and that employers in most American companies more or less dictate employment relations. There are,
however, advantages to this, since the obstacles to restructuring any

given labor-management relationship are fairly negligible. Where there are no unions, managers are more or less free to set up work and the employer-employee relationship however they wish to. It is true that where there are unions, the Wagner Act pertains, and legal obstacles to particular forms of employee representation apply.[32] For instance, the law prevents employers, even in collaboration with employees, from being involved in any way in the establishment of a worker representative body. If employees want any form of collective representation, they are more or less stuck with a particular kind of representation because they are obliged to follow the procedures laid out in the Wagner Act for electing a union. The Wagner Act discourages employers and employees from establishing new kinds of worker representation mechanisms.[33] This is not to say, however, that there are no alternative forms of worker representation and associated labor-management relations. On the contrary. When employers and unions have agreed to the creation of new forums for labor-management consultation or interaction, the unions involved have many incentives *not* to stick to the letter of the law. As a result, many new American structures and practices are especially impressive by international standards.

In Germany, experimentation with unfamiliar practices is not easy. The enterprise-level works councils, mandated by federal law, have an extensive set of legal rights and obligations. Their rights include veto power over management decisions that in the United States fall within the realm of management prerogative, such as overtime, hiring, or transfers. In Germany, any changes in the organization of work or production that touch on these and other issues must be brought to the works council. Moreover, the councils can and do use their extensive rights to gain leverage in those areas where their rights are less formidable, such as the introduction of new technology or the allocation of training. In extreme cases "wildcat cooperatism" can occur (i.e., the council cooperates with management-initiated organizational changes that are not endorsed by the unions). But the capacity of councils and unions to thwart management-initiated organizational changes remains substantial. Indeed, the sheer volume of regulations entailed in the Works Constitution Act, which governs labor-management relations at the enterprise level and below, makes organizational change a much more formal and drawn out process in Germany than it tends to be in the United States.[34]

Many American experiments with new HR practices that involve employees in management decision making are developed *jointly*—

often informally—by labor and management. In Germany, when labor plays a proactive role, changes in the structure of work and production tend to be developed *separately* by the works council (usually with the help of the union) and/or the employer. Innovative HR practices in the United States can capitalize on the principle that two heads are better than one. In Germany, innovative HR practices tend to represent a formal compromise between two rather different sets of plans.

German companies tend to be organized along functional lines. Cross-functional collaboration (for example, project-based management or interdepartmental teamwork), which can be found in many American firms, is fairly rare in German firms. German managers tend to think of themselves as highly qualified specialists in their particular areas of expertise rather than as all-around managers, concerned with eliciting the best possible performance from those they manage.[35] What is needed in Germany is a series of organizational reforms that will speed up the capacity to recombine resources in responding to changing environmental circumstances. Addressing these issues will entail not only the cooperation and participation of the works councils and unions but also fundamental changes in German organizational structures and managerial strategies.

Navigating the Trade-Off

If the American system of employment relations provides insufficient possibilities for labor and management to negotiate the terms of industrial adjustment, and if ingrained German organizational structures and practices and the institutions of corporate governance inhibit joint labor-management innovations, is there a trade-off between the American and German models? Do negotiation and accommodation above the enterprise level interfere with creative and truly joint ventures at and below that level? Is American decentralized joint innovation possible precisely because there is a lack of central coordination of employment relations?

There is indeed a trade-off between the benefits of a negotiated approach and the benefits of a less-structured model. Such a trade-off was manifested in the struggle between German employers and unions over the rate at which workers' wages in the new states would increase to match wages in the western states and the extent to which this rate would be tied to productivity increases. Productivity in the former East Germany is still a fraction of western levels, posing a dilemma for both labor and management. On the one hand, employers and unions alike share a deep interest in avoiding individualized, context-specific solutions to specific economic problems. Both parties want to avoid whipsawing (the erosion of central standards in one case used as a lever to erode standards in others) by the other. Both parties also recognize that their collective strength hinges on the solidarity of their members (whether union members or employer association members). On the other hand, it is obvious that company-specific agreements in the new eastern states may have at least temporary virtues. Unions and employers are trying to calibrate these conflicting needs to avoid setting damaging decentralizing precedents while allowing for the necessary deviations from standard procedures.

In the United States, the trade-off is reflected in the tension between employers' long-term interests in a well-trained workforce with broad skills, for example, and hesitation to invest in such skills for fear that employees may change jobs and make their skills available to competing companies. A recent study, for example, finds that employers in the metalworking sectors in Wisconsin regret the low level of skills among their employees but resist engaging in extensive training because of this free-rider problem.[36]

Given this trade-off, both the United States and Germany need to find locally appropriate ways of taking advantage of the benefits of essentially alien mechanisms. The key to successful industrial adjustment in the United States resides in the identification and harnessing of functional equivalents to the institutions that facilitate German industrial adjustment—structures that create incentives for the parties to negotiate over changes in how work is organized and done.

In Germany, employers need to increase cross-functional movement and coordination and deformalize labor-management cooperation mechanisms. These kinds of changes would allow employees to participate *directly* (rather than only through works councils) in management decision making and thus facilitate the cooperation between workers and managers across different parts of an organization. Changing how German businesses manage will surely entail a loosening of the structures of the enterprise-level negotiation of organizational change and adjustment. If both countries are able to navigate the trade-offs, Germans will become better at developing and harnessing new forms of joint and participative labor-management relations and Americans will find it easier to diffuse them throughout the economy.

Conclusion: What to Compare

The first part of this book will lay out the dynamics of the German model of negotiated adjustment and contrast them with the more unilateral processes of organizational change in the United States. Chapter 2 juxtaposes Germany's social market economy against the United States' free market system. It presents the broad outlines of the two political economies, pointing to a variety of supraorganizational factors that influence how ER issues are defined, strategies are developed, and interests pursued. This chapter provides a background for understanding the motivations, actions, and interactions of employees, employers, and their representatives in matters of organizational change and industrial adjustment.

Chapter 3 takes up the question of what industrial adjustment actually looks like at the level of the individual enterprise. It compares labor-management adjustment processes in those settings where new technologies have required changes in employees' skills and jobs. This chapter shows how the resources, strategies, and actions of labor and management at the local level depend on developments at the regional/industry and national levels. In Germany, the strong institutionalization of the interests of employees (for instance, in high skill levels and, thus, high wages) *ensures* that these interests are taken into account in managerial decision making, and it is this strategy making that has consistently bolstered the overall competitiveness of the German economy. In the United States, labor-management innovation is characterized by the impressive scope and flexibility of labor participation in management at the local level.

In chapter 4 the focus of discussion narrows to what may be the most crucial area of labor-management relations today and a central determinant of firm productivity: employee training and development. This chapter reveals the chief strengths and weaknesses of the German and American ways of structuring employment relations. Case studies illustrate the mechanisms underlying American experiments with training programs, which in some cases entail considerably *more* negotiation and codetermination than exists in the most impressive German cases. These cases will also illuminate the institutional mechanisms by which training innovations in Germany are diffused throughout entire industries. The broader institutional framework within which the training of the German workforce occurs encourages negotiation among and between everyone involved, which gives the German economy a powerful competitive advantage.

The second part of the book steps back to take a critical look at the resilience of the German model and begins to detail some of its chief weaknesses. Chapter 5 starts with an examination of how German employers view their ER system and the relationship between industrial relations and firm competitiveness. This is followed by a look at how American and German employers manage their employees at home as well as abroad. Interviews with managers at German- and American-owned companies operating on both sides of the Atlantic reveal the extent to which employers try to export familiar ways of managing human resources and how effective they are in this endeavor. This comparison clarifies how the ER context influences employers' approaches to workers and their collective representatives. It also raises a set of concrete costs and benefits involved in both the American and German approaches.

Chapter 6 tests the durability of the German model of negotiated adjustment against the backdrop of Germany's unification in 1990. In this chapter, it will become apparent that while in many regards the relationships among the actors look quite different in the new eastern states from relationships in the western states, those differences do not suggest a systematic erosion of the negotiated model. On the contrary, the realignment and articulation of interests in the eastern states allow for new forms of adjustment that are essentially negotiated. If the German model is viewed as a way of encouraging negotiations among parties, rather than as a particular set of institutions, it will not only survive but thrive in the coming century.

Chapter 7 addresses the question of how Germany can learn from the U.S. experience. Here, I distinguish between *institutional* rigidities with long-term economic benefits and *organizational* rigidities that impede the overall competitiveness of the German economy. This distinction lays the groundwork for a consideration of the types of initiatives that might create forums for informal, joint brainstorming and problem solving between labor and management without jeopardizing the integrity and overall social and economic benefits of the German institutional infrastructure.

The ways in which American public and private sector actors and policymakers can learn from the German model are discussed in chapter 8. This chapter begins with a recapitulation of the unfortunate negative effects of the strategies of individual American companies (and, to some extent, unions) at the macrolevel of the society and economy as a whole. This lays the groundwork for a three-part policy proposal that is intended to encourage more labor-management innovation in employment relations (and especially more investment in human resources), as well as the diffusion of such innovations throughout the economy. Finally, the chapter closes with a brief discussion of the implications of all this for how we think about the relationship between employers and employees. Here I will argue for the fusion of an organization-focused approach with a broader political economic perspective that can both accommodate and extract the most useful lessons from comparative analyses such as this one.

Just as similar political economic structures can and do produce extremely different outcomes, so too can similar outcomes arise in different political economies. This is the idea on which my prescriptions are based. Principles extracted from the German model can help suggest how to construct relationship-building mechanisms that will take advantage of the innovative strengths of U.S. workers and managers while compensating for the weaknesses of the free market. Conversely, the American experience can show how labor and management in Germany can make the most of the stability and security of their ER institutions to put aside the rules, in specified settings, for specified purposes, to promote more informal innovation and problem solving. In different ways, both countries can do more to capitalize on the principles of negotiated adjustment.

Notes

1. Works on the strengths of the German model include Andrei Markovits, *The Politics of West German Trade Unions* (New York: Cambridge University Press, 1986); Kathleen Thelen, *Union of Parts: Labor Politics in Postwar Germany* (Ithaca: Cornell University Press, 1991); and David Soskice, "Innovation Strategies of Companies: A Comparative Institutional Explanation of Cross-Country Differences," working paper, *Wissenschaftszentrum,* Berlin, 1993.

Among those praising aspects of the Japanese approach are William Ouchi, *The M Form Society* (Reading, Mass.: Addison Wesley, 1984); Ronald Dore, *Taking Japan Seriously: A Confucian Perspective on Leading Economic Issues* (Stanford: Stanford University Press, 1987); and John Paul MacDuffie and John Krafcik, "Integrating Technology and Human Resources for High-Performance Manufacturing: Evidence from the Auto Industry," in *Transforming Organizations,* ed. Thomas Kochan and Michael Useem (London: Oxford University Press, 1991).

The resurgence of the American model is noted in Konrad Seitz, *Die japanisch-amerikanische Herausforderung* (The Japanese-American challenge) (Munich: Verlag Bonn Aktuell, 1991), and Gesamtmetall, *Mensch und Arbeit: Gemeinsame Interessen von Mitarbeitern and Unternehmen in einer sich wandelnten Arbeitswelt* (Humans and work: Common interests of employees and employers in a changing work world) (Cologne: Gesamtverband der metallindustriellen Arbeitgeberverbände, 1989).

2. The concept of negotiated adjustment was put forward in John Zysman, *Governments, Markets, and Growth: Financial Systems and the Politics of Industrial Change* (Ithaca: Cornell University Press, 1983), and developed by Thelen, *Union of Parts.*

3. Research on these innovations is analyzed in Paul Osterman, "How Common Is Workplace Transformation and Who Adopts It?" *Industrial and Labor Relations Review* 47, no. 2 (January 1994): 173–188; Richard Walton, "From Control to Commitment at the Workplace," *Harvard Business Review* 63 (1985): 76–84; James P. Womack, Daniel T. Jones, and Daniel Roos, *The Machine That Changed the World: The Story of Lean Production* (New York: Macmillan, 1990); Ouchi, *The M Form Society;* and MacDuffie and Krafcik, "Integrating Technology and Human Resources."

See also U.S. Department of Labor, Bureau of Labor-Management Cooperative Programs, *Labor-Management Commitment: A Compact for Change,* BLMR 141 (Washington, D.C., 1991); Tom Peters and Robert Waterman, *In Search of Excellence: Lessons from America's Best-Run Companies* (New York: Warner Books, 1982); and James Kotter and William Heskett, *Corporate Culture* (Boston: Harvard Business School Press, 1991).

4. Typical arguments along these lines are found in Paul S. McDonough, "Labor Relations: Maintain a Union-Free Status," *Personnel Journal* 69 (1990): 108–14; Morgan O. Reynolds, "The Creative Destruction of Unionism," *Forum for Applied Research in Public Policy* 5, no. 4 (Winter 1990): 57–60; and U.S. Senate, Labor Subcommittee, Committee on Labor and Human Resources, 102d Cong., 1st sess., 12 March 1991. See, in particular, the testimony of Peter G. Nash on behalf of the National Association of Manufacturers.

5. "Concession bargaining" is documented in Jane Slaughter, *Concessions and How to Beat Them* (Detroit, Mich.: Labor Notes, 1983), and analyzed in Peter Cappelli, "Competitive Pressures and Labor Relations: The Response of the Airline Industry" (paper presented at the 2d annual Berkeley Conference on Industrial Relations, Berkeley, Calif., February 1985); and Kirsten Wever, "Towards a Structural Account of Union Participation in Management: The Case of Western Airlines," *Industrial and Labor Relations Review* 42, no. 4 (1989): 600–09.

6. Many of the problems associated with this kind of work are discussed in John Sweeny and Karen Nussbaum, *Solutions for the New Work Force: Policies for a New Social Contract* (Washington: Seven Locks Press, 1989). A study of HR practices in the service sector is analyzed in Leonard Schlesinger and James Heskett, "The Service-Driven Service Company," *Harvard Business Review* 69 (1991): 71–81.

7. Human resource and industrial relations problems in the petrochemicals sector are analyzed in great detail in John C. Wells, Thomas A. Kochan, and Michael Smith, "Managing Workplace Safety and Health: The Case of Contract Labor in U.S. Petrochemical Industry," monograph (South Park, Tex.: John Gray Institute, Lamar University System, 1991). Problems associated with the skills of the U.S. workforce are discussed in William B. Johnston and Arnold E. Packer, *Workforce 2000: Work and Workers for the 21st Century* (Indianapolis: Hudson Institute, 1987); and Cuomo Commission on Trade and Competitiveness, *The Cuomo Commission Report* (New York: Simon and Schuster, 1988). Broader competitiveness implications are touched on in Michael L. Dertouzos, Richard K. Lester, and Robert M. Solow, *Made in America: Regaining the Productive Edge* (Cambridge: MIT Press, 1989).

8. For in-depth discussions of the Fordist/Taylorist model, see Michael Piore and Charles Sabel, *The Second Industrial Divide* (New York: Basic Books, 1984); and Horst Kern and Michael Schumann, *Das Ende der Arbeitsteilung?* (End of the division of labor?) (Frankfurt: Campus Verlag, 1985).

9. Osterman, "How Common Is Workplace Transformation and Who Adopts It?" 173–188.

10. Overall trends in deregulation are analyzed in Susan Tolchin and Martin Tolchin, *Dismantling America: The Rush to Deregulate* (Boston: Houghton Mifflin, 1983). The bias against government involvement in employment relations and, more specifically, industrial policy is discussed in Richard Walton, *Innovating to Compete: Lessons for Diffusing and Managing Change in the Workplace* (San Francisco: Jossey-Bass, 1987); Milton Friedman, *Capitalism and Freedom* (Chicago: University of Chicago Press, 1963); and Seymour Martin Lipset, "Why No Socialism in the United States?" in *Sources of Contemporary Radicalism,* ed. Sewarin Bialer and Sophia Sluzar (Boulder: Westview Press, 1977). An excellent historical analysis of this phenomenon from a political economic perspective is offered by David Vogel, "Why Businessmen Distrust Their State: The Political Consciousness of American Corporate Executives," *British Journal of Political Science* 8 (1978): 45–78.

11. U.S. labor laws are described in detail by William B. Gould, *A Primer on American Labor Law* (Cambridge: MIT Press, 1986); and Michael Yates, *Labor*

Law Handbook (Boston: South End Press, 1987). Current problems with the law are analyzed in Paul Weiler, *The Law at Work: The Past and Future of Labor and Employment Law* (Cambridge: Harvard University Press, 1990). The effects of labor laws on HR practices in nonunion companies are discussed in Fred K. Foulkes, *Personnel Policies in Large Nonunion Companies* (Englewood Cliffs, N.J.: Prentice Hall, 1980).

12. The effect of Japanese HR practices on U.S. firms is the focus of Ouchi, *The M Form Society.* The Japanese-inspired model of "lean production" is laid out in Womack, Jones, and Roos, *The Machine That Changed the World.* The bias toward comparison with Japan rather than Germany is noted in Ulrich Jürgens, Larissa Klinzing, and Lowell Turner, "The Transformation of Industrial Relations in Eastern Germany," *Industrial and Labor Relations Review* 46, no. 2 (1993): 229–44.

13. Two very different, but on the whole complementary, and highly compelling analyses of the comparative value of the Japanese economy are offered by Masahiko Aoki, *Information, Incentives, and Bargaining in the Japanese Economy* (Cambridge: Cambridge University Press, 1988); and Robert E. Cole, *Strategies for Learning: Small-Group Activities in American, Japanese, and Swedish Industry* (Berkeley: University of California Press, 1989).

14. Dore, *Taking Japan Seriously,* argues that this explanation can be extended to cover relationships among companies in Japan as well. Richard Freeman and Edward P. Lazear, "An Economic Analysis of Works Councils" (Economic Department, Harvard University, and Graduate School of Business, University of Chicago, May 1992), argue that this sort of information sharing reduces costs to employers.

15. Williamson analyzes these dynamics in terms of transaction costs in his microlevel theoretical alternative to the neoclassical account. See Oliver E. Williamson, *The Economic Institutions of Capitalism: Firms, Markets, Relational Marketing* (New York: Macmillan, 1985). Transaction cost analysis concerns the terms of exchange between two or more actors. According to this approach, nonmarket mechanisms can reduce the transaction costs involved in many kinds of economic exchange. The German case addresses the issue from the other side, showing how nonmarket mechanisms can increase benefits as well as reduce costs. German employers may pay a high price in terms of high labor costs, short working hours, and relatively few working days, but they also experience the benefits of low turnover, high general skills, and peaceful labor relations.

16. Aoki, *Information, Incentives, and Bargaining,* provides a cross-national study of the diffusion of quality circles. He develops a similar argument, focusing more heavily on the role of employers and their associations.

17. The industrial relations perspective is laid out in the classic work of John Dunlop, *Industrial Relations Systems* (Carbondale: Southern Illinois University Press, 1958). The HRM perspective is clarified in Michael Beer et al., *Managing Human Assets* (New York: Free Press, 1984). The strategic choice perspective is developed in Thomas Kochan, Harry Katz, and Robert McKersie, *The Transformation of American Industrial Relations* (New York: Basic Books, 1986).

18. For an excellent analysis of these linkages and their implications for HRM theory, see Chris Brewster, "European Human Resource Management: Reflection of, or Challenge to, the American Concept?" (Cranfield School of Management, Cranfield, Bedford, England, June 1992).

The literature on human resource management usually deemphasizes the unionized sector. See, for instance, Jon L. Pierce and John W. Newstrom, eds., *Manager's Bookshelf* (New York: Harper-Collins, 1993).

19. Among the best political economic works exploring this question are Christopher S. Allen, "Regional Governments and Economic Policies in West Germany: The 'Meso' Politics of Industrial Adjustment," *Publius* 19, no. 4 (1989): 147–64; Thelen, *Union of Parts*; Lowell Turner, *Democracy at Work? Changing World Markets and the Future of Labor Unions* (Ithaca: Cornell University Press, 1991); Richard M. Locke, "The Decline of the National Union in Italy: Lessons for Comparative Industrial Relations Theory," *Industrial and Labor Relations Review* 45, no. 2 (1992): 229–49; and Gary Herrigel, "Industrial Order and the Politics of Industrial Change: Mechanical Engineering," in *Industry and Political Change: Toward the Third West German Republic,* ed. Peter J. Katzenstein (Ithaca: Cornell University Press, 1989).

20. The macropolitical strengths of the German model are analyzed in Peter Katzenstein, *Policy and Politics in West Germany: The Growth of a Semisovereign State* (Philadelphia: Temple University Press, 1987). For a discussion of the economic benefits of the model, see David Soskice, "Innovation Strategies of Companies"; and David Soskice, "The Institutional Infrastructure for International Competitiveness: A Comparative Analysis of the UK and Germany" (paper presented at the International Economic Association Conference, Venice, Italy, February 1991).

21. William Forbath, *Law and the Shaping of the American Labor Movement* (Cambridge: Harvard University Press, 1991).

22. This effort parallels emerging trends in both political science and industrial relations. Recently, various political scientists have intensified efforts to expand their theoretical model downward, so to speak, to capture events at the meso- and microlevels. See Thelen, *Union of Parts*; Locke, *The Decline of the Na-*

tional Union in Italy; and Joel Rogers and Wolfgang Streeck, eds., *Works Councils: Consultation, Representation, and Cooperation in Industrial Relations* (Chicago: University of Chicago Press in association with the National Bureau of Economic Research [NBER], forthcoming). At the same time, IR scholars have begun trying to expand their model upward through comparative studies of IR and ER systems. See Harry C. Katz, "The Decentralization of Collective Bargaining: A Literature Review and Comparative Analysis," *Industrial and Labor Relations Review* 47, no. 1 (1993): 3–22.

23. The institutionalist perspective is presented in many excellent works, including Turner, *Democracy at Work;* Wolfgang Streeck, "More Uncertainties: German Unions Facing 1992," *Industrial Relations* 30 (1991): 317–49; and Peter Berg, "The Restructuring of Work and the Role of Training: A Comparative Analysis of the United States and German Automobile Industries" (Ph.D. diss., University of Notre Dame, 1993).

24. "A Survey of Germany," *The Economist,* 21 May 1994, 5.

25. Institut der deutschen Wirtschaft, *IW Dienst,* January 28, 1993 and December 17, 1992; "A Survey of Germany," 7.

26. This trend is documented in Audrey Freedman and William Fulmer, "Last Rites for Pattern Bargaining," *Harvard Business Review* 60 (1982): 30–43.

27. The various international trends associated with this decentralization are discussed in Katz, "The Decentralization of Collective Bargaining."

28. For a discussion of the macrolevel pressures on employers, see also Maria Green, "Setting the Agenda for a New Europe: The Politics of Big Business in EC 1992" (paper presented at the Harvard Center for European Studies, Cambridge, Mass., April 1993).

29. These developments are discussed and analyzed at length in chapter 7. Helpful overviews are offered by Jürgens, Klinzing, and Turner, "The Transformation of Industrial Relations in Eastern Germany"; Michael Fichter, "From Transmission Belt to Social Partnership? The Case of Organized Labor in Eastern Germany," *German Politics and Society* 23 (1991): 21–39; and Matthias Knuth, "Employment and Training Companies: Bridging Unemployment in the East German Crash" (paper presented at the Conference of the Society for the Advancement of Socio-Economics, New York, N.Y., March 1993).

30. Thelen, *Union of Parts,* has developed this argument with reference to organized labor. She argues that the resilience of the dual system of employee representation is connected to the unions' ability to shift the focus of their activity across these two levels as necessary at critical junctures in the postwar period.

31. The contrast between the United States and Germany with respect to decentralized innovation and problem solving has been traced to differences in national, managerial, and organizational cultures as well as to differences in the labor-management relationship. See, for example, Heinz Hartmann, *Der deutsche Unternehmer: Autorität und Organisation* (The German employer: Authority and organization) (Frankfurt: Europäischer Verlagsanstalt, 1968); Gustav Hofstede, *Culture's Consequences* (Beverly Hills: Sage, 1980); and Edgar Schein, "Does Japanese Management Style Have a Message for American Managers?" *Sloan Management Review* 23 (1981): 55–68.

32. Many unionized workers in the transportation industries are covered by the Railway Labor Act of 1926 rather than the Wagner Act.

33. The chief exception to this rule is discussed in Stephen Schlossberg and Miriam Reinhart, "Electromation and the Future of Labor-Management Cooperation in the U.S." *Labor Law Journal* 43 (1992): 608–20. This issue is considered again in chapters 2 and 8.

34. The notion of "wildcat cooperatism" is introduced by Wolfgang Streeck, "Neocorporatist Industrial Relations and the Economic Crisis in West Germany," in *Order and Conflict in Contemporary Capitalism,* ed. John Goldthorpe (London: Oxford University Press, 1984). The legalism of the German IR system is discussed in Rainer Erd, *Verrechtlichung industrieller Konflikte: normative Rahmenbedingungen des dualen Systems der Interessenvertretung* (Overlegislation of industrial conflicts: normative framework conditions of the dual system of interest representation) (Frankfurt: Campus Verlag, 1978).

35. See, for instance, Peter Walgenbach, "Führungsverhalten mittlerer Manager in Deutschland und Großbritannien" (Leadership approaches of middle managers in Germany and Great Britain), *ZEW Newsletter,* no. 2 (1993). This issue is discussed at length in chapter 7.

36. The reader is referred to an excellent study on the Wisconsin metalworking sectors by Rogers and Streeck, *Wisconsin Metalworking Training Consortium.*

chapter two

Employment Relations in Context
how institutional structures influence business and labor strategies

How can the German social market economy be compared with the free market economy of the United States? First, we need to review some of the basic features of the *Wirtschaftswunder* (the "economic miracle") that brought the German model to international acclaim in the 1960s.[a] Second, we need to understand the institutions of employment relations in the United States and Germany and the ways in which they interrelate. How centralized and cohesive are interactions among the main players? What is the role of labor? What is the nature of government involvement in employment relations? This background information makes it possible to compare how German and American institutional infrastructures influence the capacity of labor and management to develop and diffuse competitive HR innovations. It will become apparent through this comparison that some organizations in the United States are particularly expert at *developing* innovations, but proven innovations are more easily *diffused* beyond the companies and workplaces where they are initially developed in Germany. This contrast has to do with how the various institutions and organizations of employment relations in the two countries support and/or undermine each other. The advantages of the German model, such as the ease of the diffusion of ER innovations, should not be attributed to these institutions per se. Rather, employers and employee representatives in Germany have

---

[a] Because chapter 6 is devoted to unification and developments in the new states, these are only touched on briefly in this chapter.

made particularly adept use of these institutions to take advantage of a unique set of national resources.

The Social Market Economy

Historical Background[1]

The *Wirtschaftswunder* began soon after the end of World War II. By 1949, signs of a robust economy were already emerging: the gross national product doubled within a year, and prices began to fall after an initial rise caused by the lifting of currency stabilization measures and import tariffs. That year, the Christian Democrats[b] won the national election and began to establish the country's social market economy, so named by Ludwig Erhard, the first economics minister. Fueled at the time by immigration flows from East Germany, West Germany possessed Europe's largest reserve of skilled labor. By the late 1950s, an internationally unprecedented export-oriented growth spurt was well under way. National income as well as wages and salaries had more than doubled since the end of the war. Under a series of coalition governments, first dominated by the CDU and then by the SPD in 1969, economic growth continued more or less unabated into the 1970s.

It was during this time of economic growth that codetermination, the best-known feature of labor-management relations in Germany, came into existence. The legal foundations for codetermination were established in the early 1950s, but the roots of the system can be traced back to nineteenth- and early twentieth-century German history. Through participation on supervisory boards and works councils, the institutions of codetermination allow labor a significant role in decision making in the arena of strategic management and at

---

[b] For most of the postwar period, the three main political parties in Germany were the Christian Democrats (a coalition of the national *Christlich Demokratische Union,* or *CDU,* and the Bavarian *Christlich Soziale Union,* or *CSU*), the Social Democrats (the *Sozialdemokratische Partei Deutschlands,* or *SPD*) and the Free Democrats (*Freie Demokratische Partei,* or *FDP*). Since the 1970s, the Green Party (*Die Grünen*) has played an influential role, particularly in the politics of some of the states. Since unification, the Democratic Socialist Party (*Partei des Demokratischen Sozialismus,* or *PDS,* the former Socialist Party of East Germany) has also been prominent in state politics in the eastern part of the country.

the workplace. In 1951, the terms of supervisory board representation for labor in the iron, coal, and steel industries were enacted into law. A 1952 extension of this legislation allowed minority board representation for labor representatives in large companies (more than 500 employees) in other industries as well. Works councils were also mandated in 1952. (The councils, like the unions, had played prominent roles in pre-Nazi Germany). Legislation in 1972 and 1976 extended the codetermination rights of the councils, the range of companies required to have a council (all firms with 5 or more employees), and worker representation on supervisory boards of companies with over 2,000 employees to parity (50 percent).[2]

With this legislation, the unions' and councils' rights were firmly enshrined in German law. Several factors favored labor's position in the immediate postwar period. One was the liberal influence of the British on the political economy of the Ruhr Valley, the industrial heartland of West Germany. Another was that the labor movement, unlike big business, which had collaborated with the Nazis, had been disbanded by Hitler in the 1930s. Many of labor's most prominent leaders had been killed, interned in concentration camps, or forced into exile.[c] Although these factors may have strengthened the unions' political position just after the war, the government was run by the relatively conservative Christian Democrats rather than labor's closer ally, the SPD. Thus the codetermination laws of the early postwar period were by no means pure reflections of labor's agenda. Indeed, both big business and the unions strenuously opposed the Works Constitution Act, which created the works councils. Employers feared the councils would interfere with managerial autonomy; unions feared the councils would compete with them. (As discussed in chapter 5, both fears turned out to be largely unjustified.)

Rapid growth allowed for healthy wage increases and a highly stable IR system characterized by a low strike rate that was the envy of Europe and the United States well into the 1970s. Labor-management cooperation extended from the workplace to the national level. Labor, business, and government representatives met

---

[c]Hitler began building the Dachau concentration camp three months after taking power, with the intention of imprisoning Socialists, Social Democrats, and labor activists.

regularly to coordinate strategies and discuss the future of the economy.[d] In the early 1970s, however, unfamiliar and apparently intractable economic problems began to emerge in all the advanced industrial countries. Like most of Europe, West Germany was particularly reliant on oil from the Middle East and therefore vulnerable to the OPEC price increases that occurred in the early and late 1970s. In the 1950s and 1960s, the West German government had actively recruited southern European workers to help meet extraordinarily high levels of demand for labor. However, unemployment began to creep up to match higher European levels. The extensive social security system began to appear equally expensive. By 1982, in West Germany, the real growth rate was zero, and both inflation and unemployment were high by historical German standards. In real terms, investment and private consumption were lower than in the previous year.[3] The SPD's junior partner—the FDP, which had been less and less willing to follow the SPD's domestic policies as problems continued to emerge—withdrew from the governing coalition in 1982, paving the way for the election of Helmut Kohl and the ascension of another CPU-FDP coalition.

Kohl promised a political economic reversal *(Wende)* that was to include a major trimming of government expenditures as well as the privatization of various public sector concerns, such as Lufthansa airlines, the railroads, and the postal service. In fact, however, there was little reversal. By 1988, Kohl was being widely criticized for having failed to accomplish much of anything during his tenure, and West Germany's growth rate was slower than those of other major European powers, including Britain and France. Public dissatisfaction with the Kohl government expressed itself in part in the growth of far-right extremist (neo-Nazi) parties, especially the so-called Republicans *(Republikaner)*.

International contingencies in 1989—the imminent collapse of the Soviet empire and Mikhail Gorbachev's efforts in the direction of ending the cold war—came to Kohl's political rescue. These events made possible the unification of East and West Germany, and Kohl was able to reconsolidate his political base by rallying both

---

[d]The highly publicized, national-level concerted action forum dissolved after employers mounted a particularly harsh campaign against the unions' drive for an extension of the codetermination laws in 1976.

German populations behind this long-yearned-for event. On July 1, 1990, the currencies of East and West Germany were united, and unification proper followed on October 3, 1990. Promising that unification would entail more economic gains than costs, Kohl was able to win over the majority of the voters in the new states and remained in power.

Comparative Perspective

Table 2-1 presents background figures on the German economy for most of the postwar period. As this table shows, Germany is a densely populated country and becoming more so as a result of immigration. The most recent waves of immigration have come from Eastern European states and countries of the former Soviet Union.

Employment is concentrated in manufacturing (see also Exhibit 2-1). This is reflected in the industrial concentration of Germany's largest companies, which include Daimler-Benz, Volkswagen, and Siemens in the metalworking sector (automobiles, electrical and electronic products) and Hoechst, BASF, and Bayer in the chemicals and pharmaceuticals industries.

Union membership is high by international standards. About 40 percent of the total workforce is unionized while 15 percent of the U.S., 15 percent of the Japanese, 6 percent of the French, and 50 percent of the British workforces are unionized.[e] The main industrial unions are federated in the *Deutscher Gewerkschaftsbund,* or *DGB* (see Table 2-2). By far the largest unions are the metalworking union *(IG Metall)* and the public sector union *(ÖTV)*. The chemical workers union *(IG Chemie),* the service union *(HBV),* and the media union *(IG Medien)* also play significant political roles in the DGB and the German economy. As shown in Table 2-2, total union membership was somewhat bolstered by the incorporation of the new states.[f]

As shown in Exhibit 2-2, the system of codetermination covers most German workers in one way or another. With the previously mentioned exception of small private sector companies with fewer

---

[e] It is extremely difficult to compare union influence and representativeness across countries, as union membership means different things in different settings.

[f] The percentages have fluctuated since unification, in part because of high levels of unemployment in the new states.

Table 2-1
Background Figures, West Germany, 1960–1991
(000's except where otherwise indicated)

	1960	1970	1980	1989	1991
Population	55,433	60,651	61,538	62,063	64,074
Pop. per sq. km.	223	224	247	250	258
Foreign-born pop.	686	2,601	4,453	4,846	5,882
Pop. growth rate	−326	−76	−93	−16	+13
Net immigration	395	574	312	980	587
Working pop.	26,501	26,452	26,874	27,742	29,684
Female working pop.	9,854	9,510	10,092	10,794	11,965
Agricultural employment	3,541	2,370	1,437	1,039	1,045
Manufacturing employment	12,722	12,797	12,174	11,337	12,065
Services employment	4,634	4,566	4,722	4,970	5,291
Other employment	5,603	6,719	8,514	10,397	11,283
Unemployment rate	1.3%	0.7%	3.8%	7.9%	6.3%

Source: Adapted from *Statistisches Jahrbuch 1993* (Statistical yearbook) (Stuttgart: Statistisches Bundesamt, 1993).

than five employees, all companies are legally required to have works councils, although in fact only about two-thirds of them do.[4] While unions provide the first channel of worker representation in most of Europe, works councils provide the second channel, as detailed in

Exhibit 2-1
Composition of German GDP, 1991*

Manufacturing	38.4%
Services	29.4%
Trade and Transport	14.4%
State Expenditures, Private Income	13.7%
Agriculture and Fishing	1.3%
Other	3.7%

*Total GDP: 2,782.4 billion DM

Source: Adapted from *Tatsachen Über Deutschland* (Facts about Germany) (Frankfurt: Societätsverlag, 1992).

Exhibit 2-3. Workers in larger companies also have representation on supervisory boards, which are not as involved in practical management affairs as American boards of directors except when important issues such as mass layoffs or mergers occur. The country's strong labor representation has bolstered a highly stable IR system. In the 1980s, the average number of employee work days lost annually to industrial conflicts in large firms was only about 50,000, with the exception of 1984, when a bitter and long strike occurred in the metal industries over the length of the work week. In 1993, the average number of work days lost to strikes, per 1,000 workers, was 5.6 in Germany, compared with 69.4 in the United States, 4.0 in Japan, 64 in France, and 125.6 in Great Britain.[g]

Tables 2-3 and 2-4 compare the German economy with that of the United States, Japan, France, and Great Britain. Table 2-5 shows

---

[g] The strike rate in the United States has dropped markedly since the early 1980s, however, as the political and economic position of organized labor has been increasingly compromised.

Table 2-2
DGB Union Membership, 1993

	Total membership (000's)	East as % of total	Women as % of total	% of total DGB
Construction	777	42.5	12.3	6.6
Mining	507	38.2	9.4	4.3
Chemicals	877	23.9	25.8	7.4
Railroads	527	42	20.3	4.5
Education	360	51.9	68	3.0
Agriculture/ Landscaping	135	68.5	33	1.1
Services	737	47	68.9	6.2
Wood/Plastics	239	34.6	24.6	2.0
Leather	42	33.4	52.4	0.4
Media	245	25.9	34.4	2.1
Metal	3,628	27.3	20.9	30.7
Restaurant and food	431	37.6	42.6	3.7
Public sector	2,138	44.4	47.2	18.1
Police	201	27.5	11.5	1.7
Postal	612	24.7	42.4	5.2

Table 2-2 (continued)

	Total membership (000's)	East as % of total	Women as % of total	% of total DGB
Textiles	348	30.1	63.4	2.9
TOTAL	11,804	35.2	33	100

Note: Numbers have been rounded, and therefore do not always total 100 percent.

Source: Adapted from *Gewerkschaftsjahrbuch 1993* (Union yearbook) (Cologne: Bund Verlag, 1993).

Exhibit 2-2
Extent of Coverage of Codetermination Rights, 1992

Form of Codetermination	Workers Affected	Industry
No codetermination	3.4 million	Small companies (<5 employees)
Workplace representation by personnel council	3.6 million	Public sector
Workplace representation by works council	9.3 million	Private sector
33% representation on supervisory board	0.6 million	Small incorporated firms
50% representation on supervisory board	0.5 million	Iron, coal, and steel industries
49% representation on supervisory board	4.0 million	Large private sector companies (2,000 + employees)

Source: Adapted from *Tatsachen über Deutschland* (Facts about Germany) (Frankfurt: Societätsverlag, 1992).

Exhibit 2-3

Works Councils in Europe

	Germany	Belgium	Denmark	Spain	France	Great Britain	Greece	Ireland	Italy	Luxembourg	Netherlands	Portugal
Works councils												
Conditions of existence	5 workers	>100	>35 if firm or majority of workers want	>50	>50	none	Private sector: >20 if union; >50 if nonunion	none	>15	150	35	no size
Composition	elected	6–22 elected, employer chairs	equal worker management	5+	3–15 elected, employer chair	—	3–7 workers	—	union delegates	6–16	no	3–11
Role												
information	yes	yes	—	yes	yes	—	yes	—	yes	—	yes	yes
consultation	yes	yes	—	—	yes	—	yes	—	—	yes	yes	yes
codetermination	—	—	—	yes	—	—	—	—	—	—	—	—
social funds	yes	—	—	—	yes	—	—	—	—	—	—	—
other	yes	—	—	yes	—	—	—	—	yes	—	—	—
negotiations	—	—	—	—	—	—	—	—	—	—	—	—
cooperation	—	yes	yes	—	—	—	—	—	—	—	—	—
Meeting/Facilities	paid time	paid time/month	paid time	15–40 hours	—	—	2 hours/week	—	8 hours/month	—	60 hours/year	40 hours/month
Health and Safety Committees												
Conditions of existence	>50 workers (single rep. if 20–50)	>50	>10 group >20 committee	>100	>50	none	>50 workers (single rep. if 20–50)	20 workers	none	none	none	none

Source: Joel Rogers and Wolfgang Streeck, "Workplace Representation Overseas: The Works Council Story" (paper presented at the Working under Difference Rules Conference, National Bureau of Economic Research, Washington, D.C., 1993).

Table 2-3
Background Data for Five Major Industrial Countries, 1993

	United States	Germany	Japan	France	Great Britain
Area/ sq. km. (000)	9,373	357	378	552	244
Pop. in millions	254	80.5	123.9	57.5	57.5
GNP per capita	22,240	23,650	26,930	20,380	16,550
Economic growth	3.2	−1.3	1.3	0	1.4

Source: Adapted from *Aktuell '93* (Current '93) (Dortmund: Harenberg Lexikon Verlag, 1993).

solid per capita GDP growth and relatively high levels of GDP growth and capital formation as well as a consistently positive trade balance and a high rate of savings. Inflation and unemployment rates are about average for this set of countries even though German un- employment has been driven up by the collapse of the economies of the new states (see Tables 2-5 and 2-6). While total taxes as a per- centage of GDP are high in Germany (see Table 2-4), this is ac- counted for in part by the astronomical costs of integrating the econ- omy of the former East Germany (discussed at length in chapter 6).

It is axiomatic that much of Germany's postwar economic mira- cle can be attributed to a variety of highly successful export indus- tries. In absolute terms, Germany has consistently been either the largest or second largest exporter and importer worldwide, alternat- ing only with the United States (see Table 2-7). Since the U.S. econ- omy is several times larger than that of united Germany, these figures are particularly impressive. Germany's key export industries include mechanical engineering, autos, precision instruments and optical goods, and chemicals and pharmaceuticals. Manufactured goods have typically accounted for about 75 percent of exports.

Table 2-4

Basic Economic Indicators for Five Major Industrial Countries
(Various Years)

	United States	Germany	Japan	France	Great Britain
per capita GDP* 1991	22,130	19,770	19,390	18,430	16,340
GDP growth av. 1983–92	2.7	2.7	4.1	2.2	2.2
Real GDP growth av. 1960–89	3.2	3.7	6.3	3.7	2.4
1988–89	0.9	2.6	5.2	2.6	0.8
Real per capita GDP growth av. 1960–89	2.0	2.6	5.3	2.3	2.1
1988–89	(0.1)	2.8	4.9	2.1	0.5
Fixed capital formation as % of GDP av. 1960–89	18.1	22.5	31.3	22.6	18.2
1989–90	16.1	21.2	32.2	21.2	19.2
Trade balance as % of GDP av. 1960–89	(0.6)	2.7	1.1	0.3	(0.5)
1988–89	(1.5)	5.5	0.7	—	(2.7)
Net savings as % of GDP av. 1960–89	7.0	12.7	20.7	13.4	7.4
1988–89	2.2	13.8	19.8	8.5	4.4

Table 2-4 (continued)

	United States	Germany	Japan	France	Great Britain
Total taxes as % of GDP 1991	27	39	30	41	36

*U.S. $ purchasing power.

Source: Adapted from *Organization for Economic Cooperation and Development, Historical Statistics 1960–1989* (Paris, 1992); *The Economist,* 25 December 1993, 72; 8 January 1994, 66.

The prominence of the manufacturing sector is paralleled by the rather weak development of the service sector in Germany. Table 2-8 shows the percentages of the working populations in the manufacturing and service industries in Germany, the United States, Japan, France, and Great Britain. One reason for the underdevelopment of

Table 2-5
Consumer and Producer Prices for Five Major Industrial Countries
(Average Annual % Increase 1960–1990 and Increase 1989–1990)

	United States	Germany	Japan	France	Great Britain
Consumer price increases					
1960–90	5.1	3.5	5.6	6.6	8.0
1989–90	4.4	2.7	3.1	3.4	9.5
Producer price increases					
1960–90	4.3	2.8	n/a	5.4	7.6
1989–90	4.9	1.5	1.6	(1.2)	5.9

Source: Adapted from *Organization for Economic Cooperation and Development, Historical Statistics 1960–1990* (Paris, 1992).

Table 2-6
Inflation Rates for Five Major Industrial Countries
(1990–1992 and average 1983–1992)

	United States	Germany	Japan	France	Great Britain
1990	5.4	2.7	3.1	3.4	9.5
1991	4.2	3.5	3.3	3.2	5.9
1992	3	4	1.6	2.4	3.7
average annual rate 1983–92	3.8	2.2	1.8	4.4	5.5

Source: Adapted from *Aktuell '93* (Current '93) (Dortmund: Harenberg Lexikon Verlag, 1992); *The Economist*, 25 December 1993, 72.

the service industries in Germany is the existence of such restrictive regulations as the *Ladenschlußgesetz* of 1956 (literally, the shop-closing-law), which prohibits shopkeepers from opening their stores after 7 PM on weekdays, after 1 or 2 PM on Saturdays (except one Saturday a month), and at any time on Sundays. While there has been much discussion about the restrictive effects of this law, unions, small retailers, and even some large ones have consistently defended it.[h]

If the unemployment rate has tended to be the envy of the rest of Europe, it is still higher than in the United States or Japan (see Table 2-9), although the figures for the former West Germany were distorted by the inclusion of the eastern economy (see Table 2-10). (In mid-1994 Western Germany's unemployment rate was still well below the European union average, at 8.3 percent.)[5] While apprenticeship training is viewed as a means of avoiding unemployment and between 66 and 75 percent of those who finish school enter apprenticeship programs, unemployment is split about evenly between people who had apprenticeship training and those who did

---

[h] In 1990, the law was amended to allow stores to remain open until 8:30 PM on Thursdays.

Table 2-7

Five Largest Importers/Exporters, 1991

	United States	Germany	Japan	France	Great Britain
Imports in millions of U.S. $	507,255	389,024	234,103	230,257	210,003
as % total of world imports	13.8	10.6	6.4	6.3	5.7
in U.S. $ per capita	2,007	4,864	1,889	4,036	3,661
Exports in millions of U.S. $	397,448	402,639	314,395	212,868	185,120
as % total of world exports	11.2	11.3	8.8	6.0	5.2
in U.S. $ per capita	1,573	5,034	2,537	3,731	3,227

Source: Adapted from *Statistisches Jahrbuch für das Ausland, 1993* (Statistical yearbook for foreign countries) (Stuttgart: Statistisches Bundesamt, 1993).

not.[i] As a result of a combination of national and international factors, including the relatively small size of the German service sector and increasing competition in manufactured goods from newly developed and developing countries, German manufacturing industries have experienced higher levels of unemployment than other segments

---

[i] In the early 1990s, there has been an increase in the percentage of those finishing school opting for college rather than apprenticeships in the western part of the country. In the new states, the demand for apprenticeships significantly outstrips supply.

Table 2-8

Percentage of Working Population Employed in Various Industries, 1991–1992

	United States	Germany	Japan	France	Great Britain
Agriculture	2.9	3.5	6.4	5.1	2.2
Mining	0.6	0.8	0.9	0.3	0.8*
Manufacturing	17.5	31.6	24.4	20.2	26.2
Electrical, Gas, and Water	1.4	0.9	0.5	0.9	1.1*
Construction	6.1	6.7	9.6	7.1	6.8*
Trade, Rest's and Hotel	20.6	14.7	22.3	16.7	20.1*
Transport, Storage, Communic.	5.7	5.7	6.0	6.4	5.7*
Finance, Insurance, Business Services	11.3	8.3	8.5	10.2	11.2*
Community, Social, Personal Services	34.1	27.8	21.8	33.1	30.6
Other	—	—	0.5	—	1.1

*1989

Source: Adapted from International Labour Office, *Year Book of Labour Statistics: 1992* (Geneva, 1992).

Table 2-9
Unemployment Rates for Five Major Industrial Countries, 1971–1992

	United States	Germany	Japan	France	Great Britain
1971	5.8	0.7	1.2	2.7	2.8
1976	7.6	4	2	4.4	4.8
1981	7.5	4.5	2.2	7.4	9
1986	6.9	7.6	2.8	10.4	11.6
1989	5.2	6.8	2.3	9.4	6.1
1992	7.3	6.3/14.8*	2.1	10	10.8

*Former West/Former East

Source: Adapted from Organization for Economic Development and Cooperation, *Labour Force Statistics 1971–1991* (Paris, 1991); *Statistisches Jahrbuch für das Ausland, 1993* (Statistical yearbook for foreign countries) (Stuttgart: Statistisches Bundesamt, 1993).

of the economy (see Table 2-11). Moreover, the labor force participation rate, and particularly the female labor force participation is low in comparison to other advanced industrial countries (see Tables 2–12 and 2–13).

Table 2-10
Unemployment in the Former East Germany, 1991

	Total	Female	Older employees*	Foreign-born employees
1991	1,689,366	791,686	504,116	208,094
1992	1,808,300	826,531	661,470	254,201

*50–65
Source: Adapted from *Aktuell '94* (Current '94) (Dortmund: Harenberg Lexikon Verlag, 1993).

Table 2-11

German Unemployment by Skill, Sector, 1992

	Total	%	Female	%
Total unemployed	1,783,608	100.00	830,903	100.00
With appren- tice training	933,560	52.30	421,054	50.70
W/o apprentice training	850,048	47.70	409,849	49.30
Manufacturing	369,458	20.70	148,423	17.90
Wholesale/Retail trade	181,945	10.20	105,359	12.70
Finance/Insurance	14,846	0.80	9,094	1.10
Other services	199,399	11.20	121,265	14.60

Source: Adapted from *Statistisches Jahrbuch 1993* (Statistical yearbook) (Stuttgart: Statistisches Bundesamt, 1993).

Germany's economic performance has been criticized as resting on prohibitively high labor costs. Nevertheless, from 1960 through the 1980s increases in hourly earnings were roughly comparable in Germany, Japan, and France. Increases in unit labor costs were significantly higher in France and Great Britain than in Germany, and only slightly lower in the United States and Japan (see Table 2-14). From the 1980s into the 1990s, average gross hourly earnings in Germany increased much more than in the United States, but similarly sharp increases occurred in the other three advanced industrial states (see Table 2-15). As shown in Table 2-16, in the middle of the 1980s, real average compensation in manufacturing began to outstrip compensation in the United States, Japan, France, and Great Britain. While Germany's unit labor costs were considerably higher than in the United States, so were Japan's. In addition to high labor costs, Germany also has a comparatively short working week. The effects

Table 2-12

Total Labor Force Participation Rates in Five Major Industrial Countries, 1971–1990

	United States	Germany	Japan	France	Great Britain
1971	69.6	69.3	71.7	68.1	74.6
1976	71.7	67.3	70.5	69.0	76.6
1981	74.5	66.2	72.0	68.8	76.1
1986	76.7	65.5	72.4	67.6	75.9
1990	78.5	—	74.3	65.2	78.6

Source: Adapted from Organization for Economic Cooperation and Development, *Labour Force Statistics 1969–90* (Paris, 1991).

of the unions' push for the thirty-five-hour week in the 1980s are illustrated in Table 2-17. Health and other social insurance payments contribute to high labor costs in Germany (see Table 2-18). German workers work shorter weeks, take more vacation days, and are more often absent from their jobs than workers in the United States, Japan, France, and Great Britain (see Table 2-19).

Germany also suffers in the comparison to other advanced industrial countries when government outlays for social services are considered. For example, social expenditures by the government as a percentage of GDP and on a per capita basis have tended to be between two and three times what they are in the United States (see Table 2-20).

Employment Relations in Germany and the United States

Relative Centralization and Cohesion

Three features of the German and American ER systems capture the essence of the contrast between the systems. Each feature has to do with institutional structure. The first concerns the relative *centralization and cohesion* of the institutional infrastructure of employment relations. The second has to do with the *position of organized labor*

Table 2-13

Female Labor Force Participation Rates in Five Major Industrial Countries

	United States	Germany	Japan	France	Great Britain
1973	52.7	50.3	54.1	51.2	57.2
1978	59.3	51.6	54.2	54.8	61.2
1983	63.4	52.5	57.2	55.8	60.2
1988	68.3	55.4	58.3	56.9	66.0
1992	70.2	*	62.0	58.5	68.3

*The number for Western Germany is not included in this statistical series. It is estimated that the female labor force participation rate for both parts of the country in mid-1994 is 58 percent ("A Survey of Germany," *The Economist,* 27 May 1994, 6).

Source: Adapted from Organization for Economic Cooperation and Development, *Labour Force Statistics 1971–91* (Paris, 1993).

in the political economy, particularly, the extent to which unions (and works councils in Germany) are stable and secure as national institutions. The third concerns the *nature of government involvement* in the economy in general and in employment relations in particular.

The fact that business and labor are viewed as social partners in Germany signals the centrality of both institutions to the political economy as a whole. The government does not take action or make policy on any question of major concern to labor and management without consulting with both parties. The process of distributing the costs of unification, for instance, requires constant, close collaboration with both social partners, which occurs under the ægis of the solidarity pact, a semiformal agreement on the broad outlines of national social and economic policies among the major political economic actors. Both business and labor appeal to the public for support of their positions and causes. They may conduct national advertising campaigns, for example, to win public support for their respective collective bargaining aims. This in itself testifies to the

Table 2-14

Manufacturing Labor Costs for Five Major Industrial Countries
(Average Annual % Increase, 1960–1989 and Increase, 1988–1989)

	United States	Germany	Japan	France	Great Britain
Real hourly earnings					
1960–89	0.3	3.3	3.9	3.1	− 0.9
1988–89	− 1.8	1.3	3.4	0.2	—
Unit labor costs					
1960–89	4.3	4.9	4.2	7.5	10.6
1988–89	0.7	− 0.4*	0.9	− 0.1	4.8

*1987–88

Source: Adapted from Organization for Economic Cooperation and Development, *Historical Statistics 1960–1989* (Paris, 1991).

Table 2-15

Average Gross Hourly Earnings for Five Major Industrial Countries, 1983–1991
(in $ US 1985)

	1983	1986	1989	1991
United States	93	102	110	117
Germany (former West)	93	104	118	133
Japan	94	103	113	127
France	89	103	115	126
Great Britain	89	107	134	155

Source: Adapted from *Statistisches Jahrbuch für das Ausland, 1993* (Statistical yearbook for foreign countries) (Stuttgart: Statistisches Bundesamt, 1993).

Table 2-16

Average Compensation, Unit Labor Costs, Average Annual Hours Worked in Manufacturing for five Major Industrial Countries, 1950–1991
(Index: 1982 = 100)

		United States	Germany	Japan	France	Great Britain
Real average compensation in manufacturing	1950	—	21.6	19.2	26.6	42.9
	1960	—	39.0	34.6	40.5	54.6
	1970	—	70.4	67.5	66.3	71.9
	1980	99.3	101.3	96.8	97.7	97.6
	1986	106.2	109.7	108.7	105.3	111.8
	1991	104.2	123.5	121.6	110.2	118.7
Unit labor costs in manufacturing	1950	—	17.6	24.6	26.6	15.0
	1960	—	20.4	24.4	32.2	23.4
	1970	—	34.2	33.4	36.2	28.7
	1980	88.1	121.2	106.7	125.2	118.1
	1986	102.5	119.5	155.2	116.7	91.3
	1991	109.8	184.6	185.8	150.0	133.0
Average annual hours worked in manufacturing	1950	107.6	137.3	107.4	119.8	117.3
	1960	105.5	123.8	117.3	119.8	116.3
	1970	104.0	112.5	106.1	115.7	109.2

Table 2-16 (continued)

		United States	Germany	Japan	France	Great Britain
Average annual hours worked in manufacturing	1980	102.0	101.4	100.8	105.8	100.5
	1986	104.5	97.4	100.4	99.1	109.9
	1991	104.6	92.9	97.0	99.1	99.1

Source: Adapted from Department of Labor, Bureau of Labor Statistics, "Output per Hour, Hourly Compensation and Unit Labor Costs in Manufacturing; Fourteen Countries or Areas" (Washington, D.C.: 1950–1969, 23–31; 1960–1989, 22–30; 1992, 14).

Table 2-17
Decreases in Hours Worked and Increases in Hourly Pay for the Nonagricultural Workforce by Gender, 1979–1992
(Index: 1985 = 100)

	1979	1984	1989	1992
Average weekly hours worked	103.3	100.5	98.6	95.8
Men only	103.9	100.4	98.7	96
Women only	100.8	100.5	98.1	95.2
Average hourly wages	77.4	96.3	116.5	137.6
Men only	77.4	96.3	116.4	137.3
Women only	76.7	95.9	117.1	139.1

Source: Adapted from *Statistisches Jahrbuch 1993* (Statistical yearbook) (Stuttgart: Statistisches Bundesamt, 1993).

Table 2-18

Manufacturing Labor Cost Components for Five Major Industrial Countries, 1988 (% of total labor cost)

	Base Wages	Health, Unempl't, Old Age, & Other Social Insurance (legally mandated)	Social Insurance (not legally mandated)	Training
United States	70.8	7.1	10.9	0.1
Germany (former West)	56.3	16.5	4.3	1.5
Japan	83.8	7.9	4.5	0.4
France	52.2	19.2	8.5	1.7
Great Britain	73.1	7.3	4.2	1.3

Source: Adapted from *Statistisches Jahrbuch für das Ausland, 1993* (Statistical yearbook for foreign countries) (Stuttgart: Statistisches Bundesamt, 1993).

critical position employment relations are seen as occupying in the life of the nation.

By American standards, labor and business in Germany are highly coordinated and centralized. Business is organized along two parallel lines—employer associations and industry associations. (See Exhibit 2-4 for a comparison of the major institutions of employment relations and their primary functions in the United States and Germany.) Both employer associations and industry associations are joined again in national confederations. The national and peak confederation of employer associations, the *Bundesvereinigung der Deutschen Arbeitgeberverbände,* or *BDA,* coordinates policies on national ER issues, while individual industry-specific employer associations bargain with the unions over wages and working conditions.

Table 2-19

Hours Worked, Vacation, Holidays, and Absenteeism in Five Major Industrial Countries, 1993

	United States	Germany	Japan	France	Great Britain
Hours worked	40.0	37.5	42.0	39.0	38.8
Vacation	12	30	11	25	27
Holidays	11	10	14	10	8
Absenteeism*	3.0	9.0	1.7	8.2	6.8

*Percentage of total scheduled hours

Source: Adapted from *New York Times*, 13 February 1994, F5.

Organized labor is centralized in the DGB, which consists of just sixteen industrial unions. Bargaining is conducted at the regional level for each industry, and collective bargaining agreements cover between 80 and 90 percent of the German workers. Historically most large companies have paid wages well above the minima established by contract. Industrial sectors are defined loosely. The metalworking industry, for instance, includes software companies, automakers, and machine tool manufacturers, among others. About two-thirds of Germany's workers are represented by works councils, although many small and medium-sized enterprises do not have them. The councils are not allowed to strike, but as shown in Exhibit 2-4, they do engage in continuous negotiations with management about the implementation of collective bargaining contracts, which are called framework agreements because they only establish the loose parameters within which more detailed agreements are reached by individual employers and councils. This negotiation at the enterprise level (or lower) is called "codetermination at the workplace" because the councils have the right to codetermine certain kinds of decisions with management. The councils have veto power over management decisions concerning basic personnel matters, such as hiring, firing, and overtime, and can appeal to a nationwide system of labor courts

Table 2-20
Social Expenditures for the United States,
Germany, Japan
(1970, 1980, 1986)

	1970	1980	1986
United States			
% GDP	4.4	6.8	7.5
$ per capita	215	803	1,307
Germany (former West)			
% GDP	12.1	18.6	18.5
$ per capita	358	2,280	3,010
Japan			
% GDP	2.9	6.8	8.4
$ per capita	57	692	1,441

Source: Adapted from *Statistisches Jahrbuch für das Ausland, 1993* (Statistical yearbook for foreign countries) (Stuttgart: Statistisches Bundesamt, 1993).

if management evades or undermines them. On a range of other issues, such as changes in how work is organized or how jobs are defined, the councils have the right to be consulted and informed. In practice, they can use their veto power in personnel matters to gain leverage on other issues.

The labor courts were established after World War II solely to adjudicate disputes between labor and management in the two-channel system of employee representation, which indicates the high priority the government placed on smooth and fair labor-management relations, as well as the very public nature of that relationship. The extent to which works councils can and do take full advantage of their formal rights at the enterprise level varies tremendously, as will become clear in chapter 3. Perhaps the most critical variable influencing a council's effectiveness as the independent representative of employees is its relationship with the union. Federal law guarantees all employees one week's training per year, in many cases union-offered training seminars that are available both to councils and to

Exhibit 2-4

Private Sector Labor-Management Relations in the United States
and Germany

	United States		Germany	
	Institution/ Organization	Function	Institution/ Organization	Function
MACRO (economy)	150 craft and industrial unions covering 12 percent of private sector workforce	primarily lobbying for legislation	association of employer associations federation of 16 industrial unions	coordinate policy on all major political and economic issues
MESO (industry)	a few weak industry-wide employer associations (e.g., coal) a few major industrial unions	coordinate bargaining; minimize infighting	industrial unions employer associations	annual collective bargaining framework agreements
MICRO (firm)	many craft and other non-industrial unions companies	periodic collective bargaining over wages, hours, and working conditions	works councils companies unions	ongoing negotiations on firm-specific implementation of agreements codetermination; consulting with works councils

members at large. This provides an important tie between the two institutions. Depending on a variety of factors having to do with the firm in question and the state in which a council sits, the councils (and in some cases noncouncil employees) are usually entitled to attend significantly more training programs than one, which helps to strengthen the ties between councils and unions.

Codetermination at the workplace is paralleled by codetermination at the level of companies' supervisory boards, which oversee the strategies and policies of senior management. Labor representatives on supervisory boards can be members of the union and/or of the works council, or outsiders chosen by either the union or the council or both. As shown in Exhibit 2-3, in the iron, coal, and steel industries, the unions are granted parity codetermination, that is, an equal number of labor and management representatives and a neutral chair. In large firms in other industries, labor receives between one-third and one-half of the seats on the board, and the board's chair is chosen by management. While the supervisory boards are less powerful and less concerned with the day-to-day business of running a firm than American boards of directors, they influence strategies that directly affect the welfare of employees, for instance, the nature and location of future investments. In fact, any managerial decision affecting a large number of employees (usually fifty or more) tends to be negotiated at this level.[6]

None of these institutions and organizations can fulfill its functions in isolation from the others. If it were not for the centralized industrial unions with which they bargain, employer associations would have nothing to do. If the employers were not coordinated centrally for the purposes of collective bargaining, there would be no basis for their national confederation and no clear mandate for the BDA. If the councils did not implement framework agreements to fit the circumstances of individual workplaces, the unions would be far more involved with the specific and minute details of collective bargaining agreements with individual companies or groups of employers, and a single agreement appropriate for both IBM and Daimler-Benz would be inconceivable. If bargaining concerned detailed, minute issues, it would not be possible for the unions to concentrate their resources on developing broad strategies to guide the labor movement according to their distinctive vision of the political economy. Conversely, if the German unions engaged in enterprise-level bargaining, most works councils would be out of a job.

The structure of financial institutions also affects the nature of industrial relations. Most banks are considerably more involved in industry than are American banks and carry out many of the functions that are legally relegated to different kinds of financial institutions in the United States. Many companies still operate with a house bank or group of banks. While close ties between the banks and employers mean that the banks are directly involved in some basic business decisions, they also allow for far-sighted strategies based on three- to five-year (rather than three- to six-month) plans.[7] The stock market plays only a marginal role. Employers' preference for bank funding over share capital from financial markets also reflects a certain risk aversion.

American employment relations are considerably more fragmented and decentralized than German employment relations. The steady and precipitous decline in union membership rates (from about 33 percent of the workforce in the late 1950s to 15 percent in the early 1990s) has increased the insecurity of individual unions as organizations and the union movement as an institution. As shown in Exhibit 2-4, at the national level the employers are organized (for instance, in the National Association of Manufacturers, or NAM, and the Chambers of Commerce) primarily for the purposes of lobbying. They do not usually come together around issues of concern to them *as employers*. At the same time, industry associations are not generally concerned with defining or defending the interests of member firms as employers. This lack of coordination is paralleled by the loose organization of the unions. The American Federation of Labor and Congress of Industrial Organizations (AFL-CIO) has about 150 member unions that range from craft unions representing workers with specific skills to industrial unions representing workers throughout a company and smaller unions representing workers at one or a few companies (see Exhibit 2-5 for the largest AFL-CIO affiliated unions). Even these categories are only roughly accurate because many industrial unions represent workers in a diverse array of industries. Coordinated collective bargaining was common in some industrial sectors during the first several postwar decades, but had significantly diminished by the early 1980s.[8]

Most labor-management relations take place at the enterprise, or microlevel, in the United States. At this level, representatives of the union and management negotiate agreements that dictate the terms and conditions of employment for the two- or three-year life of the contract. During that period of time, the labor-management relationship consists almost exclusively of determining through grievance

Exhibit 2-5

AFL-CIO Affiliated Unions with More Than 400,000 Members, 1991

Teamsters (IBT)	1,379,000
State, County and Municipal Workers (AFSCME)	1,191,000
Food and Commercial Workers (UFCW)	997,000
Service Employees (SEIU)	881,000
Automobile, Aerospace Workers (UAW)	840,000
Electrical Workers (IBEW)	730,000
Teachers (AFT)	573,000
Machinists and Aerospace Workers (IAM)	534,000
Carpenters	494,000
Communication Workers (CWA)	492,000
Steelworkers (USWA)	459,000
Laborers	406,000

Source: Adapted from Bureau of the Census, Economics and Statistics Administration, *U.S. Statistical Abstract, 1993* (Washington, D.C., 1993).

procedures that are laid out in the agreement whether or not the parties are adhering to the contract. When the parties involved in negotiation fail to reach agreement, they usually turn to outside mediators or arbitrators. In most conventional labor-management relationships in the United States, there is no forum for the kind of ongoing negotiations that characterize enterprise-level industrial relations in Germany.

The nature of union membership is also quite different in the two countries. Under the American system of exclusive representation, which was created by the Wagner Act, no more than one union can represent the workers at a single bargaining unit, as defined by the National Labor Relations Board (NLRB), and workers cannot become union members at will. Rather, the employees at a given enterprise or workplace must follow an elaborate set of procedures leading to an election supervised by the NLRB. If the union wins the election by a simple majority, it becomes the exclusive representative of all employees at the workplace, regardless of how they voted. By the same token, if the union loses, employees who wanted to be represented by the union cannot be. This model of unionism is quite unlike those of most other advanced industrial countries, where workers become members of unions as a matter of individual choice. It assumes that the natural state of affairs is for workers *not* to be represented collectively, while labor laws in most other advanced industrial countries—certainly those with mandated works councils—assume the opposite.

Labor's Institutional Security

In the labor-management relationship, the strength of American unions lies in job control: management grants the union detailed control over how jobs are structured and carried out, in return for the unimpeded right to control investment decisions and other strategic managerial prerogatives.[9] Ironically this strength, which was the pivot of dramatic union growth in the 1930s, is now one major source of the labor movement's weakness. Because contemporary production methods entail considerable flexibility in how jobs are defined and carried out, it is precisely the job control aspect of worker representation that American employers most strongly object to. Yet unions that recognize the need for flexibility and forfeit job control give up a major source of bargaining leverage on the faith that new forms of influence through increased labor participation in decisions about work or production organization will be forthcoming and will benefit employees. In the early 1980s when the recession forced many unions to make economic concessions (often in return for more participative labor-management relations), militant unionists argued that union leaders who agreed to such changes had been coopted by management. Since then, the stigma of cooptation has loomed large for all union leaders under pressure to change how they represent members' interests. An increase in the number of companies attempting to get out of collective bargaining contracts and sometimes trying to avoid or break unions altogether only strengthened the cooptation argument in the 1980s. As union representation became harder and harder to achieve over the 1980s, labor's institutional security was further undermined.

Strong unions that engage in innovations around less traditional issues and are able to command high wages and good working conditions are in a better position to be cooperative than weaker unions that have more to lose. However, many of these strong unions have played a more traditional adversarial role in labor-management relations that is increasingly associated with long and bitter strikes. Thus, they are viewed in the public press as obstacles to the competitiveness of American industry. Under these circumstances it is hard for the unions to find reasons to negotiate over the problems and processes of industrial adjustment with employers.

The position of German labor is much more secure. Instead of job control, councils exercise wide discretion in influencing how employees are deployed and moved within a given enterprise—that is, in structuring the internal labor market. Rather than threatening labor's strength, cooperation with management has created possibilities for enhancing employee influence at the point of production. The unions are thus able to define and represent employee interests in a way that maintains, if not strengthens, their national standing and public acceptance. Under these circumstances, it makes sense to negotiate adjustment rather than resist it.[10]

U.S. employers also face uncertainties that do not confront employers in Germany. Partly because contracts are enterprise specific, many U.S. firms see no alternatives to competing on the basis of labor costs. Thus, they pursue competitive strategies that minimize their dependence on human resources rather than enhance employee influence and managerial decision making.[11] Because of the nationally mandated nature of works councils and the broad coverage of collective bargaining agreements in Germany, many of the costs of labor are taken out of competition among domestic companies. This creates incentives for employers to develop high labor-value-added strategies (that is, compete on the basis of the value added to products and services by highly skilled employees), which in turn help to keep German companies competitive on international markets. Because the returns to such strategies usually appear in the medium or long term, the risks can be considerable. Investments in labor, for example, may be drained by employee turnover. For these reasons, among others, only a few employers in the United States have adopted these strategies and many firms that were identified with them have recently been forced to abandon them.[12]

An additional source of insecurity for U.S. employers is the system of financial regulation, which places stockholders in a powerful position and thereby encourages strategies with short-term payoffs. The more stable, long-term relationship between German companies and banks, along with the comparatively minor role of nonbank stockholders, promotes a longer strategic time horizon. High labor costs encourage German employers to make the most efficient use possible of their human resources. This usually translates into ER strategies that place a premium on skills and labor-value-added to production processes.[13] These strategies depend on the negotiation of adjustment processes with the representatives of labor, which reinforces the institutional security of the unions and councils.

How the Government Intervenes

German employers accept government intervention in employment relations because of the special character of that intervention, which is very different from the American idea of government regulation. The involvement of the German government can be characterized as extensive but not intensive. The U.S. government's role is nearer the reverse. In both cases, the nature of intervention is somewhat paradoxical.

On the one hand, for example, the U.S. government remains uninvolved in a range of matters that are regulated by public policy in other advanced industrial countries. It typically does not adjudicate disputes between labor and management at the enterprise level or ensure that employees be able to exercise their rights to collective representation. The NLRB can, for example, require employers to reinstate workers who have been fired because of union activity or insist that both sides bargain in good faith, but its influence on the practices of both unions and companies is limited. Penalties on employers for failing to abide by the law (in union election campaigns, for instance) are negligible. In matters concerning violations of health and safety regulations, the Occupational Health and Safety Administration (OSHA) lacks the resources to inspect sites that may be in violation of the law and tends to impose minor penalties on those who flout it.[14] While most European governments provide and administer basic social benefits like health insurance, the U.S. government does not. Most collective bargaining contracts provide for at least a partial employer payment for health insurance.

On the other hand, when the U.S. government does intervene, its involvement is intensive, detailed, and controlling.[15] For example, under the system of exclusive representation, the NLRB not only runs the union election but also establishes precisely which workers can and cannot be part of the bargaining unit. The detailed side of the government's regulation of industrial relations is also manifested in the Wagner Act's rules concerning the substantive areas over which the parties are (and are not) permitted to bargain and its de facto preclusion of certain kinds of employee participation plans. The intensive nature of labor regulation has become so onerous that firms often go to great lengths to prevent unionization in the first place. Even leaders of the AFL-CIO have argued that labor might do better in an entirely unregulated economy.

If the U.S. government's involvement in ER is intensive, the German government's intervention is extensive, consisting of a loose set of policies and laws that encourage, but do not require, the parties to negotiate adjustment. The state has played a crucial part in promoting the development of infrastructural industries since the late 1800s and early 1900s, and German industry continues to be characterized by a system of "organized finance capitalism" that was initially structured by the state, as reflected in the highly coordinated national-level peak associations. Contemporary legacies include the preference for long-term investment and the presence of the banks on company boards.[16]

As Peter Katzenstein has noted, the German political economy is dotted with "parapublic institutions" that augment the activities of individual actors in the private sector.[17] Parapublic institutions are more than simple interest groups: they are explicitly chartered by the government to perform important public functions. For instance, the chambers of commerce and industry (Deutscher Industrie und Handelstag, or DIHT) are charged with organizing and administering crucial aspects of the apprenticeship training system, even though it is a public sector system. Because they are parapublic institutions, these organizations carry significant obligations to balance the priorities of national economic competitiveness against the need for social peace, but the precise definition of their tasks and how they are to be implemented are more or less left up to the organizations themselves. This unintrusive and indirect form of regulation can be seen in the labor court system (a public institution) in which labor and business each appoint one-third of the judges and the courts' interpretations are widely regarded as fair and just. Thus, the German government's involvement is extensive but not intensive. Framework regulation encourages the parties to negotiate outcomes that are both mutually and socially acceptable, but the substance of labor-management relations is determined by the parties and labor and management autonomy remains sacred.

Innovations in Employment Relations

The Diffusion of Innovations in Germany

The centralization of employment relations, the institutional security of labor, and the framework nature of government intervention in Germany come together to create a set of circumstances that is particularly conducive to the *diffusion* of certain kinds of organizational innovation. The structure of the political economy actively promotes lines of communication and information exchange both vertically (between central bodies and their local representatives) and horizontally (across organizations and institutions). This structure is related to, but not the same as, the relatively centralized nature of labor-management relations. It may be possible to imagine a highly centralized ER system with minimal contact among worker representatives at different enterprises or HR managers in different industrial sectors. In Germany, however, the linkages that tie together the ER system are strongly developed along vertical and horizontal lines. (Chapter 3 examines the concrete nature of these connections.) What makes these linkages—especially the horizontal ones—so important is their impact on the way in which changing forms of HR management are taken up and implemented on a cross-organizational and cross-sectoral basis.

Paradoxically, the institutional constraints that may appear to be anticompetitive from an American standpoint actually help labor and management diffuse particularly competitive HR practices. This is best illustrated through the government-launched Humanization of Work program *(Humanisierung der Arbeit, or HdA),* which was initially designed to address ergonomic improvements in working conditions. In the 1970s under the banner of the HdA program, a number of impressive innovations in employment relations occurred in the form of workplace and collective bargaining agreements that dealt with the introduction of new technologies, the reorganization of work, and the uses of performance-measuring data made possible by the computerization of work. The ways in which unions, works councils, and companies made use of the government program illustrate the close ties among the actors, their security as institutions and organizations, and the organized flexibility of their long-term interactions within the political economic framework.

Under the HdA program, both unions and companies were able to apply for government funding for pilot programs to "humanize" work. In some cases, the unions, works councils, and companies worked together to develop and implement work reorganization plans. In others, either the company alone or (more usually) the union, acting through the works council, would broach the issue unilaterally. While the programs were substantially government funded, some companies and unions also contributed to them. Because the programs were well financed, labor-management relations around the projects involved few distributive struggles,[j] and because the concept of humanization is broad, the parties were free to interpret it in a variety of ways. While some HdA projects focused on ergonomic issues, others tackled the introduction of new technologies, which had become an increasingly important issue, the reorganization of work and production (or service delivery), and training and further training measures.

The unions, led by the IG Metall, saw in the HdA projects a means for conveying a concerted technology strategy. Among other things, they emphasized the improvement of employee skills and wages as part of employers' reorganization of work.[18] Union-inspired experiments at particular companies were transferred by union officials and the works councilors they worked with to other companies. Principles that emerged from these experiments were embodied in regional collective bargaining agreements.[19] Strategies that worked for some unions were adopted by others. Both the development and the diffusion of the HdA experiments hinged on interrelationships among numerous institutions and organizations.[20] Critical connections included those between (a) the government and the unions, councils, and companies that started pilot projects; (b) the IG Metall and other unions that adopted similar technology strategies; (c) the unions and the councils at the various HdA sites; (d) the companies

---

[j]The labor-management relationship in Germany is generally a cooperative one, especially in comparison with the United States, but there can be sharp confrontations. Over the past decade, hostilities have flared up regularly, especially in the metalworking sector over the issue of working time reduction and in the printing industry over issues of technological change.

and employer associations that were involved in negotiations with the unions about the implementation of HdA projects; (e) the works councils at different workplaces within companies where HdA experiments were running or being considered; and, of course, (f) the unions, individual works councils, and companies that implemented the projects. (For more details regarding some of the HdA experiments, see the discussion of the Cologne branch of the Commerzbank in chapter 3 and the section on the VW-IG Metall technology agreement in chapter 4.)

The Development of Innovations in the United States

Almost all of these linkages are weak or entirely missing in the United States. Nonetheless, unions and managements in a wide variety of service and manufacturing industries have developed highly participative and cooperative labor-management innovations. In May 1981, *Business Week* published a cover article entitled "The New Industrial Relations" that heralded a new age of cooperative labor-management relations and increasing levels of employee and union participation in management decision making. Since then a heterogeneous spectrum of impressive cases of labor-management cooperation have resulted in many innovations in how employment relations are structured and carried out at the level of the enterprise. Examples cited in the business press come from the automobile, aerospace, communications, steel and electronics industries, as well as a variety of other sectors. The "new" relationships between the management at NUMMI (the joint General Motors–Toyota venture in California) and the United Auto Workers (UAW), GM's Saturn Corporation and the UAW, AT&T and the Communication Workers of America (CWA), Boeing and the International Association of Machinists and Aerospace Workers (IAM), Xerox and the Amalgamated Clothing and Textile Workers Union (ACTWU), and Bethlehem Steel and the United Steelworkers of America (USWA) are among those most frequently cited. Indeed, some of these cases of ER innovation (or, more specifically, labor-management cooperation) are widely cited abroad as examples of international "best practice."[21] Perhaps the most impressive example is GM's Saturn Corporation. At Saturn, the union was involved in everything from the design of the plant and the car to pricing and distribution policies. At Western Airlines (which was absorbed into Delta Air Lines in 1986) each of the four unions was granted a seat on the company's board of directors, profit sharing, and an Employee Stock Ownership Plan (ESOP) as well as various sorts of workplace-level employee participation in management decision making. Through the Alliance Program, AT&T and the CWA have pioneered far-reaching and long-term training and development innovations.[22]

Clearly the incentive for labor and management to become involved in new IR practices must be powerful. For a U.S. union, innovation usually means the abandonment of at least some aspects of job control in the absence of any guarantee of alternative sources of leverage. Even if this obstacle can be overcome, others emerge. The auto industry illustrates the limits of the "new" industrial relations in the United States. The UAW, which historically has played a leading role in the labor movement, has been more involved than any other U.S. union in the new IR experiments and innovations. UAW concessions helped the Chrysler Corporation out of its deep financial troubles and led to more labor participation in management in the late 1970s. UAW concessions, in exchange for increased labor participation, also helped Ford move from record losses to record profits (and quality levels) in the early 1980s. Moreover, the UAW helped pioneer the Saturn experiment with GM. However, while various locals in the union continue to be immersed in the development and implementation of a range of labor-management innovations, support for a new IR strategy among the union's leaders has waned. Key figures identified with early forays into new forms of labor-management relations have retired, and current leaders (including the president of the union) have fairly traditional views of the labor-management relationship. At present, the central UAW leadership appears more interested in shoring up labor's rights under the Wagner Act than in moving beyond that legal framework. Annual UAW conventions have revealed a broad base of support for the renewal of the more traditional adversarial stance. Even within the union locals closely identified with innovations, there remains skepticism about the basic principles underlying the new industrial relations.[23]

At the same time, employers seem equally skeptical. All three of the big auto companies engage in confrontational, "arm's length" practices alongside their more cooperative, participative experiments, and at the corporate level none has made a commitment to long-term employment security. Within GM, different divisions and managerial factions have different opinions of cooperation with the UAW, just as within the UAW there exist movements both for and against the sort of experiments represented by NUMMI and Saturn.

If there is no consensus within each of these organizations, there certainly is little agreement between them regarding the new IR.

New forms of labor-management relations also remain controversial at higher levels of the labor movement and business community. In the early 1980s, the AFL-CIO established the Committee on the Evolution of Work (CEW, a subcommittee of the executive council) to look into the implications of changes in work and the organization of work and production. The CEW issued a report in 1985 urging unions to experiment with new ways of integrating members' views in local policy making, organizing new members,[24] and presenting themselves in the public media. But the recommendations were vague and did not address the key questions about labor participation in management decision making that underlie the change the committee was to analyze. As a result of the continuing decline in the percentage of workers unionized, the committee was reconvened in the late 1980s, but deep ambivalence over the advisability of a less traditional and adversarial stance toward employers left it unable to reach any consensus.[k]

Currently the Collective Bargaining Forum is the only regular joint consultation arena between labor and business leaders at the national level. Every few months, the forum brings together top business and labor representatives to consider and debate issues of mutual concern, including matters related to the new industrial relations. One of the issues the forum is considering is the way in which some type of works council could be adapted to a U.S. setting, but to date the forum has not been able to publish more than highly general statements about the need for more cooperation and collaboration between business and labor.[25] The larger business community has limited interest in exploring alternative ways of structuring the union-management relationship because unionized companies form only a minority constituency in key central business associations. Collective bargaining at the level of the enterprise plays up the (competitive) conflicts of interest among employers and minimizes their collective interests. Therefore, even with significantly higher rates of unionization, the cost of labor would remain a competitive factor

---

[k] See chapter 8. The CEW was reconvened in early 1993 with a view to being able to exert substantive influence on the first Labor Department sympathetic to unions since the late 1970s.

among employers, and national employment relations would remain fragmented.

Like the German case, then, the U.S. ER landscape has a peculiar paradoxical quality. The lack of institutional linkages makes it difficult for parties to institute innovations that run counter to the relationship fostered by the highly competitive domestic market. That is, the existence of a variety of impressive HR innovations at workplaces in a range of industries suggests a particularly innovative private sector, but these innovations tend to remain isolated because of the lack of the sorts of institutional linkages that characterize Germany's social market economy. If the private sector in Germany is particularly adept at spreading HR innovations once they have been proven effective, Americans seem to be especially good at developing them against impressive odds.

Conclusion and Caveat

Four institutional features in Germany combine to create a hospitable environment for a negotiated approach to industrial adjustment: (1) the centralized organization of labor and management and important aspects of labor-management relations; (2) the institutional security of organized labor; (3) the extensive but not intensive nature of government intervention; and (4) the linkages that tie together and transfer information and communications among the various actors in the ER system. Centralization takes many of the costs of labor out of competition, which enables unions and employers to act with a certain amount of restraint. Labor's secure position in the political economy also encourages union moderation. Public sector and parapublic forums in which labor and management negotiate different aspects of employment relations create regular contact around consensual goals between representatives of labor and management from the micro- to the macrolevel of the economy. These features not only promote negotiation over the terms of institutional and organizational change but also facilitate the diffusion of innovations across workplaces, enterprises, and even industries.

The fragmented character of employment relations in the United States, the insecurity of labor, and the detailed, restrictive character of government regulation—especially in the area of labor-management relations—reinforce unilateral tendencies in the business community and create for both employers and unions disincentives to the pursuit of a more negotiated approach. Most employers find it hard to make the cost of labor a low bargaining priority. The government's role in collective bargaining creates huge incentives for many companies to avoid becoming unionized if at all possible. Because exclusive union representation is more or less the only form of independent collective employee representation available to American workers, even employers who want to engage in regular negotiations with some alternative collective body cannot do so. Industrial adjustment, then, is either negotiated within the confines of an outdated and narrowly prescribed set of rules (the Wagner Act) or determined more or less unilaterally by employers. However, employer unilateralism heightens conflicts between the labor movement and the business community, which creates further obstacles to a negotiated approach. In light of these facts, HR, IR, and ER innovations in a variety of industrial sectors are all the more impressive. At the same time, these institutional features explain the limited extent of such innovation and experimentation.

While the success of the negotiated approach to industrial adjustment is unimaginable in the absence of the key institutional features identified above, an exogenous variable also played a critical role. This factor is the steady and continuous nature of change in international markets from the 1950s into the 1980s. Certainly during this time markets changed and companies and industries had to adapt products and processes—in other words, to engage in industrial adjustment to a dynamic environment—but the nature of that change was continuous, whereas today it is discontinuous and less predictable.[26]

The tendency of German companies to base strategies on their products rather than actual and potential markets and to avoid risky investments makes more sense under environmental conditions of continuous and relatively slow change than it does at a time when everything about the environment is increasingly unpredictable. Under current circumstances, the payoffs of slow, steady, long-term strategies are diminishing, and the conspicuous absence of German firms among the international leaders in most high technology industries is increasingly worrisome. Companies that have been associated with the core strengths of the German economy for decades—such as Daimler-Benz and BASF—are now facing losses and casting about for new strategies. Thus, from quality circles to lean production, American and Japanese managerial techniques have developed enormous caché among German business leaders.[27] (For example, both BMW and Mercedes are pursuing Japanese-style nonunion strategies in their new U.S. operations.) In other words, the deterioration of the more stable international production regime of the 1960s, 1970s, and early 1980s is calling into question the continued effectiveness of some of Germany's core institutions. The German penchant for *Technik* and painstaking attention to product detail, which is founded on a solid human resources base of highly skilled, functionally specialized labor, can no longer guarantee success in international markets. Stable, conservative institutions, including the highly specialized apprenticeship training system and the extension of collective bargaining contracts to all companies in a given industry, are increasingly being called into question.

The negotiated pattern of adjustment, then, faces two central challenges. First, can it step up its pace of adjustment? Second, can the nature of negotiation become a topic of negotiation? These issues are taken up in the second half of this book. First, however, it remains to lay out in greater detail the day-to-day practice of negotiation at the level of the workplace, the central role of worker skills and employee training in German employment relations, and the way in which German employers and managers themselves understand the negotiated model of adjustment.

Notes

1. This section is based in part on Andrei Markovits, *The Politics of West German Trade Unions* (New York: Cambridge University Press, 1986); Peter Katzenstein, *Policy and Politics in West Germany: The Growth of a Semisovereign State* (Philadelphia: Temple University Press, 1987); and Susan Stern, *Meet United Germany: Handbook 1991–92* (Frankfurt: Frankfurt Allgemeine Zeitung GmbH Information Services in association with Atlantik Brücke e.V., 1991).

2. True parity representation exists only in the iron, coal, and steel industries (the sectors covered by the first and most comprehensive codetermination law), because in large firms in other industries tie votes are broken by a representative of management. A 1990 amendment to the Works Constitution Act introduced further minor alterations, including the extension of the terms for works councilors from three to four years and a broadening of the rights of high-level management employees in the councils. See Manfred Bobke-von Camen, "Novellierung des Betriebsverfassungsrechts" (Updating the works constitution act), *WSI Mitteilungen* 1 (1989): 16–24.

3. See Collin Randlesome et al., *Business Cultures in Europe* (Oxford: Heinemann Professional Publishing, 1990).

4. See Walther Müller-Jentsch, "From Collective Voice to Co-Management,"

in *Works Councils: Consultation, Representation, and Cooperation in Industrial Relations,* ed. Joel Rogers and Wolfgang Streeck (Chicago: University of Chicago Press, in association with the National Bureau of Economic Research, forthcoming).

5. "A Survey of Germany," *The Economist,* 21 May 1994, 5.

6. For a discussion of the effectiveness of codetermination on the supervisory boards, see Jutta A. Helm, "Codetermination in West Germany: What Difference Has It Made?" *West European Politics* 9, no. 1 (1986): 32–53. See also Audrey Freedman and William Fulmer, "Last Rites for Pattern Bargaining," *Harvard Business Review* 60 (1982): 30–43.

7. See Christopher S. Allen, "Ideas, Institutions, and Capital Investment in the United States and West Germany: The Politics of Banking and Stock Market Regulation" (paper presented at the annual meetings of the American Political Science Association, Washington, D.C., August 1994).

8. See Freedman and Fulmer, "Last Rites for Pattern Bargaining," 30–43.

9. See Harry C. Katz, *Shifting Gears: Changing Labor Relations in the U.S. Automobile Industry* (Cambridge: MIT Press, 1985); Joel Rogers, "Divide and Conquer: The Legal Foundations of Postwar U.S. Labor Policy" (Ph.D. diss., Princeton University, 1984).

10. See Lowell Turner, *Democracy at Work: Changing World Markets and the Future of Labor Unions* (Ithaca: Cornell University Press, 1991); "SOS beim DGB" (SOS at the DGB), *Focus,* 7 June 1993, 120.

11. See Thomas Kochan and Paul Osterman, *The Mutual Gains Enterprise: Setting the Agenda for Workplace Innovation* (Boston: Harvard Business School Press, 1994).

12. David Soskice, "The Institutional Infrastructure for International Competitiveness: A Comparative Analysis of the UK and Germany" (paper presented at the International Economic Association Conference, Venice, Italy, February 1991); Kirsten Wever, Peter Berg, and Thomas Kochan, *Employee Development in the U.S. and Germany: Coordinating Interests in Employment Relations,* Economic Policy Institute Monograph (Washington, D.C., 1995).

13. See also Horst Kern and Michael Schumann, *Das Ende der Arbeitsteilung?* (End of the division of labor?) (Frankfurt: Campus Verlag, 1985).

14. For instance, in 1985, the average manufacturing establishment in the United States paid only thirty-four dollars per violation in OSHA penalties. See David Weil, "Enforcing OSHA: The Role of Labor Unions," *Industrial Relations* 30 (1991): 20–36.

15. The onerous nature of government regulation in the United States is not limited to the realm of labor law. In finance, for instance, the operational principle is one of free markets; yet throughout American history, episodes of market failure have produced substantial government intervention in the financial system. In response to the Great Depression, for instance, the Securities and Exchange Commission was developed to regulate stock transactions and the Glass-Steagall Act was passed to regulate banking activity. Indeed, the Great Depression led to the introduction of the precise, detailed regulation that later generations of free market advocates who decry regulation have attacked. The dominant pattern of financial regulation has been a repeated lurching between extremes, which can be seen during the period of financial deregulation in the 1980s. See Kirsten Wever and Christopher S. Allen, "Financial Systems and Corporate Governance in Germany: Institutions and the Diffusion of Innovations in Comparative Context," *Journal of Public Policy* 13, no. 2 (1993): 183–202.

16. See Andrew Shonfield, *Modern Capitalism* (New York: Harper and Row, 1965); and Alexander Gershenkron, *Bread and Democracy in Germany* (Ithaca: Cornell University Press, 1989).

17. Katzenstein, *Policy and Politics in West Germany.* See also Markovits, *The Politics of West German Trade Unions.*

18. Siegfried Roth and Heribert Kohl, eds., *Perspektive Gruppenarbeit* (Perspectives on group work) (Cologne: Bund Verlag, 1988).

19. Reinhard Bispinck, "Entgelt nach Qualifikation" (Pay for performance), working paper, Wirtschafts- und Sozialwissenschaftszentrum des Deutschen Gewerkschaftsbundes, Düsseldorf, Germany, 1991, 17. Thomas Klebe and Sigfried Roth, "Information Ohne Grenzen—Globaler EDV-Einsatz und neue Machtstrukturen" (Information without borders—global electronic communication and new power structures), in *Information Ohne Grenzen: Computernetze und internationale Arbeitsteilung* (Information without borders: computer networks and the international division of labor), ed. Thomas Klebe and Sigfried Roth (Hamburg: VSA Verlag, 1987); Roth and Kohl, *Perspektive Gruppenarbeit;* and Reinhard Bahnmüller, Reinhard Bispinck, and Werner Schmidt, "Weiterbildung durch Tarifvertrag—am Beispiel der betrieblichen Umsetzung des Lohn- und Gehaltsrahmentarifvertrages I der metallindustrie in Nordwürttemberg/Nordbaden" (Further training through collective bargaining contracts—the example of enterprise-level implementation of the wage framework agreement I of the metalworking industry in North Württemberg/North Baden), *WSI Mitteilungen* 44 (1991): 171–80.

20. Cole develops a related argument about the diffusion of quality circles in Japan, Sweden, and the United States, citing the fragmented American institutional structure and, in particular, the lack of central coordination among employ-

ers as key reasons for the failure of QCs to diffuse widely in the United States. See Robert E. Cole, *Strategies for Learning: Small-Group Activities in American, Japanese, and Swedish Industry* (Berkeley: University of California Press, 1989).

21. See, for instance, Gesamtmetall, *Mensch und Arbeit: Gemeinsame Interessen von mitarbeitern and Unternehmen in einer sich wandelnten Arbeitswelt* (Humans and work: common interests of employees and employers in a changing work world) (Cologne: Gesamtverband der metallindustriellen Arbeitgeberverbände, 1989).

22. On Saturn, see Saul Rubinstein, Michael Bennett, and Thomas Kochan, "The Saturn Partnership: Co-Management and the Reinvention of the Local Union," in *Employee Representation: Alternatives and Future Directions,* ed. Bruce Kaufman and Morris Kleiner (Madison, Wis.: Industrial Relations Research Association, 1993). On Western, see Kirsten Wever, "Toward a Structural Account of Union Participation in Management: The Case of Western Airlines," *Industrial and Labor Relations Review* 42, no. 4 (1989): 600–09. Other cases are discussed in Eileen Applebaum and Rosemary Batt, *The New American Workplace: Transforming Work Systems in the United States* (Ithaca, N.Y.: ILR Press, 1994).

23. See Katz, *Shifting Gears;* Thomas Kochan, Harry Katz, and Robert McKersie, *The Transformation of American Industrial Relations* (New York: Basic Books, 1986); Harry Katz and Charles Sabel, "Industrial Relations and Industrial Adjustment in the Car Industry," *Industrial Relations* 24 (1985): 295–315; Rubinstein, Bennett, and Kochan, "The Saturn Experiment"; and Turner, *Democracy at Work.*

24. See American Federation of Labor and Congress of Industrial Organizations, Committee on the Evolution of Work, "The Changing Situation of Workers and Their Unions" (AFL-CIO, Washington, D.C., 1985).

25. U.S. Department of Labor, Bureau of Labor-Management Cooperative Programs, *Labor-Management Commitment: A Compact for Change,* BLMR 141 (Washington, D.C., 1991).

26. Some have argued that the critical change in markets dates from an earlier point in the 1970s. See Michael Piore and Charles Sabel, *The Second Industrial Divide* (New York: Basic Books, 1984); and Kern and Schumann, *Das Ende der Arbeitsteilung?* There is widespread consensus, however, that the change has to do with the erosion of mass production techniques and associated methods of managing human resources, as discussed in chapter 1. See Iain Campbell, "New Production Concepts? The West German Debates on Restructuring," *Labour and Industry* 2, no. 2 (1989): 247–80.

27. See *Manager Magazin,* 9 September 1993.

chapter three

Organizational Innovation at the Enterprise

how management and labor navigate change at the workplace

How is it that works councils can be effective, independent representatives of employees while also helping ease change processes through negotiated adjustment?[1] What prevents them from becoming the instruments of management, like many of the American company unions of the 1920s?[2] Do joint adjustment processes simply *look* negotiated while in fact being dictated by the employer? Are the councils effective in representing employee interests? This chapter is devoted to the concrete day-to-day processes of change and adjustment at the workplace. American experiences are held up against those of the works councils, managers, and unions involved in the local operations of five companies in Germany: a branch of the Commerzbank (one of Germany's three largest banks), Betrix Cosmetics, a Digital Equipment Corporation software distribution and servicing outlet, one of the major production facilities of Bayer (the pharmaceuticals giant), and the central operations of Henkel, a producer of cleaning, personal care, and other chemical products. The cases were selected to cover a range of industrial sectors and a variety of local private sector labor-management relations.

The German literature on works councils is somewhat skeptical of the councils' independence and effectiveness. Many analysts hold that the councils are overworked and insufficiently prepared to develop effective, proactive (as opposed to reactive) strategies in countering rationalization, technological development, and other associated organizational changes. Analysts have argued that because the effects of contemporary rationalization cannot be projected far into the future (because technology changes so fast), the councils are unable to anticipate personnel changes and develop strategies to deal with these changes. Because the attainment of full-fledged codetermination at the workplace has been one of the chief goals of the German labor movement since the 1970s, most German research has taken this goal as a starting point and has shown how the legal rights of the works councils do not provide sufficient political clout for true codetermination.[3]

The problem with relying on this account for the purposes at hand lies in its basic assumptions. The question of how employee representation affects the *economic* well-being of the enterprise (or the nation) has been of little interest to a research community that assumes the legitimacy of such representation is a political phenomenon that requires no further justification. The criteria this body of writing has established for effective and independent employee representation make little sense in the United States, where workers' political rights to representation at the firm and industry levels remain contested.

The councils described in this chapter are impressive in their independence from management and their effectiveness in defining and representing employee interests, especially in comparison with typical American local unions. In large part because of the way in which they are embedded in the institutional infrastructure of employment relations, these councils are able to support employers' adjustment goals and simultaneously defend the interests of their members. Moreover, the councils are able to contribute to industrial adjustment processes as they are defined by the employers themselves. Through the case studies, the councils' microeconomic contributions as well as their broader social impact will be revealed.[4]

Workplace-level Employment Relations in Germany

Works Council Independence and Effectiveness

The case of Betrix Cosmetics, a cosmetics producer outside of Frankfurt that employs about 1,000 employees, shows how a works council can articulate, communicate to management, and press for employee interests that conflict with the interests of management. Because the cosmetics industry is in the chemical branch, the unionized workers at this plant are represented by the IG Chemie, a union usually associated with an accommodationist stance toward management. However, the council at Betrix, led by a forceful, well-spoken feminist, is proactive and sometimes confrontational.

The company produces a full line of cosmetics, soap, and beauty products. It employs mostly low-skilled, blue-collar women. More than 80 percent of these are members of the IG Chemie, and a minority of the white-collar workers at the company also belong to the union. Relations between the union's central offices and the Betrix council are strained. Central union representatives believe the council chair is too activist and confrontational. Historically, relations between management and the council have been conflictual. The industrial adjustment challenges that Betrix faced led to the introduction of a manufacturing resources planning (MRP) system and the modernization of assembly-line operations involving the filling of containers and the packaging of finished products. These changes were instituted over a five-year period, from 1985 to 1990.

The activism of the council can be seen in its responses to the changes proposed in production and process technology. During interviews, both management and works council representatives agreed that the company was thrown into chaos for several months when the MRP software was introduced. Everyone also agreed that this had to do with the lack of adequate training for employees using the new software. The council demanded considerably more training than management believed necessary, and in the end it pressured management into offering further training and orientation seminars to lower and mid-level managers using the software.

The periodic introduction of adjustments to the filling and packaging assembly lines spurred the council to develop a plan for job rotation and related cross-training. The council chair first began to push for job rotation in the mid-1980s but without success. Management rejected the idea out of hand. However, in March 1990, after the company had been bought by Revlon, the American cosmetics giant, management began to discuss regularly with the council the possibility of linking job rotation with greater work flexibility. This change of heart was the result of the American parent company's threats to move production to other European facilities unless productivity improved by about 50 percent within a year. At the time of this research, jobs were being defined, and employees and management were jointly designing a rotation schedule.

The most striking aspect of the Betrix case is the council's ability to make employee interests heard, given an initially uncooperative management and no union support. By the end of this research, it appeared likely that job rotation would be introduced on the assembly line. The council chair's strategy of relentlessly pressing for better training and less monotonous forms of work organization looked like it might finally pay off.[a]

The case of Digital Equipment Corporation's (DEC) Cologne branch illustrates in a different way the ability of a council to articulate and effectively champion employee interests while building a base of political support for itself and the union. At the time of this research, the Cologne branch of DEC employed about 500 people engaged in developing, selling, and servicing software and hardware. Those employees who are represented by a union belong to the IG Metall. The majority of workers are highly skilled technicians and computer scientists, many with advanced degrees. As the subsidiary of an American company, DEC-Cologne has refused to join the employer association and therefore is not covered by the collective bargaining contract between the IG Metall and the employer association.

Prior to 1986, the union had almost no presence at DEC-Cologne. When an activist (albeit neophyte) works council was elected in that year, however, contacts between the local union administration and the council grew stronger. As part of a strategic push, starting in the 1980s, to gain skilled, white-collar members, the IG Metall appointed representatives throughout the country to work with interested council members at certain firms to learn more about the needs of white-collar employees and to help the councils use their rights and powers at the enterprise level. DEC was one of the targeted companies. At DEC-Cologne, industrial adjustment challenges were related primarily to the continuous, rapid development of new software.

The works council was concerned about the lack of adequate training for employees when new software products were released. The council also raised concerns about the length of the work week and other basic issues, such as the lack of regularized job descriptions or any formalized compensation package or performance appraisal system. The union representative assigned to the council by the Cologne branch of the IG Metall helped the council to codify its de-

---

[a]About a year later, Procter & Gamble, another large American personal-care products company, bought Betrix, and there were plans for further production reorganizations. At the time of this writing, no major changes had been introduced.

mands and make significant strides in the areas of training, compensation, job descriptions, and assessment, as well as other issues. (The union played a similar role at other DEC operations throughout Germany.)

Prior to the 1986 council election, council members had been afraid to identify themselves too closely with the union. At that time only 2 percent of the employees were union members. In the 1990 council elections, the councilors ran on an IG Metall slate and publicized the union's role in helping them to make significant gains over the previous four years. By then, 10 percent of the employees were unionized, and the councilors were reelected handily. In April 1992, the union was able to coordinate a brief "warning strike." This was not formally a strike because the works councils are legally prohibited from striking. Employees picketed the facility between the earliest and latest starting times on the flexible work schedule. Largely as a result of that mobilization, membership in the union jumped to over 20 percent.

In the spring of 1993, the central works council in Munich, where DEC-Germany is headquartered, decided to coordinate a national series of warning strikes to pressure DEC into formally instituting HR policies (such as those won at DEC-Cologne) throughout its German operations. The company's refusal to meet with the council to discuss these issues had led to a further politicization of DEC employees. Union membership had jumped to 50 percent at DEC-Cologne and to 80 percent in some of the company's facilities. Widespread employee dissatisfaction then led the works councils, in cooperation with the IG Metall, to demand a company-specific collective bargaining agreement. After a hugely successful series of "strikes" in May and June of 1993 at DEC facilities across the country, the company agreed to conclude a collective bargaining contract with the union. Union officials described the contract as being better than the industry contract in virtually every regard.[b]

The councils' willingness to learn and apply the union's political tactics allowed the union to project its influence in an industry in which it is only weakly represented and whose employees' needs and

---

[b] In 1994, DEC-Germany reorganized its operations and claimed that the contract was null and void under the company's new structure. At the time of this writing, the European works council for DEC was developing plans to pressure DEC's U.S. headquarters into reversing its reorganization.

interests it is still learning to define. Within the space of half a decade, the Cologne council was able to transform itself from an ineffectual and unskilled collection of individuals into a popular and politically astute collective body. The local and central councils' strategy of using the union's resources to force the company to develop HRM procedures has enhanced their overall stature, popularity, and capacities.

A somewhat different strategy was pursued by the works council of the central Cologne branch of Commerzbank, one of Germany's three largest banks. This branch employs 640 people in a variety of white-collar professional, technical, and clerical jobs. About 60 percent of the employees are women, most of whom hold low-skilled positions. About 33 percent of the bank's workers are unionized. The headquarters of the HBV, the main service union in Germany, has a technology department that advises works councils about technological changes and their personnel implications and helps them to develop strategies for meeting these challenges. The council for the Cologne branch of the Commerzbank needed the union's services in the mid-1980s when the bank began to introduce a new computer system that was to be accompanied by an increasingly sharp division of labor between front and back office personnel. (Similar technological changes were being introduced at other branches of the bank.)

Before the new system was introduced, customer service representatives did some of the data entry involved in processing account transactions, and data entry personnel sometimes covered for customer service personnel. With the introduction of the new system, the bank planned to separate out and rationalize all data entry work. The council, fearing that jobs would be redefined to require lower skill levels, went to the union for help. Together with the HBV's technology department, the council held a series of working sessions in which employees developed an alternative plan for reorganizing work. The sessions involved works council representatives from various sub-branches of the Cologne office who met for several months to develop their alternative strategy. (This was one of the HdA projects discussed in chapter 2.) The plan included cross-training and increased skills for the low-skilled data entry workers. The idea was to increase the number of employees able to perform all the tasks required by a given customer rather than separate the tasks into higher and lower skill levels. Knowing that management would only consider the plan if it made economic sense, the council took care to show how its plan would increase productivity and customer satisfaction.

Ultimately the central works council in Frankfurt, where the bank is headquartered, decided the plan required too much leverage on the part of local works councils to be effectively implemented at most branches. According to the central council's technology specialist, the council of the Cologne branch was unusually skilled at negotiating with management and making full use of its rights under the Works Constitution Act. Thus, the Cologne plan was not implemented, and the agreement that management finally reached with the central council was less impressive and fairly conservative, guaranteeing only that there would be no job loss as a result of the new system.

This case illustrates not only some of the strengths but also one of the generic weaknesses of works councils. The Cologne council was unable to realize its strategy because the Commerzbank's rationalization scheme was highly centralized. Nonetheless, the case shows how a council can anticipate organizational change and act effectively to make the interests of its members known to management. While the central council's technology representative believed that the Cologne council would have been more successful in reaching its goals if it had been able to act alone at the local level, he noted that without the council's strategy as a bargaining chip, the agreement he was able to attain in the end would have been less favorable.

How Managers See the Councils and Their Contributions

What about the council's ability to add value to production and service-delivery processes? Although there is no evidence in the DEC case that management perceived the council as adding value, the picture is not as clear in the Commerzbank case. There, while the council claimed it could prove that its scheme for reorganizing work would have brought increases in productivity and the quality of service delivery, managers neither confirmed nor denied this contention.

In the Betrix case, the council's claim that it could contribute to the company's overall productivity if its job rotation scheme were implemented would appear to have been accepted but not necessarily acknowledged by management. After all, as soon as management was pressured to raise productivity, it began to take job rotation seriously. While the managers interviewed at Betrix did not make this link directly, they did mention other ways in which the council had helped lower costs and improve product quality. One manager told of an employee's suggestion—brought to the attention of management by the council—that hygienic hats be worn in production rooms containing open vats of liquids and that these rooms be vacuumed more frequently to minimize the time required to scoop off debris. Others talked about similar situations in which small practical problems primarily visible to employees were brought to the attention of management, along with appropriate solutions, by the works council.

Managers at Bayer's main facility freely acknowledge that the works councils add value. Bayer, a pharmaceuticals giant, employs about 40,000 people in Germany; more than 10,000 work at its headquarters. The union representing the bulk of the company's employees is the IG Chemie. Over the past ten years, there has been extensive automation and rationalization, which has been accompanied by the need for higher level skills and employee transfers. There have been no lay-offs. Employment in the industry grew steadily until the early 1990s.[5]

The central works council's technology representative at the company's headquarters characterized labor-management relations as friendly. He attributed his own negotiating skills to the union's seminars and consulting services. In a personal interview, a management representative from the central personnel department described the company's relationship with the council as follows:

> We inform the council in a . . . timely fashion regarding all issues concerned with new technology introduction. Two or three times a year we even sit down and discuss broader developmental trends and decide how to work together in the medium and long term to change workplaces and look at what else needs to be done. We work not against, but with, the council and the employees, and that way we reach acceptance [of the new technologies].

A concrete example was offered by another manager who cited a case in which the council objected to a decision to reorganize a group of engineers. The reorganization would have narrowed the employees' skills base and reduced the firm's capacity to deploy these engineers flexibly. Management reversed the decision on the basis of the council's analysis. The manager described this as "one among many" examples of how the council's ideas "can certainly be a positive productivity factor." Speaking of works councils in general, another personnel manager said that the councils' rights to information, consultation, and codetermination led management to think through any organizational change plans that affected employees and to reject proposals that were not beneficial to the enterprise as a whole over the long term. This, he noted during the interview, was one of the features of the German IR system that strengthened overall competitiveness. "Simply stated," he said, "the works councils require of us that we manage well."

Henkel, a primarily family owned and operated producer of various chemical products, offers a somewhat different lesson about how managers perceive works councils. The company has about 13,000 employees of almost every description and skill level at its main operations. Its shares are not traded openly on the stock exchange, and the firm's management is known throughout the region and industry for its benevolent paternalism. The central council's approach to technology is considerably more passive and accepting than the approach of Bayer's main council. The council's technology representative was not very familiar with the new hardware the firm was introducing, and, expressing his faith in what he called a well-intentioned and highly successful management team, he saw no reason for a more proactive stance.

The personnel and technology directors at the company viewed the passivity of the council as a decidedly mixed blessing. Both directors pointed to the advantages of being able to count on the council's acceptance of management initiatives, which was predictable, the personnel director noted, because "most of them [the council members] have been around from time immemorial, and we know them inside out—and for that matter, that's true in the reverse as well." At the same time, both directors saw a trade-off between passive acceptance and the ability to grasp the need for flexibility, rapid response to dynamic markets, and a faster pace of change in the future. "Times are changing, and flexible and quick responses to market changes will become increasingly important," the personnel director said. "A slow council that's not on top of these issues and that's more interested in stable forms of interaction and predictability can become a hindrance. In the future, we might need a more active council that can work with us in anticipating the momentous changes occurring in the international marketplace today."

Works Councils in Context

These five cases show the crucial role unions usually play in helping works councils to develop and implement labor's strategies. The union's central role in the DEC-Cologne case is self-evident. The council's popularity increased during its first term because it was able to get management to improve basic personnel policies, which provided tangible benefits to employees. These successes, however, hinged on the union's ability to teach the council tactics for exploiting its legal rights. The union in turn benefited from the council's ability to translate local successes into increased union membership.

Bayer offers a more subtle example of this symbiosis. The technology representative on the central council at Bayer learned how to deal with management on issues of technological and organizational change from the union. As a member of a regional committee on technology and another on skills development, he also learned from fellow councilors at other firms. In this case, we can see not only the importance of the institutional ties between the local council and the central union but also the importance of the connections among works councilors.

In order to develop its internal labor market and retraining scheme, the works council at the Cologne branch of the Commerzbank needed the help of the union's central technology department (as well as the government's HdA program). Informal local committees of works councilors from different banks in the Cologne area also influenced the council. Like the Betrix council chair, the councilor championing the work reorganization scheme at the Cologne branch claimed to have gained her tactical and organizational skills through attending local committee meetings that dealt with political issues, including women's rights issues. Some of these were coordinated by the union. At the same time, the head of the union's technology department attributed the fact that membership at the Commerzbank was higher than at the other two largest German banks (roughly 33 percent as opposed to about 25 percent) to the visibility the union gained through its work with the Commerzbank's councils nationwide. The union's ties to the councils at other large banks were not as extensive or close.

At Betrix the union intentionally did not become involved in helping the council to develop its local strategies. In fact, union representatives chastised the local council chair for excessive activism. Even so, the council chair claimed her union training in earlier decades—when the IG Chemie was considered more activist—and her involvement in ecology issues and the women's rights movement were indispensable to her ability to articulate members' interests and develop effective strategies for achieving them.

In short, to the extent that these councils did identify and pursue independent interest representation strategies, they were able to do so substantially as a result of their connections to the union movement and various other social movements and institutions.

Lessons from the Five Cases

Exhibit 3-1 will reveal the three themes that emerge from these cases. First, works councils can provide an effective independent voice for employees. They are more than simply reactive institutions; they develop strategies in their efforts to shape local outcomes. The extent to which the councils in these cases were able to achieve the ends they sought varied across cases. Indeed, at Henkel the council appeared to have no strategy at all. But it appears that the councils *can* make strategic choices and vigorously follow through without the help of a union.

Second, as managers themselves acknowledge, works councils can

Exhibit 3-1
Comparing the Five Councils

	I Does the council make effective strategic choices?	II Does the management perceive benefits from the council?	III Is council choice/effectiveness tied to central/other institutions?
Betrix	yes	maybe	some
Commerzbank	yes	no	yes
DEC	yes	no	yes
Bayer	yes	yes	yes
Henkel	no	no	no

act in ways that tangibly benefit local management interests, both short term and long term. Councils can take specific actions that directly enhance the microeconomic performance of firms. Moreover, by their mere existence and by virtue of the rules and regulations defining and underpinning them, councils constrain management decision making in a variety of ways. Although some of these constraints, such as the extra time needed to make decisions that require council consultation or approval, are undoubtedly costly to management, some benefit employers.[6] As the managers at Bayer noted, the councils' information and consultation rights force management to carefully plan and justify any organizational changes.

Third, this indirect process of adding value is made possible by the councils' *embeddedness* in the institutional framework of German industrial relations. There does not appear to be one clear dynamic connecting enterprise-level employee representation and labor-management relations with the broader (national, industrywide, and regional) institutional network that structures German industrial relations. Thus, while these cases support the idea, prominent in the German literature, that works councils cannot strategically shape outcomes or achieve full codetermination at the workplace simply on the basis of their legal rights, they also show there is more to representing employee interests than legal rights. For a council to carry out its job effectively, it must be able to capitalize on cognitive resources such as the capacity to plan, strategize, and anticipate. To do this, the council must be able to draw on external resources, particularly the union. Representatives of the HBV claim that close relations with their councils provide by far the largest source of new members. The DEC case also shows how the union can gain members, and even a collective bargaining contract with a company that does not belong to the employer association, through its link to the council.

The employers' views of the works councils also must be understood in the context that shapes their strategies and actions. Because bargaining occurs at the industry level through employer associations, individual companies need not worry about some costs as competitive factors. This allows employers to focus on the potential gains to be achieved through cooperation with works councils on issues not directly regulated by collective bargaining. Consequently, some of the managers interviewed thought the councils enhance productivity, quality, and ultimately, profits. While DEC attempted to pursue a more unilateral strategy and refused to join the employer association, thus incurring the ire of the union and ultimately the council, that strategy appeared to be problematic. With the help of the union, the council was able to extract most of the gains that it would have received through the industry contract. Given the successes the council has had when it has followed the activist and somewhat confrontational path laid out for it by the union, it seems improbable that management would be able to elicit the council's full cooperation even if it chose to change its stance. This case is certainly no argument for a unilateral, maverick approach to labor-management relations in Germany.

Local Adjustments in the United States

Successful ER Innovations

A quick perusal of the American business press in the late 1980s and early 1990s will reveal the growing American interest in new, more cooperative labor-management relations that can enhance the competitiveness of American firms and industries. The range of companies engaging in innovations is so broad that the country as a whole can be characterized as the international leader in ER innovations. No one doubts the capacity of these labor-management innovations to add value to management adjustment processes.[7] If managers did not believe that participative ways of structuring employment relations at the point of production would ultimately enhance profits, they would not pursue this path. Nonetheless, as will become clear in the discussion that follows, both labor and management in the United States are profoundly skeptical of departures from traditional strategies. Much of this skepticism can be traced to various features of the ER context within which the parties operate.

To date, the team production approach, which has its roots in the Scandinavian sociotechnical job design experiments of the 1970s, represents the most widely successful model of ER innovations available in the United States. It can be found in the auto, steel, electronics, and telecommunications industries, among others. Unlike the lean production approach, which has gained international renown through the publication of *The Machine That Changed the World,* team production explicitly engages workers in management decision making and thus frequently involves union participation in efforts to reorganize work and production.[8] Two well-known cases illustrate the impressive range of activities encompassed by the team approach.

At the high-performance plants of Xerox and Corning (where

the Amalgamated Clothing and Textile Workers Union and the American Flint Glass Workers Union, respectively, represent the employees), joint union-management innovations are characterized by independent and effective representation of the workers' interests and a clear contribution to the company's bottom line. In both cases, production is organized around teams in which employees on the line are involved in helping to determine the structure of their jobs.

At one of Corning's high-performance plants, teams are fully autonomous; team members cross-train and rotate through a variety of jobs. Members communicate directly with managers and workers in other departments, including engineering, human resources, and marketing. In a manner similar to that required by the German Works Constitution Act, the company regularly shares information with its employees about the economic situation of the plant. Teams are involved in hiring new team members, and through their work in defining tasks, they influence their own compensation, which is based on skills. Roughly 15 percent of workers' time on the job is devoted to ongoing training. The effects on the company's bottom line have been impressive, although "total quality management," introduced in 1982, did not really take hold until the union became involved and negotiated a shared vision of the program's design and implementation.[9] The company reports that its high-performance plants have reduced scrap levels by almost one-half and increased productivity levels by almost one-third. Returns on investment have also increased significantly.

Some of Xerox's operations have been equally impressive. The union has been involved in the design and implementation of high-performance operations from the start. At Xerox's Webster, New York, facility, the basic work unit involves managers and workers from different levels of the company hierarchy and different functional areas. Labor-management "decision rings" address plantwide operational problems as they arise. Engineering functions have been pushed downward in the organization. The mechanism for internal company training is extensive and has involved employee development in a variety of problem-solving techniques, quality practices, and methods of presenting material at meetings, among other things. The joint labor-management decision-making structure reaches to the top of the organization. The highest level of worker participation occurs in two committees, the executive and policy committee and the joint planning committee; at the plant level, the plant advisory committees include shop-floor workers as well as managers and union leaders. Extensive long-term research at Xerox has found significant evidence of the productivity and quality benefits associated with the joint participation mechanisms.[10]

Internal Contradictions in Successful ER Innovations

As impressive as these experiments may be, many of them are characterized by odd internal contradictions that have to do with how they are situated in the U.S. ER system as a whole. Lines of conflict run between labor and management, between local plant or workplace management and central or corporate management, and between local and national unions. These continuing tensions can be best illustrated by what is perhaps the most famous labor-management innovation in the United States—the Saturn Corporation of GM.

GM involved the UAW in the earliest stages of Saturn's plant and auto design.[c] Because the plant was treated as a separate corporation within GM, it was somewhat isolated from the more conflictual labor-management relations at other GM plants until late 1994. Any changes in production or work require consensus decision making, which in turn requires union participation. This provides the union with an unusual and powerful source of leverage. Moreover, because employees forfeit their seniority within the GM system when they join Saturn, they have a particularly strong interest in the survival and economic success of their division. Since 20 percent of their pay is contingent on Saturn's economic success, they also have a strong stake in the profitability of the company. This translates into an interest in broad and continuous training because Saturn production is based on semiautonomous teamwork. In the 1991 collective bargaining contract, the UAW local was able to institutionalize a fairly substantial measure of training. The minimum training for all employees and managers is 5 percent of annual working hours. The 1993 contract links the contingent portion of employees' (including managers') pay to ongoing training—that is, all employees (labor and management) suffer financially if a certain amount of training is not undertaken.

Various developments at Saturn illustrate the tensions among and between local and central labor and management. It was because the local union was uncertain of management's commitment to extensive training—even though that training lies at the core of the

---

[c]The Saturn experiment is described further in the next chapter.

experiment—that the UAW insisted on tying training to pay, including the pay of management. Other persistent tensions have to do with the introduction of a third crew of workers. The local union is in favor of a third crew. Demand for the car is high, and workers have had to work significant overtime hours. Management is not as anxious to introduce a third crew as it would involve a series of costs that the company would prefer to defer at the moment.[11]

There are continuing tensions between the local and national union. A 1993 strike at GM's Lordstown facility left Saturn without parts and threatened to interrupt production. This was at a time when demand for the car was high, and workers were already putting in significant overtime. Saturn's local union leader was understandably unhappy with the effect of the Lordstown strike, which in fact may have targeted Saturn as a means of gaining leverage over GM, thus laying bare an inevitable conflict of interest between local and national union leaders. Given GM's layoff of about 74,000 workers over a three-year period in the early 1990s, the overall relationship between GM and the UAW is strained, and it is impossible to isolate Saturn completely from these conflicts.

Union ambivalence about Saturn has also emerged around the question of how extensive union participation in management decision making should be. One of the defining aspects of the Saturn experiment is that managerial decisions from the shop floor to the level of plant management are reached by consensus with 50 percent input from labor. Early in 1993 an internal union referendum revealed that over one-fourth of Saturn's employees were dissatisfied with the process by which the union counterparts of mid-level managers are chosen. Twenty-nine percent of the workers wanted these representatives to be elected exclusively by the union membership rather than jointly selected by the union and management. The joint appointment of the people in these positions, however, is Saturn's distinguishing feature: labor and management run the operation based on negotiation and consensus. Moreover, if the union's representatives in these positions were not jointly selected, GM would probably stop permitting the union to participate in the selection of the nonunion counterparts in these positions.

Conflicts between Saturn's management and GM's headquarters have also arisen from time to time. In late 1992, GM gained a new senior management team. After a series of major shake-ups in GM's corporate management, the company announced it would bring the Saturn Corporation back into the GM fold in 1993. By linking Saturn's fate more closely with that of GM's more traditional plants, senior management raised the possibility of a return to traditional business-as-usual practices. Managers at Saturn were able to prevail on GM's corporate headquarters to reverse its position and leave Saturn's independent status intact. But more recent developments once again threaten to undermine Saturn's independent status. In October 1994, the head of General Motors' North American operations, G. Richard Wagoner, announced the company's decision to place Saturn in a new small car group. GM's rationale is that in order to cut costs, Saturn must share engineering and manufacturing processes and economies of scale with other GM small cars. The absorption of Saturn into the mainstream of GM is strongly favored by the union's top negotiator with the company, Stephen Yokich, who is on record as opposing the expansion of Saturn's operations while other GM plants are scheduled to close.

Not surprisingly, Saturn management, dealers, and union leaders are unhappy with GM's decision. Michael Bennett, the local UAW president, laments the waning commitment to "the Saturn process," [12] and dealers believe that selling other products under the Saturn label could conflict with Saturn's independent mission. Saturn's president, Skip LeFauve, has clearly been denied the possibility of increasing Saturn's output, which he has strongly urged on GM's corporate leadership, and will have to settle for running the small car group that has yet to be created.

Saturn's engineering, production, and work processes are fundamentally different from processes at most of GM's plants. Therefore, it is hard to imagine how much of the innovations developed at Saturn can be sustained as GM proceeds with its consolidation plans. The continued ambivalence of management (especially at the corporate level) inevitably fuels the continued ambivalence of the union (especially the national union), and vice versa. There is no way to secure the roles and functions of either party at the local level because the institutions of employment relations foster an entirely different mode of labor-management relations. Saturn illustrates the complexity of the challenges facing American unions interested in a new form of industrial relations.

Similar problems have defeated or severely curtailed numerous other labor-management experiments with new forms of work and production organization. Extensive employee involvement at Eastern Air Lines fell to pieces when the company announced plans for large pay cuts in the mid-1980s without consulting its union counterparts.

At Western Airlines, programs for labor participation in management (including profit sharing, 33 percent employee stock ownership, four union seats on the company's board of directors, and employee participation programs for ground personnel) were disbanded when the carrier was bought by Delta Air Lines (a mostly nonunion carrier). A joint training fund established by the Machinists Union and Boeing languished unused for years as a result of both parties' uncertain commitment to joint forms of labor-management relations.

Many of these problems could be addressed more easily, or would not even arise, in a different ER environment. It would not be possible for an acquiring company in Germany to disband unilaterally extensive mechanisms for employee participation in management decision making, as occurred at Western Airlines. No German automaker would announce an important decision like the admittedly short-lived decision of GM's new management to end Saturn's status as a separate corporation without prior consultation with the union and the works council. Such a matter would have been raised with the supervisory board, which is made up of employees as well as managers. The national UAW's ambivalence about participation in the Saturn project appears very American from a German union's standpoint. The operative question in Germany is not *whether* but *how* to engage in participative management. The principle itself has become widely accepted because experience has shown that organized labor can profit from participative management.

Conclusion: Negotiation versus Unilateralism at the Local Level

It is not simply the subjective preferences of labor and management that determine their pursuit of unilateral or negotiated adjustment measures and the success of their efforts. If it were, the Saturn experiment would not appear to be rather tenuous still, after a decade of operation and other cases of labor-management innovation would not have failed or slid into obscurity. Indeed, based on subjective preferences alone, there might not be effective works councils at companies like Betrix Cosmetics, DEC-Cologne, or the Commerzbank, where managers at best follow the letter of the law with regard to engaging works councils in negotiations over the processes of organizational change.

This chapter has offered a highly stylized outline of how enterprise-level ER innovations develop in Germany and the United

States, and it has provided examples of the linkages (or lack thereof) between and across various ER organizations and institutions. The cases presented here have shown how, and to some extent why, German and American labor and management pursue particular avenues in their dealings with each other. In Germany, labor and management have learned to use the institutional framework within which they operate. Unions, which initially opposed separate enterprise-level works councils, have learned how to make themselves indispensable to the councils and thus guide the councils' approach to management. Employers, who initially opposed enterprise-level works councils with extensive formal rights, have learned to use the councils to engender employee acceptance of organizational changes that managers have had to justify to the councils. The councils themselves have learned to use their legally guaranteed leverage in some personnel-related areas to influence other issues over which they have limited formal leverage.

It is clear that the extent to which labor and management in Germany can successfully pursue non-negotiative strategies is limited. Of course, they can refuse to negotiate as DEC did, but there the consequences were not auspicious. The Betrix case showed how economic circumstances may force employers who prefer not to negotiate to do so. On the other hand, companies and unions in the United States that prefer to negotiate can find it difficult to do so within the fragmented and decentralized institutional context of employment relations. The best intentions of the parties at Saturn have not been enough to dispel deep-seated mistrust and ambivalence on both sides at higher levels.

Notes

1. Parts of this chapter are based on Kirsten Wever, "Learning from Works Councils: Five Unspectacular Cases from Germany," *Industrial Relations* 33 (1994): 467–81.

2. See Sanford Jacoby and Anil Verma, "Enterprise Unions in the United States," *Industrial Relations* 31 (1992): 137–58.

3. See Birgit Mahnkopf, "Training, Further Training and Collective Bargaining in the Federal Republic of Germany" (Wissenschaftszentrum, Berlin, 1990); Hans-Willi Hohn, *von der Einheitsgewerkschaft zum Betriebssyndikalismus* (From unitary unions to enterprise syndicalism) (Berlin: Edition Sigma, 1989); Hermann Kotthoff, *Betriebsräte und betriebliche Herrschaft: eine Typologie von Par-*

tizipations mustern im Industriebetrieb (Works councils and enterprise rule: A typology of participation patterns at the enterprise) (Frankfurt: Campus Verlag,
1981); Klaus Bartölke et al., *Neue Technologien und betriebliche Mitbestimmung*
(New technologies and enterprise-level codetermination) (Opladen: Westdeutscher
Verlag, 1991); Reinhard Hoffmann, "Erweiterung der innerbetrieblichen Mitbestimmung durch Arbeitsgruppen" (Broadening enterprise-level codetermination
through work groups), *Gewerkschaftliche Monatshefte*, no. 12 (1968): 719–26;
Hans Matthöfer, "Die Bedeutung der Mitbestimmung am Arbeitsplatz und im
Betrieb für die Bildungsarbeit der Gewerkschaften" (The meaning of codetermination at the workplace for the training work of the unions), *Die Neue Gesellschaft*
15, no. 1 (1968): 37–46.

4. See also Richard Freeman and Edward P. Lazear, "An Economic Analysis
of Works Councils" (Department of Economics, Harvard University and Graduate
School of Business, University of Chicago, May 1992).

5. In the mid-1990s, some of Germany's large chemical concerns began considering substantial layoffs for the first time in postwar history.

6. Sorge and Streeck explain this virtuous relationship at the level of the
political economy, showing how the German IR system forces employers to follow
high wage/skill/labor-value-added competitive strategies. See Arndt Sorge and
Wolfgang Streeck, "Industrial Relations and Technical Change: The Case for an
Extended Perspective," in *New Technology and Industrial Relations,* ed. Richard
Hyman and Wolfgang Streeck (London: Basil Blackwell, 1988). The present analysis reveals the concrete manifestation of this dynamic in a variety of different
workplace settings.

7. Thomas Kochan, Harry Katz, and Robert McKersie, *The Transformation
of American Industrial Relations* (New York: Basic Books, 1986); Eileen
Applebaum and Rosemary Batt, *The New American Workplace: Transforming Work
Systems in the United States* (Ithaca, N.Y.: ILR Press, 1994); Larry Mishel and
Paula Voos, eds., *Unions and Economic Competitiveness,* (New York: M. E. Sharpe,
1992); and Alan S. Blinder, ed., *Paying for Productivity: A Look at the Evidence*
(Washington D.C.: The Brookings Institution, 1990).

8. See James P. Womack, Daniel T. Jones, and Daniel Roos, *The Machine
That Changed The World: The Story of Lean Production* (New York: Macmillan,
1990). For a comprehensive survey of team and lean production experiments in
the United States and a discussion of the origins of both kinds of ER innovation,
see Applebaum and Batt, *The New American Workplace.*

9. See Applebaum and Batt, *The New American Workplace,* 143.

10. See also Joel Cutcher-Gershenfeld, "The Impact on Economic Performance of a Transformation in Workplace Relations," *Industrial and Labor Relations Review* 44, no. 2 (1991): 241–60.

11. Many of these observations are based on field work in progress by Saul Rubinstein, Sloan School of Management, Massachusetts Institute of Technology. See also Saul Rubinstein, "Rethinking Labor and Management: Saturn and the UAW; The Governance and Supervision of High Performance Team Based Work Systems" (Ph.D. diss., Massachusetts Institute of Technology, forthcoming); and Saul Rubinstein, Michael Bennett, and Thomas Kochan, "The Saturn Partnership: Co-Management and the Reinvention of the Local Union," in *Employee Representation: Alternatives and Future Directions,* ed. Bruce Kaufman and Morris Kleiner (Madison, Wis.: Industrial Relations Research Association, 1993).

12. Quoted in *The Wall Street Journal,* 5 October 1994, 4.

chapter four

Industrial Adjustment and
Skills Development

how employee training processes and outcomes
reflect and influence adjustment strategies

Advanced industrial countries cannot maintain or improve the competitiveness of their firms, and thus the standard of living, by competing with low-wage producers in developing countries. To do well
in the international economy, companies and industries must compete on the basis of some comparative advantage. Typically, this is
advanced technology and/or the quality of their human resources.
Using either of these sources effectively requires access to the other,
but usually one of these resources of competitive advantage is emphasized over the other. For example, German firms have developed
and profited from what is perhaps the best-trained workforce in the
world, especially in the manufacturing industries; on the other hand,
American companies have pioneered in high technology. At this
point, Germany would do well to expend more resources on high
technology sectors, and the United States would do well to expend
more resources on training. The German economy is strikingly weak
in a number of young growth sectors (for example, biotechnology,
supercomputers), while the American workforce is underskilled and
undereducated.

The German vocational education system, which is the most ad-
mired in the world, rests on the sorts of institutional linkages described and analyzed in the first three chapters. The American education system produces the most highly innovative and creative college
and university graduates in the world. But private sector experiments
with continuous further training and ways to deliver training to
workers suggest tenacious problems in these areas. Solving these
problems will be increasingly important to the well-being of the
economy, not only in manufacturing but also in the services.

For this reason, it is important to understand how new skills are passed on to employees in the United States and Germany and how the contexts within which companies and employee representatives operate influence their HR strategies. What are the institutions involved in training? To what extent do employers in the United States and Germany engage in initial (vocational) training and further training? These questions raise two prominent and interrelated problems with company training in the United States. The first is the sparsity of supraenterprise institutions that are capable of coordinating, standardizing, and/or delivering further training. The second is the widespread lack of formal employee voice in decisions about what training is delivered, how it is carried out, and who receives it.[1]

The Extent and Nature of Training in the United States and Germany

Vocational Education

American vocational education is more school-based than company-based. Each state establishes curriculum requirements and occupational standards and enforces those standards. Because there is no standardized national curriculum or certification process for secondary vocational education, the content and quality of vocational education varies tremendously across the states. At the microlevel, vocational training tends to focus on specific skills that are tailored to the needs of individual local firms. Performing well in a high-school vocational education program is not associated with any advantage in the labor market. Post-secondary vocational education also offers little in the form of higher-paying jobs or occupational status. Therefore, it is not surprising that the number of students enrolled in post-secondary vocational training has decreased steadily since 1982.[2]

American companies and unions are not usually formally involved in the school-based portion of vocational training. Although labor and management representatives are involved in establishing standards and training content of apprenticeships on an industry or firm basis, current industrial apprenticeship programs cover a very small and declining proportion of new entrants into the labor force. Only 3 percent of a given cohort of students leaving school in the United States take an apprenticeship, while 66 to 75 percent do so in Germany.[3] In any case, U.S. apprenticeships tend to provide training in a narrow, rather traditional set of skills that reinforces an obsolete division of labor.

U.S. vocational training, then, reflects the way in which employee representation is viewed. The leverage unions have over employees comes through job control—the detailed ordering of job classifications attached to wage scales and seniority rules. In the event of an economic downturn, workers with the lowest seniority may be laid off, while workers with higher seniority are retained. Job control is an effective defense against arbitrary hiring, firing, or transferring, but it can impede the development of flexible internal labor markets in which workers can be reassigned to other parts of the operation when needed. Job control can be (though it is not always) incompatible with the sorts of broad, general skills associated with high-performance work systems.[a]

In Germany, on the other hand, vocational education is quantitatively the most important feature of the educational infrastructure. Between two-thirds and three-quarters of all German workers receive two to three years of vocational training. Each student involved in vocational training spends three to four days a week on the job and one to two days a week in the classroom.[4] Apprenticeships are available for hairdressers, bank tellers, metal workers, health-care workers, laboratory technicians, photographers, and more than 400 other professions. Thus, the quality of the German workforce at entry level is higher than the quality of the workforce in the United States. German apprentices must pass an examination on completion of their training in order to receive a certificate indicating that they have met national standards for their particular occupation.[5] The standards are established by national tripartite boards that consist of representatives from labor unions, employer associations, and the economics ministry of the government. Local parapublic chambers of industry and commerce (in which membership is compulsory) and craft chambers ensure the standards are implemented. These chambers are responsible for determining the suitability of firms for providing training, monitoring the training contracts of member companies, advising

---

[a]Unions and managements in the auto, aerospace, and airline industries, among others, have come up with ways of combining the seniority principle with internal labor market principles that allow for a more flexible deployment and redeployment of workers than is typically associated with traditional IR practices.

management on how to improve training, arbitrating conflicts between apprentices and employers, administering final competency exams, and supporting external training centers and consortia for small and medium-sized firms.[6] Most apprentices receive jobs in the companies in which they have trained.[7]

Unlike apprentices in the United States, German apprentices enjoy clear advantages in the labor market. The system is defined and administered jointly by labor and management. Employers and the chambers of commerce and industry carry out most of the tasks involved in training apprentices. Employees' needs are voiced not only through works councils at the enterprise level but also through labor representatives in the chambers. Thus, an apprentice's knowledge base is explicitly tied to the needs of the local employer and to the employee's needs for broadly applicable skills.

Further Training

The lack of American national data makes it difficult to compare the extent and nature of further training in Germany and the United States. A 1989 survey by the Society for Human Resource Management does provide a few insights into the further training practices of U.S. firms.[8] Managerial and supervisory training appear to be the highest priorities of the member firms the society surveyed. Sales and technical/professional training were ranked first and second in importance. The types of training offered by the largest percentage of firms were line supervisory and management skills, communication skills, and computer literacy skills. Most of the companies surveyed claimed to have increased their training activities over the last five years. A quarter of the firms surveyed provided remedial training in basic writing, math, and reading skills. This development parallels growing public concerns over the quality of basic education. There is no way to know if there has been a real increase at the national level in further training. Thus, there is no way of determining whether or not further training is concentrated in remedial skills or higher level skills that are compatible with or responding to the requirements of high-performance work systems.

In Germany, most firms are engaged in some type of further training, and the extent of involvement increases with the size of the firm. National surveys indicate that firm expenditures on further training have increased over the last decade. Employers have cited the introduction of new technologies as one of the most important reasons for engaging in further training, indicating their emphasis on competitiveness through human resources. Overall, German companies put less emphasis on management training than American companies do.[9]

Clearly the data leave many things unexplained. For instance, what are the mechanisms in the United States and Germany underlying the initiation of further training? How do the relationships among the parties involved affect the way in which training is viewed, designed, and implemented?

The Institutionalization of Employer and Employee Interests

Employer Interests

The fragmentation of business interests in the United States makes it risky for employers to offer further training in more general problem-solving skills—the kinds of competencies that are required for extensive teamwork, cross-functional cooperation, and those other aspects of work that are associated with high levels of trust, employee commitment, productivity, and quality. The problem is that such broad skills can be of use to other employers, and employers with these skills can be poached by free riders.[10] Thus, lacking any mechanism for removing the costs of training from competition, most employers tend to deliver narrow, firm-specific skills. Although most companies could benefit from HR investments in broad problem-solving skills, they cannot afford to invest in them because training needs are determined and implemented unilaterally.[11]

The free-rider problem can be avoided in Germany because centralized employer associations and chambers of commerce and industry help to ensure the standardization of skills across companies. Employer groups and think tanks generate volumes of research and case studies on the costs of and justifications for further training.[12] At the industry level, labor-management committees help to articulate supraenterprise interests. To reduce training costs for small and medium-sized firms, chambers of industry and commerce support regional training centers for further training. As membership in these chambers is compulsory, the costs of financing these centers are equalized across enterprises. Thus, all these institutions encourage and sustain collective employer policies and strategies.

Employee Voice

If it is hard for U.S. companies to develop joint labor-management training strategies, the same can be said for the unions. Jurisdictional conflicts between craft unions, and even between noncraft unions competing to represent the same bargaining units, dampen the extent of cooperation between unions. Although the unions tend to favor an increase in the quantity of training, they lack a coherent vision of the type of skills that should be developed in the American workforce as a whole. Partly as a result of their limited resources, American unions have not generated much research on the kinds of skills employers are likely to need in the future. Without this, it is difficult for the unions to anticipate future skills needs and to take actions to ensure these needs are met in accordance with members' interests.

Organizational and institutional insecurity only compounds the problem. Currently only about 12 percent of the private sector workforce is unionized. The remaining 88 percent of the private sector workforce has no representation at all and is not covered by any collective bargaining contract. (In Germany, 80 to 90 percent of the workforce is covered by collective bargaining contracts because companies are either members of an employer association and thus signatories to an industry contract or covered by the contract by political fiat.) This low level of unionization can be traced in part to the American model of employee representation, under which it does not make sense for workers to become members of unions that are not their exclusive bargaining representatives.[13] At the same time, most U.S. unions derive their legitimacy from the local representation of employees' economic interests through collective bargaining. Thus, many of them lack the time and resources to focus on broader, long-term proactive strategies.[14] Strategic shifts are politically risky for many of them, which explains the difficulty of developing strategies that trade off local job control for greater participation in management decisions that affect employees' long-term interests in training and development.

In Germany, the unions develop and deliver training for works councilors at union headquarters, special training centers, and regional offices. Part of this training consists of teaching works councilors how to think about and negotiate with management about further training. The DGB (the union confederation) and some individual unions run consulting centers to provide assistance to works councils dealing with the introduction of new technology. Research institutes that are attached to or closely associated with the unions provide a steady stream of research and scholarship to help guide unions and councils in their efforts to define employees' training-related interests and implement them in workplace agreements.[15]

The ability of unions and works councils to pursue further employee training so actively hinges on their security as organizations and institutions. Union membership is steady at about 40 percent of the working population, which means that German unions are not as pressed to expend significant resources on direct recruiting of new members as American unions are. Furthermore, because membership is voluntary and requires no special election, it is easier for German unions to recruit new members than it is for American unions. The notion that an employer might try to do away with or bypass the union altogether is seen as odd in Germany. The works councils' institutional security is based on their legally mandated status.

This security enables labor to concentrate on defining and advocating long-term employee interests. Thus, German unions began to promote active works council involvement in the area of skills development and the structuring of internal labor markets in the 1970s.[16] This action was accompanied by a shift in the unions' rhetoric that signaled a transition from "quantitative" to "qualitative" collective bargaining goals, with skills considerations and influence over internal labor markets at the top of the list of issues to be targeted. Employee involvement in training is defined on the basis of labor's broad socioeconomic interests, while the concrete implementation of enterprise-level technological, organizational, work-process, and skills changes is tailored to the immediate requirements and resources of the local parties.

Examples from the United States

Saturn

Some American unions and companies have developed impressive experimental training and further training programs. The programs of General Motors' Saturn Corporation were developed as a part of an innovative experiment that changes the very nature of the employment relationship.[17]

Saturn's governance structure was intended to make the union a "full partner." The corporate culture was explicitly based on consensus decision making and the sharing of authority through joint union-management groups. Departing radically from past practice, GM invited the UAW to participate in the corporation's design. Joint union-management committees, operating under consensus guidelines, determined site selection, choice of technologies, supplier selection, retail dealer selection, pricing, business plans, training, budgeting, quality systems, job design, product development, recruitment and hiring, organizational structure, and engineering and process design. In its first two years of production, Saturn achieved higher consumer ratings in initial vehicle quality, satisfaction after one year of ownership, and service than any other domestic car line. In the mid-1990s employment was over 7,000 and included 5,300 UAW members, relocated from 136 GM locations in thirty-four states.

One of the defining features of the Saturn experiment is its heavy reliance on the skills of its employees. Over 600 self-directed work teams, called work units, of six to fifteen members are Saturn's basic building blocks. The members of each team are cross-trained to do all of the jobs within the team's jurisdiction, and members rotate through the jobs based on a schedule they themselves determine. There are only two job classifications: operating technician and maintenance technician. This contrasts sharply with the extensive classifications found in traditional GM plants. The members of all production teams are operating technicians; maintenance technicians are the members of skilled trades teams. Teams manage their own budgeting, quality control, housekeeping, safety and health, maintenance, material and inventory control, training, job assignments, repairs, scrap control, vacation approvals, absenteeism, supplies, record-keeping, work planning, and scheduling. They also do their own selection and hiring from a recruiting pool that consists of active and laid-off GM/UAW employees. Seniority is not the basis for selection.

The training of all team members is extensive when compared to training in more traditional plants. New employees receive up to 700 hours of training before they start building cars. The training includes team management and participation skills as well as the technical aspects of auto production. Therefore, work-team organization, problem solving, decision making, conflict resolution, labor history, budgeting, business planning and scheduling, cost analysis, manufacturing methods, ergonomics, industrial engineering, job design, accounting, record-keeping, statistical process control, design of experiments, and data analysis are all part of the training. Saturn's commitment to training was reinforced in 1991 contract negotiations, when the union proposed tying training to the contingent portion of pay. All Saturn employees, both union and management, have an annual training goal of 5 percent (92 hours) of the annual work schedule. A portion of compensation is at risk if the goal for all employees is not met. In 1992 the portion was 5 percent. By 1995 it was 20 percent.

Clearly Saturn entails labor participation in management decision making—especially decisions concerning workers' skills—at a level that is virtually unparalleled inside or outside the auto industry. Nevertheless, the national UAW remains somewhat ambivalent about the Saturn experiment, partly because it must represent the interests of auto workers at Saturn, at other GM plants, and throughout the auto industry. The union's interests in these three arenas are often different and sometimes conflicting. For instance, while the national union increased its level of participation in the area of further training throughout the 1980s, it has not pressured automobile companies for the types of institutional arrangements that exist at Saturn. If union participation in the training process is to lead to training in broad, general skills, it must be supported by work structures that make greater use of these types of skills, a pay system that links greater skill acquisition to higher income,[b] and a job security system that is not tied to narrow job definitions. These are all defining features of the Saturn experiment. However, because job control is the union's primary source of strength, that approach continues to dominate in many plants and provides little incentive for local unions to pursue extensive participation in training matters.[c]

The Petrochemicals Industry

For every success story, there are many examples of joint training efforts that were never properly undertaken, stalled once under way,

---

[b] "Pay for knowledge" schemes do exist in the automobile industry, but they are usually in specific areas of a plant and have not replaced the traditional system of job classification and seniority.

[c] American unions' attachment to the seniority principle, combined with the policy of employment-at-will, also has negative consequences for training policies. The current employment guarantee covering union workers in the auto industry does not apply during periods of declining demand. It therefore encourages layoffs as a means of demand adjustment, which discourages investment in general skills. Even plants that are taking steps to involve labor representatives more deeply in the training process will find it difficult to generate the broad, general skills necessary to adapt to new market demands without changes in other areas of the employment system.

failed to be fully implemented, or slowly slid into obscurity. The perverse effects of the fragmented institutional infrastructure of employment relations in the United States are nowhere more clearly illustrated than in the petrochemicals industry. The use of contract workers to perform maintenance, renovation, and other specialized tasks has become a major source of controversy in this industry.[18] Frequent, often fatal, accidents have been linked to the inadequate training of these workers. Yet because of the way employee and employer interests are structured, labor and management continue to eye each other with the mistrust that has become a defining feature of American industrial relations. Following a major explosion in 1989, in which twenty-three workers were killed, the Occupational Safety and Health Administration (OSHA) commissioned a report examining the role of contract construction workers and the training they received. The study uncovered two common problems: a lack of trust in the labor-management relationship and a lack of institutions at the micro- and mesolevels, either inside or outside the firm, that can provide the impetus for changes that would benefit both labor and management.

In the past decade, plant owners have allocated an increasing amount of work to outside contractors and a decreasing amount to regular employees, even though contract employees are less educated, younger, and have higher turnover rates and shorter tenure in the industry and with their employers than company employees. For managers, contract workers are less expensive than company employees. If contractors are responsible for such managerial functions as training, employers may not be liable for workers' compensation premiums in the event of accidents.[19] Although the contract workers were performing some of the more risky work in the facilities studied, according to the report, they received significantly less safety training than plant employees. Furthermore, their training was less effective in reducing the probability of injury than that provided regular employees. Because the fastest growing sector of the contract workforce is nonunion, traditional union apprenticeships are also less common among contract workers.

Management has tended to reject union leaders' claims that HR strategies are increasing the risk of fatal accidents. In fact, most managers openly endorse the decline of unionization. At the same time, unions have done little to develop their own initiatives to improve safety and health. In short, the inadequacies of training and their implications for the risk of accidents are the result of a cycle of deteriorating labor-management relations in the industry.

The OSHA study concluded that there were ways to address these problems. The creation of regional training and certification programs, cosponsored and managed by the contractors, owners, and labor representatives active in the construction and the petrochemicals industries, is one possible solution. However, it seems unlikely that the cooperation required to do this will emerge any time soon in this industry. A second possibility is a government requirement for the creation of labor-management safety and health committees as well as communication programs that include representatives of the contract workers on site. But this too would require substantial cooperation. A third possibility involves workers exposed to comparable risks receiving comparable training. For this to occur, OSHA would need to work with industry and labor representatives to develop and implement reasonable training standards, and to date the government has been unwilling to undertake such an initiative. It would appear that a solution to the training problem in this industry will require institutionalized negotiations among the parties at the micro- and mesolevels.

The low level of trust between labor and management in this industry can again be traced to the broader structure and nature of employee representation and corporate governance. The fact that nonunion contract workers play such a critical role in the industry reflects the low level of unionization among American workers generally. This lack of unionization also accounts for the relatively small percentage of workers who have had formal apprenticeships. Those workers who are union members belong to several different (mostly craft) unions, which do not often cooperate closely with one another. The construction unions tend to favor an adversarial rather than cooperative style of labor-management relations, in part because of the rapid increase in nonunion construction during the 1980s. Similar fragmentation exists on the employer side, as the question of which employer has accident liability indicates. In short, the petrochemicals industry is characterized by a typically American lack of institutionalized channels of enterprise- or industry-level negotiations and cooperation and the prevalence of competitive and adversarial relations not only between labor and management but also within each camp.

Examples from Germany

The Volkswagen Technology Agreement

The key differences between further training experiments in the United States and Germany have less to do with the content of the experiments than with the processes by which they come into being, are sustained, and change over time. These processes have a lot to do with how employee voice is institutionalized.

The strength of the dual system of employee representation[d] in Germany must be understood in the context of the overall sociopolitical standing of the labor movement. The unions' widespread legitimacy is accepted as a matter of course. While questions may be raised about how they represent their members' interests, there is no serious question about employees' and society's need for unions. Thus, German unions are able to seize the initiative in defining the relationship between further training, new technology, and the organization of work, and successful further training experiments can be diffused fairly easily across companies and even industries. Moreover, while the works council is embedded in German law, most German employer association representatives and managers also see it as, in the words of the personnel manager at Bayer, a "positive productivity factor." Against this backdrop, unions and councils can focus on their respective strengths and bolster each others' strategies and capacities.

In the 1987 technology agreement between VW and the IG Metall, which is particularly powerful and activist in its definition of members' interests (a rare enterprise-specific contract), labor seized the initiative in defining the issue of further training and setting the agenda for how to address it.[e] The contract was one of the first collective bargaining agreements to address the issue explicitly, and

---

[d]The term "dual system" is used to refer to the system of employee representation, which involves unions and works councils, as well as to the system of vocational training and education, which involves schools outside the workplace and private sector companies.

[e]VW is a relatively rare case because the company is covered by a company-specific contract rather than the industry metalworking agreement. The union has tried to make sure that the terms of the VW agreements are in line with and/or better than those elsewhere in the industry and usually is successful in this regard. Company-specific contracts and provisions have become more popular among employers in the 1990s and are discussed at greater length in chapters 6 and 7.

this case is especially impressive because of the union's and the works council's efforts to define training needs independently of management's technology-driven requirements. The agreement came about as the result of the HdA project that the VW works council and the IG Metall initiated with the backing of the Research Institute for Employee Development. The project was financed in part by VW's central personnel office and in part by a federal grant to the IG Metall. The thrust of the union's strategy was to involve the employees in decisions about how rationalization would take place, how new technologies would be introduced, and how consequent changes in skills and qualifications would be dealt with. Under the terms of the agreement, the works council would receive information about changes in production and work organization before the changes were introduced and therefore could develop alternative plans and/ or bargain over the terms of change. As a result, the council at VW's Kassel works developed a training package that delivered a broad understanding of the new technological systems and how they fit into the overall production system at VW. Specific technical skills were dealt with only after a course of general training. While management at first resisted the broad side of the training package, over time it has dropped its objections to it.[20]

The NW/NB Metalworking Agreement

Because the IG Metall represents employees at companies throughout the metalworking industries, it has been able to carry the principles underlying the innovations at VW to other enterprises. The union's ambitious 1988 Nord Württemberg/Nord Baden collective bargaining contract with Gesamtmetall significantly aided the diffusion of new ways of organizing training. The contract, which was spearheaded by one of the most activist and forward-thinking offices of the IG Metall, is to "make possible the deployment of human resources in multiple areas, as well as furthering the maintenance and broadening of employees' existing qualifications."[21] Together with two parallel contracts for neighboring regions the agreement covered almost one million workers. Because of the success of many of the IG Metall's innovations, experiments in further training spilled over into other regions and industries.[22]

DEC-Cologne

The case of DEC-Cologne, discussed in chapter 3, illustrates how unions can influence further employee training without the cooperation of the employer. At DEC-Cologne, the symbiotic nature of the dual system's central union-local council relationship was crucial to success. Although the Cologne branch is not a member of the employers' association and is not bound by the regional metalworking collective bargaining contract, the works council, concerned about the lack of adequate training when new software products were released and other basic HR issues, was able to codify its demands and make significant strides in the areas of training, compensation, job descriptions and assessment, working time, and other issues, with the help of the union. On its own, the works council might have had trouble finding out what training standards were normal for its industry. But the union was able to provide this information and help the council develop strategies for pressuring DEC's management to enhance its employee training and other HR measures. The effectiveness of this strategy at DEC-Cologne was partly due to the fact that the central IG Metall also had representatives working closely with other DEC branches. The horizontal and vertical linkages between the labor representatives at DEC and in the industry more broadly were pivotal in this case.

The HBV's Technology Strategy

Taking advantage of the availability of government funds for HdA pilot projects, HBV used its ability to act as a consultant to the works councils to develop a training strategy similar to that of the IG Metall. As a part of the project, HBV's technology department head helped the local works council at the Cologne branch of the Commerzbank develop a work reorganization plan that included further training innovations. (See chapter 3 for a discussion of the reorganization plan.) The plan, developed as an alternative to the bank's plans for increasing the division of labor with the introduction of a new computer system, would have broadened the skills required of front *and* back room employees. Although the plan was not implemented, a compromise plan did focus on buffering the impact of the new technology on employees and guaranteed no job loss as a result of the introduction of the new computer system. Thus, workers were protected from the possible negative repercussions of the bank's original plan for reorganizing work and skills.[f]

---

[f] As noted in chapter 3, this case illustrates the limits to local labor maneuverability in the face of centralized corporate decision making. The central works council

As in the case of DEC-Cologne, the union's role at the Cologne branch of the Commerzbank was pivotal. Without HBV's technology department, the works council would not have been able to conceptualize an economically realistic alternative to the bank's plan. It was the union that helped coordinate the weekly planning sessions among works councilors from sub-branches in the Cologne area at which the employees' alternative plan was developed. Frequent communication between the Cologne works council and the bank's central works council in Frankfurt also played a role in helping the local council and HBV shape their strategy.

Conclusion: Institutions and the Incentive to Train

Certainly labor and management in the United States are capable of developing highly successful work and production reorganization experiments that entail extensive, productivity-enhancing training, but these experiments are far from widespread. Because there is no way to centralize or coordinate training expenditures above the microlevel, U.S. employers underinvest in training for fear of losing employees to competing firms. This is especially problematic for small and medium-sized American firms, which engage in less employee training than large companies in the first place. Employment-at-will in the United States reduces the loyalty of employees to their firms and increases the chances that they may shift to another employer. As a result, American firms, unlike German firms, invest disproportionately in managers rather than lower-level professional, technical, clerical, and skilled blue-collar employees. U.S. employers also tend to favor fairly narrow, often firm-specific skills. While this limits the poaching problem, it curtails the adoption of flexible manufacturing processes. Because there are many mechanisms for centralizing and coordinating training in Germany, there are fewer firm-specific skills to begin with, and poaching is less of a problem. In the United States, the lack of a mesolevel forum for employer consultation and collaboration on industrywide technology and HR strategies exacerbates the bias against investment in broad general training and thus flexible manufacturing processes. Since collective bargaining

---

was not in a position to push through the Cologne council's fairly aggressive training strategy because councils at the bank's other locations would not have had the resources to implement it.

with unions only affects a fraction of the companies in most industries, and since it is carried out at the level of the enterprise rather than the industry, collective employer action *seems* to be unwarranted.

Because American unions cover a small and declining portion of the workforce, they cannot compensate for the employers' inadequate provision of ongoing training for the incumbent workforce. Moreover, the unions' continued lack of institutional security supports allegiance to the principles of job control. Unlike their German counterparts, American unions are institutionally encouraged to focus on the local, short-term economic interests of their members. This reinforces the tendency toward training in narrow skills that do not necessarily enhance the careers of their members in particular or the productivity of the nation's human resources over the long term. The way in which employee voice is institutionalized, together with the minimal extent to which it is institutionalized, explains why American unions are seldom able to initiate changes in employee skills or the organization of production and work, to diffuse experiments with such changes within or across companies (or industries), or to turn the issues of work organization and skills into vehicles for strengthening their positions *vis-à-vis* employers. The dual system of worker representation in Germany supports the development and implementation of broader visions of skills and work organization in the unions and to some extent in the councils. For this reason, organized labor in Germany offers employers both incentives to negotiate and a great deal to negotiate about.

Notes

1. This chapter is based in part on Kirsten Wever, Peter Berg, and Thomas Kochan, *Employee Development in the U.S. and Germany: Coordinating Interests in Employment Relations,* Economic Policy Institute Monograph (Washington, D.C.: 1994).

2. See Stephen J. Hamilton, *Apprenticeship for Adulthood* (New York: Free Press, 1990); John Bishop, "The Productivity Consequences of What Is Learned in High School," working paper #88-18, Center for Advanced Human Resource Studies, Cornell University, Ithaca, N.Y., 1988; and Thomas Kochan and Paul Osterman, "Human Resource Development and Utilization: Is There Too Little in the U.S.?" working paper, Sloan School of Management, Massachusetts Institute of Technology, Cambridge, Mass., 1990.

3. See Lisa Lynch, "The Private Sector and Skill Formation in the United States: A Survey," working paper 3125-90-BPS, Sloan School of Management, Massachusetts Institute of Technology, Cambridge, Mass., 1990; and Walther Müller-Jentsch, "From Collective Voice to Co-Management," in *Works Councils: Consultation, Representation, and Cooperation in Industrial Relations,* ed. Joel Rogers and Wolfgang Streeck (Chicago: University of Chicago Press in association with the National Bureau of Economic Research, forthcoming).

4. Müller-Jentsch, "From Collective Voice to Co-Management," places the percentage at about three-fourths; the more commonly estimated figure is two-thirds.

5. For an excellent survey of the history of the "dual system" of apprenticeship training and its reforms, see Karlwilhelm Stratmann and Manfred Schlößer, *Das Duale System der Berufsbildung: Eine historische Analyse seiner Reformdebatten* (The dual system of occupational training: A historical analysis of reform debates) (Frankfurt: Verlag Gesellschaft zur Förderung arbeitsorientierter Forschung und Bildung, 1990).

6. For a comprehensive explanation of the apprenticeship training system, see Wolfgang Streeck et al., "The Role of the Social Partners in Vocational Training and Further Training in the Federal Republic of Germany," IIM working paper, Wissenschaftszentrum, Berlin, 1987.

7. The reader is referred to Dietmar Harhoff and Thomas Kane, "Financing Apprenticeship Training—Evidence from Germany," NBER discussion paper no. 4557 (National Bureau of Economic Research, Cambridge, Mass., 1993). The authors analyze the postapprenticeship movement of workers across firms and conclude that some companies subsidize others in this process. A certain small but steady percentage of workers may leave the company they trained with to work elsewhere for an average wage premium of about 9 percent. However, the authors also explain why the German system makes it economically worthwhile to train even in the face of this poaching problem. In any case, the poaching problem is considerably more significant in the United States.

8. Society for Human Resource Management, "1989 Training/Retraining Survey" (Alexandria, Va., Society for Human Resource Management, 1990).

9. See Institut der Deutschen Wirtschaft, *Finanzierung der Weiterbildung* (Financing further training) (Cologne: Deutscher Institutsverlag, 1990); Bundesministerium für Bildung und Wissenschaft, Martin Baethge, et al., "Betriebliche Weiterbildung: Forschungsstand und Forschungsperspektiven Aus Sicht von Arbeitnehmern" (Enterprise-level further training: State of the research and research

perspectives from the perspective of employees), in *BMBW Studien* (Bonn, 1990); and Reinhard Bahnmüller, Reinhard Bispinck, and Werner Schmidt, "Weiterbildung durch Tarifvertrag—Am Beispiel der betrieblichen Umsetzung des Lohn- und Gehaltsrahmentarifvertrages I der metallindustrie in Nordwürttemberg/Nordbaden" (Further training through collective bargaining contracts—The example of enterprise-level implementation of the wage framework agreement I of the metal-working industry in North Württemberg/North Baden), *WSI Mitteilungen* 44 (1991): 171–80.

10. For a discussion of the free-rider problem, see Gary Becker, *Human Capital* (New York: National Bureau of Economic Research, 1965).

11. Leonard Schlesinger and James Heskett, "The Service-Driven Service Company," *Harvard Business Review* 69 (1991): 71–81; John Sweeny and Karen Nussbaum, *Solutions for the New Work Force: Policies for a New Social Contract* (Washington: Seven Locks Press, 1989); William B. Johnston and Arnold E. Packer, *Workforce 2000: Work and Workers for the 21st Century* (Indianapolis: Hudson Institute, 1987); and Paul Osterman, "How Common Is Workplace Transformation and Who Adopts It?" *Industrial and Labor Relations Review* 47, no. 2 (1994): 173–88.

12. See Uwe Göbel and Winfried Schlaffke, eds., *Die Zukunftsformel: Technik—Qualifikation—Kreativität* (The formula for the future: Technology—skills—creativity) (Cologne: Deutscher Institutsverlag, 1987); Günter Siehlmann, ed., *Weiterbildung im zwischenbetrieblichen Verbund* (Further training in cross-employer consortia) (Cologne: Deutscher Institutsverlag, 1988); Institut der Deutscher Wirtschaft, *Finanzierung der Weiterbildung;* Reinhold Weiß, *Die 26-Mrd.-Investition—Kosten und Strukturen betrieblicher Weiterbildung* (The 26 billion DM investment—Costs and structures of enterprise-level further training) (Cologne: Deutscher Institutsverlag, 1990); Boy-Jürgen Andresen, Gernold Frank, and Ulrich Jürgens, *Zukunftsorientierte Personalentwicklung: Neue Produktionskonzepte und formen der Mitarbeiterqualifizierung* (Future-oriented personnel development: New production concepts and forms of employee training), IW Beiträge 158 (Cologne: Deutscher Institutsverlag, 1990); Werner Faix et al., *Der Mitarbeiter in der Fabrik der Zukunft: Qualifikation und Weiterbildung* (The employee in the factory of the future: Qualification and further training), IW Beiträge 143 (Cologne: Deutscher Institutsverlag, 1989); and Bundesverband der Deutschen Industrie, Bundesvereinigung der Deutschen Arbeitgeberverbände, Institut der Deutschen Wirtschaft, *Hochschule 2000: Wirtschaft und Wissenschaft im Dialog* (Polytechnics 2000: economy and sciences in dialogue) (Cologne: Deutscher Institutsverlag, 1990).

13. See also Roy Adams, "Union Certification as an Instrument of Labor Policy: A Comparative Perspective," in *Restoring the Promise of American Labor Law*, ed. Sheldon Friedman et al. (Ithaca, N.Y.: ILR Press, 1994), 260–72.

14. Selig Perlman characterized American unions as "business unions" that pursued a "bread and butter" (or economistic) agenda unlike many of their European counterparts that agitated for deep social reforms. See Selig Perlman, *A Theory of the Labor Movement* (New York: Kelley, 1928).

15. Helmut Rose, "Zur Ökologie der Arbeit: 10 Jahre Bilanz: Innovations- und Technologie beratungsstelle der *IG Metall* Hamburg" (On the ecology of work: A ten-year inventory of the innovation and technology consulting center of the Hamburg IG Metall) (Institut für Soziologische Forschung, Munich, October 1989). See also Bahnmüller, Bispinck, and Schmidt, "Weiterbildung durch Tarifvertrag"; Klaus Heimann and Eva Kuda, eds., *Handbuch Berufliche Bildung: ein praktischer Ratgeber* (Handbook on occupational training: A practical primer) (Cologne: Bund Verlag, 1989); Reino von Neumann-Cosel and Rudi Rupp, eds., *Handbuch für den Wirtschaftsausschuß: ein praktischer Ratgeber* (Handbook for the economic subcommittee of the works council: A practical primer) (Cologne: Bund Verlag, 1988); Heinz Dachrodt, *Unternehmensführung und Betriebsrat* (Enterprise management and the works council) (Cologne: Bund Verlag, 1988).

16. Michael Lacher et al., *Die Fort- und Weiterbildung von Montagearbeiter/innen* (The training and further training of assembly workers) (Recklinghausen: Forschungsinstitut für Arbeitsbildung, 1987); and Gerhard Kakalick, "Qualifizierungsprogramm für Produktionsarbeiter im Zusammenhang mit der Einführung neuer Technologien im Volkswagenwerk Kassel" (Training program for production workers in connection with the introduction of new technologies at the VW Kassel Works) (paper presented at Neue Technologien, Lernen und Berufliche Weiterbildung, Universität Bremen, Bremen, Germany, February 1989).

17. This discussion is based on research conducted by Saul Rubinstein, and reported on in Kirsten Wever, Rosemary Batt, and Saul Rubinstein, "Workers' Participation in Work Organization in the United States," Report for the International Labour Organization (Geneva: International Labour Organization, 1993).

18. John C. Wells, Thomas A. Kochan, and Michael Smith, "Managing Workplace Safety and Health: The Case of Contract Labor in the U.S. Petrochemical Industry," monograph (South Park, Tex.: John Gray Institute, Lamar University System, 1991).

19. Ibid., 9–10.

20. See Kakalick, "Qualifizierungsprogramm für Produktionsarbeiter"; Lacher, *Die Fort- und Weiterbildung von Montagearbeiter/innen;* and "Weiterbildung durch Tarifvertrag."

21. Reinhard Bispinck, "Entgelt nach Qualifikation" (Pay for performance), working paper, Wirtschafts- und Sozialwissenschaftszentrum des Deutschen Gewerkschaftsbundes, Düsseldorf, 1991, p. 17.

22. Bahnmüller, Bispinck, and Schmidt, "Weiterbildung durch Tarifvertrag"; and Thomas Klebe and Sigfried Roth, "Information Ohne Grenzen—Globaler EDV-Einsatz und neue Machtstrukturen" (Information without borders—global electronic communication and new power structures), in *Information Ohne Grenzen: Computernetze und internationale Arbeitsteilung,* ed. Thomas Klebe and Sigfried Roth (Hamburg: VSA Verlag, 1987).

chapter five

Negotiation versus Unilateralism

why german managers like
collective employee representation

Because private sector companies are in business to make money, and collective employee representatives are in the business of trying to get as large a share as possible of that money, there is, of course, a basic conflict of interest between employers and employees. No matter how "social" the market economy, then, an American might expect that German employers would prefer not to have to deal with collective employee representatives.[1] While German employers in the immediate postwar period fiercely resisted works councils, their resistance had less to do with the councils' role as enterprise-level employee representatives than with the fear that the councils would simply become the political instruments of the unions.[2]

However, the differences between the political economic structures of the social market economy of Germany and the free-market economy of the United States are reflected in, among other things, a different set of managerial preferences. To understand how these differences in managerial preferences affect employers, we need to know what German managers think of their ER institutions. Is their world view consistent with the institutional logic laid out in the first four chapters of this book? What sort of variation exists in the viewpoints of different managers and employer association representatives in different industries?[3] How do the day-to-day mechanics of employee representation affect the implementation of technological change and associated changes in the organization of production, work, and skills? How do the approaches and beliefs of managers in German-owned and American-owned companies differ? What are the advantages and disadvantages of the policies and corporate cultural factors that are specific to German- and American-owned companies? Finally, what are the trade-offs between the negotiated approach and the unilateral approach? How do managers themselves perceive the German ER system in relation to the U.S. system?

The Value of Works Councils

Five Themes

Representatives of employer association and German managers at all levels in a wide array of large and medium-sized companies are strikingly unanimous as to what they like about their system of worker representation.[a] The same five themes were volunteered again and again throughout the interviews: (1) the relative merits of working with works councils versus unions; (2) the ability of the works councils to ease the conflict of interest between employers and employees; (3) the benefits of negotiating with strong bargaining partners; (4) the advantages of the German system of industrial relations over the American system; and (5) the contributions works councils can make under contemporary economic pressures. There was a remarkable amount of overlap in the basic substance of their comments. No one I talked with even implicitly contradicted any of the remarks falling into these five categories. Comments not specifically related to the five themes were consistent with and in general supported or implied them. Interviewees did not differ substantially across industrial sectors or levels of the organizational hierarchy.[4]

Works councils versus unions. All the German managers interviewed agreed that it was easier to deal with works councils than with unions. The councils, the managers thought, were more pragmatic and less ideological than the unions and could ease organiza-

---

[a] These interviews were conducted with supervisors, mid-level, and top managers at six large companies (over 2,000 employees) in the cosmetics, computer software, electronics, pharmaceuticals, chemical detergents, and banking industries, as well as with representatives of the employer associations for these industries and representatives of the BDA, the central federation of employer associations. Both personnel managers and managers from other parts of the organizations were asked how employee representation at the workplace level affects industrial adjustment at the level of the enterprise (see Appendix 1). The loose interview format allowed those interviewed a great deal of latitude in deciding what to discuss.

tional adjustment processes by convincing employees to accept necessary changes, particularly changes in technology.

> On a day-to-day basis, the councils play an important role in the implementation of technology and training. They know the needs of the company and are closer to the problems of the employees and how jobs actually get done than managers are. For that reason, it wouldn't be such a good idea for managers to work entirely without the councils. But the main point is that because of this connection to the work, it's better to deal with the works council than the union.
> *(Employer Association Representative, Printing Industry)*

> We can say that this [give and take between management and the council] happens more pragmatically than ideologically, because it's practitioners who are sitting there, who understand the effects of technology in practice in the day-to-day workplace. So it's important that it be the councils and managers who are involved in these daily negotiations, and not the unions and employer associations, which . . . naturally have to engage in the representation of ideological interests.
> *(Public Relations Manager, Bayer)*

These comments reflect the way in which the dual system insulates the enterprise from political negotiations, including negotiations over wages, which are then institutionalized in regional and industrywide collective bargaining. Through their comments, managers and employer representatives show how the dual system plays up the confluence of interests between the parties at the workplace, while giving expression to the inherent conflict of interest between labor and management through collective bargaining.

How councils ease conflicts of interest.

> If the goal is working together, then [the system] works . . . [W]ithout unions, and in the last twenty years without works councils, the economic situation in Germany would not be as good as it is. . . . If there were no works council [institution], then there would have to be other instruments that could resolve . . . problems to the satisfaction of both sides.
> *(Plant Manager, Bayer)*

When [management] cannot know the woman on the line . . . in the interest of a good workplace climate of relations . . . the employees need interest representation that can serve as a conduit [and that] can also from time to time competently tell management where to get off. My personal experience . . . with [our council chair] is that [often my solutions to problems] were changed when she was consulted so that both sides could endorse the solution.

(Acting Chief Operating Officer, Betrix Cosmetics)

Other comments along these lines contained specific praise for the councils' ability to mediate and ease tension between employer and employee interests. None of the interviewees, even those who described their relations with the works council as confrontational or conflictual, saw the institution of the works council as exacerbating these basic tensions or leaving them unaffected.

The benefit of strong negotiating partners. All the comments on this point favored dealing with strong negotiating partners.

A strong works council is always good, can implement what it wants to, and can also defend itself against the union. We always say . . . that we need strong unions and strong works councils. We have relative industrial peace only because everyone in the system is strong. As soon as one party is weakened, the [social] contract can no longer be upheld.

(Representative, Gesamtmetall)

When the works council is in too deep, this makes things difficult for management because when the works council [fails to grasp complex issues] it gets scared, and when it gets scared we can't deal with them. The more competent the council, the easier it is to deal with them.

(Director of Personnel, Henkel)

Strong negotiating partners may wield more power than weak ones, but they can also deliver what they promise. The costs involved in bargaining with a strong negotiating partner appear to be outweighed by the costs of not being able to rely on the integrity and competence of the negotiating partner. The strength of the works councils and unions as bargaining partners rests on their security as institutions, based both in law and in the broad social and political legitimacy of the labor movement. Thus, this appreciation of the strength of their negotiating partners reflects how solidly these institutions are embedded in the German political economy.

The advantages of the German system of industrial relations. Despite their widespread admiration of specific aspects of American management (for instance, flexibility and innovation), German managers and employer association representatives were uniformly critical of U.S. employment relations in comparison with German employment relations.

> If there were no Works Constitution Act, then the personnel policy differences across enterprises would be much greater. . . . [Given the choice between the U.S. and German systems], I would take the German system, because it is more social and humane. American capitalism's understanding of the free market doesn't reflect my preferences. . . . I think with technological developments we need, more than in past years, . . . employees who are not only highly qualified but also motivated. . . . Manchester liberalism can't be realized in this kind of world. Basically, even in just economic terms, a progressive employer strategy will pay off better anyhow. In this regard, a preventative strategy is the best strategy. Though if we were only competing with Korea or Taiwan it would be a different matter.
>
> *(President, BDA)*

> One of the reasons why we have this [social] peace is that we have the works councils. Though at the same time, there are daily lots of problems [that] we wouldn't have if we didn't have to deal with the works councils. But [as a whole] it's a sensible system. . . . In any case, better our system than the American.
>
> *(Personnel Manager, Commerzbank)*

The managers interviewed linked the stability of their economic system to the fact that some costs of operation—including labor costs (for example, personnel policies)—are standardized across employers. They also expressed great pride in the social peace achieved through the social market economy. Their skepticism of the American system of industrial relations again reveals their view of industrial relations as rooted in the institutions of the broader political economy. In their view, industrial peace exists because conflict is channeled through collective bargaining, which assumes a strong labor movement. Centralized collective bargaining, according to the interviewees, enables employers to compete with other firms and, to some extent, with other countries on bases other than labor costs. The works councils are viewed as allies in this process.

Contemporary benefits of works councils. The fifth major theme reflected a widespread preoccupation with the problems of continual, rapid economic and environmental change. Many of the managers interviewed explicitly noted that works councils will play an increasingly critical role in the German private sector as current trends, including technological change, pressures for greater organizational flexibility, and the increasing importance of skills, escalate.

> [T]he works council is a positive productivity factor regarding new technologies. If you want to introduce new technology today, it's not enough that the employees accept it because they have to, but rather that beyond that they accept it as helpful and sensible. And this certainly only is possible when [they are not afraid of] possible effects at the workplace. . . . To get them to accept it, you need the council as an interest aggregator [that] conveys the faith that . . . this will not create problems for the employees or that when there are problems that acceptable solutions will be found.
>
> *(Personnel Manager, Bayer)*

> As a general manager (not a personnel manager), I'd rather have a system without a works council, the Works Constitution Act, and all the associated restrictions. But the U.S. system is no better than ours. . . . By its development, our system in Germany has shown itself to be more efficient. And for higher levels of industrialization [the German IR system] works better [than the American system]. As skills get more and more important, this way of organizing interests gets more and more effective. The more we develop, the better the German system looks.
>
> *(Director of Technology, Henkel)*

Again there was a widespread assumption that change must be negotiated and that there will inevitably be conflicting interests over how it is introduced.

The Impact of Institutions on Managers' Beliefs

For these managers, the negotiated model of adjustment appears to be more than an abstraction. It seems to be imprinted on the world view that motivates their thinking and actions. Thus, although some of the managers recognized they could do their jobs more quickly, and sometimes more easily, without having to deal with a council, they viewed the councils as negotiating partners capable of helping them perform their jobs, not just as government-imposed employee voice mechanisms. To make the most of these institutions, German managers prefer them to be powerful enough to be effective. Having recognized the benefits of the negotiated model of adjustment, the managers interviewed reject a more unilateral approach and suggest that the negotiated model will become increasingly attractive as international economic pressures intensify.[5]

Within the institutional infrastructure of U.S. employment relations, this view makes little sense. Consequently it is hardly surprising that many foreign investors in the United States pursue labor relations strategies that are significantly different from those they follow at home. For instance, German and Japanese companies in the United States have opted to take advantage of the possibility of operating without unions. This is fairly easy to do, especially in the case of greenfield sites located in right-to-work states.[b] Well-known Japanese examples include Honda's plant in Marysville, Ohio, and Nissan's Smyrna, Tennessee, operations. Both BMW and Mercedes-Benz are following similar nonunion strategies in the southern United States. BMW has built a $600 million plant in Spartanburg, South Carolina, that started operations in the fall of 1994. The state of South Carolina helped to coordinate hiring for BMW, screening over 60,000 applicants, of whom fewer than 600 were hired in 1994. (BMW expects to employ 1,500 workers by the end of 1996 and about 2,000 by the turn of the century.) Mercedes is building a $350 million plant in Vance, Alabama, to begin production in 1997. Mercedes is particularly interested in introducing a variety of Japanese-style management practices, inspired in part by Mitsubishi Planning Corporation, which is helping to design the facility.

---

[b] Greenfield sites are operations that are built from scratch (on a "green field," so to speak). Right-to-work states are those states with laws that make it particularly difficult for unions to organize. Roughly half the states—and most southern states—have such laws.

While most of the top executives are Germans, the manufacturing vice president and the vice president for purchasing and logistics have been hired from North American Toyota and Nissan operations, respectively.[6]

These strategies, involving a very different sort of labor-management relationship than the dominant German pattern, make sense in the U.S. context. On the other hand, there is obviously no inherent reason why managers should find employee representation per se to be bad for the enterprise; witness Saturn (among other examples). Thus, what is seen as good or bad for the company varies with the institutional context in which the good and the bad are defined.

Comparing German- and American-Owned Companies

Why Compare?

The strong influence of the institutional context is illustrated by the contrast between management policies and styles in German-owned and American-owned chemical companies. Is the difference between the German and American styles of managing—particularly managing human resources—purely a difference in style, or does it reflect objective constraints imposed by the environment? Do companies try to export policies and practices developed in the United States to Germany and vice versa? Does an American approach work in Germany? To answer these questions it was necessary to look at companies operating in Germany but owned, and to some extent run, by Americans. Determining whether or not there was a clear contrast between the two national styles, and if there was, understanding that contrast, required a comparison of substantially similar companies. I chose a group of large companies in the chemicals industry, which allowed the analysis to hold constant the effects of industrial sector and firm size on employment relations and HR policies.[7]

Three American companies—3M, and two firms I have dubbed A&B and Rey (managers at these companies requested anonymity)—and four of the largest German chemicals companies—Bayer, BASF, Hoechst, and Henkel—were chosen for the study. I also studied the wholly owned American subsidiary of Hoechst, Hoechst-Celanese.[c]

---

[c] About half of those interviewed were employed by German-owned companies operating in Germany and the other half by American-owned firms also operating in Germany. In order to determine how management practices and approaches

HR Policies at the American-Owned Companies

To American managers, the HR policies of A&B, 3M, and Rey will be fairly familiar. Within the limits set by the collective bargaining contract, compensation tends to be linked to individual performance. Though German law makes it hard to lay off or fire employees, these managers noted unanimously that employment security was not guaranteed, as it has been historically in almost all German industries, particularly the chemicals industry. (In point of fact, however, layoffs had been rare even at these American companies.) Performance appraisals were frequent (at least twice annually) and strongly emphasized individual achievement.[8] Employee development through individual goal-setting techniques was introduced at A&B and 3M in the early 1990s.

Managers recruited and selected employees carefully, looking for highly motivated individual achievers rather than people with specific types of formal training. The management career patterns at these companies also reflected the relatively unimportant role of formal skills. Managers in all three American firms reported rapid movement, by German standards, through the organizations and many lateral career moves. At A&B and Rey, mobility across functional areas was justified on the basis that general management skills were more valuable than specific functional expertise. The prevalence of cross-functional movement can be traced in part to the existence of fewer managerial levels in the American-owned firms. Managers at A&B, 3M, and Rey also reported that in comparison to colleagues at German-owned companies, they had been assigned heavy responsibilities at low levels of the organization. They linked this phenomenon to their employers' emphasis on achievement by individuals rather than by the group of employees as a collective. Finally, almost

---

could be exported from Germany to the United States, I interviewed managers at the U.S. production site of one of the German companies. All of the firms in this sample are multinationals that employ from 15,000 to about 45,000 people worldwide. Interviews were conducted with managers at all levels of the organizations and in a number of areas, including R&D, production, engineering, and human resources. With the exception of those at the American facility of the German company (see Appendix 1), most were German nationals. As with the first set of interviews, the loose, relatively unstructured format of these interviews meant that managers' comments were volunteered for the most part, rather than given in response to specific questions.

all those interviewed in these companies noted that the senior American managers of their firms had little interest in or time for the works councils.

Corporate Culture at the American-Owned Companies

All of the managers at A&B, 3M, and Rey spoke enthusiastically about what they perceived to be the unique culture of their organizations. In point of fact, however, the cultures at A&B, 3M, and Rey seemed to be quite similar. What these managers perceived as unique may have been part of the overall culture of American firms. Especially valued by these managers were the openness of communication, the informal nature of the work atmosphere, the open door policy of high-level managers, and the relatively high levels of responsibility and autonomy that were assigned middle and lower-level managers. Managers at A&B and 3M spoke of a certain "dynamism" that they associated with dense communication networks, informal, as-needed teamwork, and the rapid implementation of organizational changes. Indeed, one of the uniformly praised "American" aspects of the management approaches at all three organizations was the ability and willingness to implement organizational change quickly and decisively. A production manager at A&B described the contrast between American and German managerial approaches as: "Germans follow, Americans lead." At 3M, a personnel department head referred to the American "can-do" attitude: "Don't tell me why it won't work; make it work."

Another aspect of the cultures at the American companies that these managers noted was the effort to integrate the HR function into the rest of the organization. At A&B, the director of HR spoke of other parts of the organization as his "customers." At Rey, arguing that ideally HR management should be the concern of all managers and should not require a separate department, the HR director said, "It's my job to try to make my job superfluous." Managers at all three organizations spoke of the importance of communicating directly with employees rather than channeling contacts through the works council. At A&B and Rey, the councils were explicitly encouraged to try to solve problems directly with production managers rather than using the HR department as mediator, which is how it is usually used in German companies.

A plant manager at Rey, who had several degrees, summed up the American managerial approach to problem solving as follows: "Faced with the same problem, German managers will tend to try to rely on the skills of their workforce to solve it, while Americans will more likely develop a new management system or tinker with the technology or the organizational structure. On the other hand, I appreciate the fact that Americans value performance more highly than degrees."

German Managers' Critiques of Their American-Owned Companies

While the managers (who were for the most part German nationals) praised the informal cultures of their organizations, they also criticized certain aspects of what they perceived to be the American style and offered numerous examples of how American ways of doing things could be counterproductive and could make their work more difficult.[9] The criticisms fell into two broad categories. The first concerns a lack of thoroughness and a tendency to prefer quick fixes over long-term solutions. The second deals with the costs of failing to work constructively with the works councils.

Quick fixes and a lack of thoroughness. One common complaint centered on a lack of steady vision and common goals and the frequent "reinvention of the wheel."

> On the one hand, rapid managerial movement through the organization can help develop quick fixes to immediate problems. But then these policies often are detrimental to the building of long-term solutions to deeper problems. Ultimately this means that top management can't rely on the rest of the organization to rally in a common cause when a larger problem, or the next problem, comes up.
>
> *(Site Manager, 3M)*

Throughout the interviews, managers noted that Americans were better at quick fixes and firefighting than at the development of long-term solutions to underlying problems. The A&B manager who spoke of American managers as leaders also said, "I believe that in order to lead effectively, I also have to know where I'm going." At least two interviewees at each of the three firms noted that the short time horizon of senior management decision making often left them uncertain of where they were headed over the medium and long term. A personnel manager, a process design manager, and a plant manager at Rey and a manager of technical services at A&B, among others, complained that they were unsure of what sorts of training they should offer their employees since they did not know what kinds of jobs these employees would be doing in six months or a year.

Four managers at A&B noted that Germans and Americans at their firm had different understandings of what it means to implement a policy. These managers said the Germans tended to be more thorough and the Americans more impressionistic. A plant engineering manager gave the following example:

> We had a new slogan sent to us by headquarters in the U.S.A., apparently with the idea that each manager would do with it what seemed appropriate. But we took the thing rather more seriously and developed a program to build consensus on the precise meaning of the slogan and the best uniform way of applying it in daily work practices. That's not what the Americans had in mind.

Although this story may be slightly comical, the plant engineer was certain that similar misunderstandings had wasted significant resources over the years. An employee relations manager at A&B concluded that Germans need to learn how not to implement every directive with total thoroughness, while Americans need to learn that some directives simply cannot be implemented.

A number of other interviewees alluded to similar conflicts. One production manager at Rey argued that the American penchant for rapid implementation of change conflicted with German employees' attachment to security of all kinds: "Organizational change of any kind can be especially difficult to implement in Germany, because everyone is so intent on being secure." An HR manager at Rey recounted the following telling anecdote:

> We had a survey of employees to help us figure out how to restructure a certain department. Seventy percent of employees agreed with management's plan while 30 percent opposed it. The American manager's response was to go ahead and implement the planned restructuring. But a number of the Germans wanted time to work with the employees who opposed it.

Emphasizing a point that was key in the previous section, a chemist at A&B noted that it was much easier to implement changes when those who were affected accepted the changes and were willing to accommodate them. In his view, this sort of acceptance required independent worker representation, which might, at the same time, slow the pace of organizational change. According to one Rey production manager, "Americans will tend to introduce change first and worry about how to implement it later."

Managers also complained of a certain superficiality in the American management styles. Four interviewees at 3M and Rey spoke of "management by acronym"—the introduction of various slogans and catch phrases to help organize and channel managers' energies. While these slogans were invariably helpful and interesting in the short term, the managers noted they were usually forgotten or replaced within a few months. At Rey, all but one of the managers interviewed spoke of a "presentation culture," referring to the frequency and importance of communication and the persuasive presentation of information and policy positions at meetings, and several questioned the depth or effectiveness of this approach. One production manager complained of "flow charts everywhere." Managers at all three organizations detected a greater focus on process than on outcomes. In the words of a personnel department head at 3M: "Acronyms, presentations, and flow charts—there's nothing wrong with these things in and of themselves. But it's a problem when that's all there is, and there's no further initiative to follow through in any concerted way."

The interviewees offered a variety of examples of how the American tendency toward quick fixes could interfere with their work and with the welfare of the company. Several people at A&B and Rey claimed that their American headquarters sometimes directed them to take quick-fix actions that were simply impossible—or illegal—in Germany. Examples included laying off employees with little or no notice or justification, unilaterally introducing a compensation or job evaluation scheme that infringed on the rights of the council, and trying to institute a seven-day work week.

Failing to work with the council. Comments falling into the second category dealt with the failure of American managers to take the works councils seriously and their suspicions of the Works Constitution Act. A&B and Rey had recently reorganized specifically to minimize the extent of employee influence in the company. At Rey, reorganization into smaller business units prevented employees from gaining parity representation on the company's supervisory board. At

A&B, certain pieces of production were outsourced to keep the employee count low enough to avoid the legal requirement to relieve an employee representative on the council of full-time duties. Several managers at both organizations claimed that they were diverted from their jobs at times by the need to mediate between the works council and their American superiors. Most of the benefits of working with the works council discussed in the first part of this chapter were noted by these managers as well.

Three managers at Rey noted that one of the works councils was increasingly vigilant and suspicious because the company was not in the employer association and therefore had few direct dealings with the union. (All of these firms have several German production sites and thus several councils.) As a result, the managers noted, the amount of work they had to do to meet the council's demands for information had increased. They all believed they would be freed up to do more important things if the company simply accepted the contract and the union.[10] These same managers and three others at A&B and 3M said the American unwillingness to take the works council and the Works Constitution Act seriously involved them in time-consuming negotiations and dispute resolution procedures with the councils and the union. These managers were uneasy with the American understanding of the HR department. According to a personnel department head at 3M,

> HR is really a liaison between the company and the external world, on the one hand, and employees themselves, on the other. The American conception of the role of HR can lead to problems when top managers insist on the immediate introduction of organizational changes—changes that legally and practically require prior consultation with the works council.

Several managers at A&B, 3M, and Rey thought many Americans failed to grasp the benefits of working with strong employee representatives. Two people at Rey, for example, spoke of a colleague who was elected to the works council and whose career was then declared "dead in the water" by the Americans at the company. Over the space of several years, the manager was able to elicit the council's cooperation and help in the implementation of highly valued technological changes. After he was bypassed for promotions, the manager's German superiors brought these accomplishments to the attention of

U.S. managers, who then promoted him to a considerably more powerful position.

HR Policies and Corporate Culture at the German-Owned Companies

It is commonly accepted that German companies—especially large firms—are rather slow, lumbering organizations.[11] The interviews at Hoechst, BASF, Bayer, and Henkel confirmed this notion. Management in these firms tended to be less dynamic, more stable, and more collectively oriented than at Rey, A&B, and 3M. The works councils' primary contacts were with the HR or personnel department rather than production managers. The HR departments in these companies played a much more central role in negotiations with the works councils than they did in their U.S. competitors. Indeed, the relationship between the HR department and the works council was universally seen as the appropriate focal point of labor-management relations.

In this set of interviews, managers echoed both the points made in the first section of this chapter and the criticisms of the U.S. approach voiced by managers at A&B, 3M, and Rey. At Hoechst, Bayer, BASF, and Henkel, the legal rights and responsibilities of labor and management and the need to maintain smooth relations with the council were more emphasized than they were at the American-owned companies. Production managers claimed that conflicts with the works councils were rare because these were preempted in early dealings between the council and personnel managers. Basic HR practices followed the guidelines of the industry collective bargaining agreement and locally negotiated supplemental agreements that emphasized collective, rather than individual, features of the employment relationship. Compensation tended not to be performance-based except for higher level managers. Until the early 1990s, employment security was assumed as given.[d] Individual performance was deemed less important than stable collective employee relations.[12] Selection processes were fairly crude, and there was a widespread belief that what really mattered was how well the company trained and integrated those who were hired.

---

[d] In the early 1990s, some companies in the chemicals industry laid off employees for the first time in postwar history.

Managerial promotions were slow, and cross-functional movement was rare.[13] Unlike the senior managers at the U.S. companies, the chief executives of all four of the German companies were chemists, a reflection of the importance of functional expertise in German-owned companies. At all four organizations, several of the managers spoke of excessive hierarchy and referred to flat organizational hierarchies as an American innovation. One production manager at BASF said that as a result of the German penchant for hierarchy, "unfortunately, in a crunch we often tend to push decision making upward precisely when it should be pushed downward."

Managers at Hoechst, BASF, and Bayer noted that labor-management relations, HR policies, and to some extent, corporate cultures at large German chemical concerns are substantially similar.[e] As the vice president of personnel at Hoechst put it, "All of our cultures grow out of a single historical tradition and rest on broader national cultural and institutional traditions."[14]

A German-Owned Company in the United States

Hoechst-Celanese, a U.S. facility of Hoechst, captures many of the sharpest contrasts between the German- and American-owned companies. Until the late 1980s, Hoechst's U.S. operation had acted as a marketing and distribution outpost for its German-made products, and its production facilities had been geared exclusively toward adding value to these products. The facilities were laid out and run according to blueprints from Hoechst's headquarters. U.S. operations followed a five- to ten-year plan, made possible by its close ties to the operations of German headquarters. Top managers were German, and all had Ph.D.'s in chemistry; engineers and general managers were not as highly valued. Four production managers described the work environment as "typically German," patriarchal, family-oriented, secure, and stable. Relations with the union were close. A manager of organizational development and training explained that

---

[e] Hoechst, BASF, and Bayer were portions of the IG Farben chemicals giant which collaborated closely with Hitler and was broken up after World War II by the occupying allied powers. This common heritage explains in part why the cultures and approaches of these three companies are so similar. The fact that Henkel's policies were also similar suggests the important role played by broader national cultural factors.

employee training tended to be extremely thorough. Layoffs were unheard of.

In 1987 Hoechst acquired Celanese, an American company, and merged the German-owned U.S. operations with the American firm, allowing the new American management team free reign. All but one of the managers interviewed at the U.S. facility had been there for over ten years, and all said that in the years since the merger almost everything about the company had changed radically. The production facility was reoriented to produce a variety of specialty products for an international market; investments in plant modernization had become substantial (by one estimate, as high as $40 million in the first two years). Five interviewees called the American managers' style "lean and mean," noting that numerous layoffs of managers and nonmanagerial employees had taken place within weeks of the merger. Most of the company's German managers were transferred back to Germany or demoted. According to interviewees, relations with the union became tense. HR managers estimated that the number of grievances filed had increased by a factor of two or three.

Two employees—a chemist and a production manager—said that with the change promotion patterns began to reward general managers rather than specialists or scientists. Seven of the managers interviewed said management responsibilities increased, as did the freedom to act without approval from superiors. A new compensation scheme tied managers' and employees' pay to performance. The time horizon of the company shrank to between three and nine months. The internal managerial labor market became more dynamic, and managerial movement through the organization became more common. Three of the company's executives resigned within a year of the interviews, which, by the pre-1987 German standards, is an astronomically high level of turnover. Exhibit 5-1 shows how one production manager who had been there for twenty-two years described the contrast between German and American management. The overlap between the "Old Way" on the one hand and the "New Way" on the other is clearly significant.

Conclusion: The Nature of the Trade-Off

It is possible to draw three broad conclusions from the interviews analyzed in this chapter. First, on the whole, German managers and employer representatives are quite content with their negotiated sys-

Exhibit 5-1

Characterization of Hoechst-Celanese Before and After the Takeover of
Celanese by Hoechst

"Old Way"	"New Way"
Specialization	General skills
Chemistry	Engineering
Long term	Short term
Top down	Employee involvement
Paternalism	Responsibility
Minimal movement on internal labor market	Maximal movement on internal labor market
Market share	Profits
Authoritative	Challenging
Focus	Diversity
Conservative capital	Aggressive capital
Low profile	High profile
Many jobs adequately done	Few jobs well done

tem of employment relations and conscious of its economic benefits.
While they admire American management, they tend to be critical
of U.S. employment relations, taking issue with the lack of predictability and the conflictual nature of labor-management relations.

Second, almost all the managers interviewed (particularly those
working at the chemical companies) are nevertheless quite conscious
of certain deep flaws in the negotiated model and certain powerful
benefits of a more American approach. They appear especially enam-

ored of what they see as a typically American capacity for rapid organizational change and managerial maneuverability.

Third, while conscious of some of the benefits of the U.S. approach, they are aware of the fact that the unilateral style of managing—like their own style—is to some extent dependent on the institutional context. Taken to extremes, many American practices and policies bump up against legal, cultural, and organizational boundaries. As many of the interviewees noted, this can be quite costly, especially when compared to a slower, more consensus-oriented, and longer-range method of managing.

Exhibit 5-2 lays out in highly stylized fashion the basic HR policy dimensions and three general organizational dimensions that can be used to contrast the unilateral stance of American companies with the negotiated approach of German companies. The differences between the two ideal-typical approaches suggests some tangible trade-offs between them. These are depicted in Exhibit 5-3.

Exhibit 5-2
Contrasting the Unilateral and Negotiated Models

Unilateral (United States)	Negotiated (Germany)
HR policies target individual achievement, allow for layoffs, rapid internal labor market movement, broad skills, cross-functional HR deployment	HR policies target collective achievement, provide employment security, involve slow movement within the internal labor market, formal skills, functional specialization
Low hierarchy/high management responsibility, discretion	High hierarchy/low management responsibility, discretion
HR department serves internal organizational customers	HR department serves employees and acts as liaison between management and labor
Unique culture of individual dynamism in the name of rapid organizational change	Common cultural and institutional heritage in the name of stability, consensus, and slow, steady adaptation

Exhibit 5-3

Trade-Offs Between the Unilateral and Negotiated Models

Potential Advantages

Unilateral (United States)	Negotiated (Germany)
Individual achievement, creativity, innovation	Collective achievement, everyone pulling in the same direction
Managerial maneuverability and discretion	Managerial accountability, employee acceptance of change
Smooth internal cross-functional collaboration	High overall competence levels
Quantitative flexibility	Stability, reliability, labor peace
Rapid organizational change in response to market/demand changes	Accommodation of constraints, thorough change once change is initiated/implemented

Potential Disadvantages

Unilateral (United States)	Negotiated (Germany)
People working at cross-purposes, reinventing the wheel	Stifling individual initiative, creativity
Hostile labor force/employee representatives	Everything takes too long
Higher employee turnover, lower commitment	Cost of keeping labor on in economic downturns
Promotions before necessary skills/ experience have been gained	Slow organizational change, lack of cross-fertilization

138

Exhibit 5-3 (continued)

Unilateral (United States)	Negotiated (Germany)
Lower overall skills level	Inadequate collaboration between various departments
Costs of ignoring labor/ environmental constraints	Excessive bureaucratization

The unilateral approach is characterized by HR policies that target individual achievement, make it relatively easy to lay off employees, entail fairly rapid movement of employees within the internal labor market, and value general aptitudes and cross-functional HR utilization. The typical American organization is thought to minimize hierarchy while maximizing managerial responsibilities and autonomy at relatively low levels, to cast the HR department as a vendor of services to internal organizational customers (but not the group of employees as a whole), and to harness a uniquely dynamic culture in the interest of facilitating rapid organizational change. There are clear advantages associated with this model. At its best, it can promote individual achievement, managerial maneuverability, and discretion; meet the HR needs of various parts of the organization; allow for quantitative flexibility and rapid organizational change in response to market changes; and contribute to innovation and creativity through cross-fertilization. At the same time, this approach can also entail costs. Different people in the organization may work at cross-purposes or duplicate each others' efforts. Organized labor, feeling excluded, may create obstacles to organizational change. Managerial discretion may minimize the expression of employee voice and thus lead to missed opportunities, employee disgruntlement, or employee turnover. Managers may be transferred or promoted into jobs for which they lack appropriate skills. Overall skill levels may be relatively low. The tendency to proceed regardless of environmental (for instance, legal or cultural) constraints can be costly.

The negotiated approach is characterized by HR policies that target collective achievement, make it relatively difficult to lay off employees, entail relatively slow movement through the internal labor market, and value formal skills and functional specialization. In the typical German organization, one finds a relatively high level of hierarchy and low levels of responsibility for middle and lower-level managers. The HR department is usually viewed as serving the needs of employees and acting as liaison between management and workers. In the interest of slow, steady adaptation to the environment, the organizational culture is usually shared throughout the industry and, to some extent, the country as a whole. At its best, the German approach can enhance overall collective achievement; ensure that organizational changes, when they occur, are fully accepted and implemented by all; promote predictability, stability, accountability, and reliability; and provide a relatively high average competence level among employees and managers. This model can have substantial opportunity costs, however. This way of managing can stifle individual creativity and initiative, significantly slow the pace of change, and diminish the effectiveness of interdepartmental or cross-functional communication and collaboration.

In short, there appear to be two broad types of trade-off between the unilateral and the negotiated approaches. The first has to do with the pace and thoroughness of organizational change. On the one hand, an organization can try to develop the capacity to adapt extremely quickly to changes. This entails certain costs, however, and change is apt to be partial, superficial, and/or short term. Alternately, an organization can try to implement change thoroughly, so as to involve all those affected in the organization. In this case, however, change will probably be slow in coming. Seen as a continuum, the American approach falls toward the former end and the German toward the latter.

The second trade-off concerns the average skills and competencies of employees, including managers. Again, at one end of a continuum one can imagine an organization in which all employees are trained thoroughly and extensively in their area of expertise. Staffing, promotion, transfer patterns, and other aspects of the organization's structure and strategy are geared toward taking advantage of a fairly sharp division of functional responsibilities that rests on a fairly high level of overall competencies and skills. This would be the German end of the continuum. While the base level of employees' competence will be fairly high, the ceiling may be relatively low, because the dominance of functional specialization can pose obstacles to the expression of individual initiative and/or cross-functional innovation. On the American end of the continuum would be an organization in which the overall aptitude of individual employees is valued over extensive formal training of any particular kind and organizational strategies and structures are not strongly influenced by a sharp demarcation of formal functional distinctions. In this type of organization, the average competency level of employees may be lower, and the lack of an extensive training screen may let in or keep on especially low performers, but the possibilities for excelling outside of any particular area of functional expertise or across two or more such areas will be relatively unconstrained.

The question raised by these trade-offs, which will be addressed in detail in chapter 7, is whether or not it is possible to combine the strengths of the two models into a unified managerial approach to employment relations in the workplace. Before addressing this substantial challenge to managers in both countries, we need to consider the pressing problem currently preoccupying Germans: the absorption and restructuring of Eastern Germany.

Appendix 1
Interviewees Data

A&B
Department Manager, Product A
Department Manager, Employee
 Relations
Clerk, Employee Relations
Manager, Employee Relations
Director, Employee Relations
Manager, Packing and Converting
Group Manager, Plant Engineering
Department Manager, Product B
Group Manager, Converting
 Technical Support

Rey
Superintendent, Methylchloroform
 Production
Manager, Process Design and
 Development
Manager, Production
Manager, Employee Development
Director, HR
Manager, Production
Manager, Plant
Manager, Production
HR Group Leader, Production

3M
General Manager, HR
Group Leader, Personnel
Module Manager, Traffic Control
 Material
Department Head, Personnel
Site Manager, Traffic Control
 Material

BASF
Director of Personnel
Plant Manager
Plant Manager
Director of Logistics
Title Withheld
Title Withheld
Title Withheld
Title Withheld
Title Withheld

Hoechst
Vice President, Production
Director, HR
Vice President, Polypropylene
   Production

Hoechst-Celanese
Project Leader, Chemicals
Production Manager, Chemicals
Manager, HR
Business Director, Pigments
Production Manager, Pigments

Chemist, Azo Pigments
Controller
Manager, Production
Manager, Technical Services
Manager, Organizational
   Development and Training

Bayer
Titles withheld by request of firm

Henkel
Titles withheld by request of firm

Notes

1. See, for example, Mancur Olson, *The Logic of Collective Action* (Cambridge: Harvard University Press, 1965).

2. See, for instance, Walter Simon, *Macht und Herrschaft der Unternehmerverbände BDI, BDA und DIHT* (Power and control of the business associations: The federation of employer associations, the federation of industry associations and the chambers of commerce) (Cologne: Pahl Ruggenstein Verlag, 1979).

3. Much of the research on German industry and most of the work in the area of labor and employment relations has focused on the metalworking industries (for instance, the automobile sector or the machine tool sector), which have historically represented the bastions of Germany's export strength and are organized by the powerful IG Metall. See Kathleen Thelen, *Union of Parts: Labor Politics in Postwar Germany* (Ithaca: Cornell University Press, 1991); Lowell Turner, *Democracy at Work? Changing World Markets and the Future of Labor Unions* (Ithaca: Cornell University Press, 1991); Gary Herrigel, "The National Context: Two Different Patterns of Regional Economic Order in a Single Nation: 1871–1945," working paper, Department of Political Science, University of Chicago, Chicago, Ill., 1992; and Ulrich Jürgens, Larissa Klinzing, and Lowell Turner, "The Transformation of Industrial Relations in Eastern Germany," *Industrial and Labor Relations Review* 46, no. 2 (1993): 229–44. To include cases in which the unions were less influential and the companies less competitive my own research was targeted at a range of other industries.

4. These findings are consistent with interviews conducted in the course of ongoing research by Lowell Turner of Cornell University, Richard Freeman of Harvard University, and Joel Rogers of the University of Wisconsin.

5. See also Rüdiger Keim and Hans Unger, *Kooperation Statt Konfrontation: Vertrauensvolle Zusammenarbeit zwischen Arbeitgeber und Betriebsrat* (Cooperation instead of confrontation: Trusting cooperation between employer and works council) (Cologne: Infomedia, 1986); Werner Faix et al., *Der Mitarbeiter in der Fabrik der Zukunft: Qualifikation und Weiterbildung* (The employee in the factory of the future: Qualification and further training), IW Beiträge 143 (Cologne: Deutscher Institutsverlag, 1989); Gesamtmetall, *Mensch und Arbeit: Gemeinsame Interessen von mitarbeitern and Unternehmen in einer sich wandelnten Arbeitswelt* (Humans and work: Common interests of employees and employers in a changing work world) (Cologne: Gesamtverband der metallindustriellen Arbeitgeberverbände, 1989); and Paul Windolf, "Productivity Coalitions and the Future of Corporatism," *Industrial Relations* 28 (1989): 1–20.

6. See *Ward's Automotive Reports,* various issues; *Automotive News,* various issues.

7. Employment relations in some sectors are more confrontational than in others, for instance, in part because of the political stance of the union and employer association. See Andrei Markovits, *The Politics of West German Trade Unions* (New York: Cambridge University Press, 1986). Smaller firms tend to have weaker works councils than larger ones, which has an impact on the tenor of labor-management relations and management HR approaches. See Hermann Kotthoff, *Betriebsräte und betriebliche Herrschaft: eine Typologie von Partizipationsmustern im Industriebetrieb* (Works councils and enterprise rule: A typology of participation patterns at the enterprise) (Frankfurt: Campus Verlag, 1981).

8. Jones argues that organizational cultures are significantly influenced by broader socioeconomic principles. This argument is consistent with the focus on individualism in the U.S.-owned firms in which the business cultures developed in the relatively free market oriented United States and with the tendency toward more collective norms in the German-owned companies in which the business cultures emerged in a more paternalistic (pre-1920) and then more social (postwar) economy. See Gareth Jones, "Transaction Costs, Property Rights and Organizational Culture: An Exchange Perspective," *Administrative Sciences Quarterly* 28, no. 3 (1983): 454–67.

9. Research on corporate culture in different national contexts has found that organizational cultures reflect not only the external environment (i.e., the institutions of employment relations) but also the broader national culture. See, for example, Nancy Adler, *International Dimensions of Organizational Behavior,* 2d ed. (Boston: PWS Kent Publishing, 1991). That this was the case here will become apparent later in this chapter. It should be noted that the criticisms offered by

managers at A&B, 3M, and Rey reflect some familiarity with, and attachment to, a more steady, paternalistic approach, even if the managers praised various aspects of the American model.

10. Kerbo, Wittenhagen, and Nagao find that employee relations in Japanese-owned companies operating in Germany are better where management has a thorough familiarity with and commitment to German labor laws. See Harold R. Kerbo, Elke Wittenhagen, and Keiko Nakao, "Japanese Corporations in Germany: Corporate Structure and Employee Relations" (Department of Social Sciences, California Polytechnic State University, San Luis Obispo, Calif., September 1993).

11. See, for instance, Heinz Hartmann, *Der deutsche Unternehmer: Autorität und Organisation* (The German employer: Authority and organization) (Frankfurt: Europäischer Verlagsanstalt, 1968).

12. In this connection, Grunert and Schernhorn find that Germans in general tend to value a "sense of belonging" more highly than a "sense of accomplishment" while the value prioritization of Americans is the reverse. See Susanne C. Grunert and Gerhard Scherhorn, "Consumer Values in West Germany: Underlying Dimensions and Cross-cultural Comparisons with North America," *Journal of Business Relations* 20 (1990): 97–107.

13. This is consistent with research conducted by Walgenbach, who finds that German middle managers are more oriented toward functional specialization, change jobs within the firm less frequently, and move less frequently across functional areas than their British counterparts. He also finds that they move more slowly through their organizations. See Peter Walgenbach, "Führungsverhalten mittlerer Manager in Deutschland und Großbritannien" (Leadership approaches of middle managers in Germany and Great Britain), *ZEW Newsletter,* no. 2 (1993): 16–19. These and related points are discussed at length in chapter 7.

14. See also Markovits, *The Politics of West German Trade Unions;* and Horst Kern and Michael Schumann, *Das Ende der Arbeitsteilung?* (End of the division of labor?) (Frankfurt: Campus Verlag, 1985). The reader will recall that managers at the U.S. firms tended to focus on what they saw as unique features of their companies. This contrast is consistent with the findings of Wilkins and Ouchi, who report that more bureaucratized companies may have less powerful cultures because their bureaucratic norms provide sufficient basis for organized action. See Alan L. Wilkins and William Ouchi, "Efficient Cultures: Exploring the Relationship Between Culture and Organizational Performance," *Organizational Culture,* special issue of *Administrative Sciences Quarterly* 28, no. 3 (September 1983): 468–81.

chapter six

Employment Relations in Eastern Germany

how the negotiated model works out of context

At the moment, immense variety and confusion characterize employment relations and the economy as a whole in Eastern Germany. In the first half of the 1990s, government, management, and labor representatives agreed that personalities and case-specific contingencies played important roles in shaping the processes and outcomes of employment relations in the new states (and, indeed, in many other spheres of social and economic life).[1] Thus, although the institutions of the former West Germany's ER system have been imposed on labor-management relations in the eastern part of the country, one cannot yet speak of an ER *system* in any meaningful sense of the word because relations between and among the many parties involved are anything but systematic.

But developments in the new states do not seriously threaten the negotiated model laid out in the previous chapters of this book. While there are certain indications of increased managerial unilateralism in eastern German employment relations, there are also signs that the negotiated pattern of adjustment is being reinforced and, more interestingly, redesigned.[2] The experiences of the new states seem to represent not the end of the negotiated model but the emergence of new conflicts requiring new sorts of negotiation that go beyond those developed since World War II in the western states. Regional variation as well as strong east/west cleavages are emerging alongside the traditional labor-management divide and, in some cases, at least temporarily replacing it. The ER situation in the former East Germany represents an uncoordinated but widespread restructuring of alliances and strategies on both sides of the employment relationship and on the part of the government that has led to the development of peculiarly eastern negotiated adjustment processes. While it is unlikely that the institutions of industrial and employment relations in the new states will be identical to those in the western states, it is clear that industrial relations in both parts of the country are likely to be changed by events in the other.

Mapping the Eastern German Landscape

The Mechanics of Unification

The Kohl government's optimistic assessment of what would be involved in integrating and revitalizing the eastern German economy was belied within a few months of unification in October 1990. While the new states offered a well-trained workforce that was eager to partake in the processes of transformation to a market economy, years of working under a command economy had sharply affected individual initiative and creativity. Moreover, the economy was structured around a small number of giant, nationally owned industrial combines that allocated resources extremely inefficiently. Financial records had been badly kept and, in many cases, were doctored by managers eager to fulfill the party's economic plan. During the 1960s, investments in enterprises and infrastructure had halted almost entirely, resulting in physical plants that were several decades out of date by any standard. Labor and employer representatives from a variety of industrial sectors estimate that between 80 and 90 percent of the people employed at many enterprises were redundant, many of them manning the vast administrative bureaucracies of East Germany. The eastern German economy offered virtually no competitive products other than those made at western-owned greenfield sites. The economic problems facing the new states at the time of unification were astounding, and the task of transforming this economy overwhelming.[a]

The Kohl government's decision (politically successful but economically questionable) to implement monetary union between the

---

[a] Mickler points out that the East German combines were organized on the basis of three separate bureaucracies: those of the "management," the union, and the party. See Otfried Mickler, "Modernization of East German Industry and the Development of New Structures of Industrial Relations in Enterprises—The Case of the Auto Industry" (working paper, Institute for Sociology, University of Hannover, October 1992).

two parts of the country in July 1990—even before formal unification—had a dramatic negative effect on the markets for eastern Germany's products. Trading partners in eastern Europe now had to pay in convertible currency, and most could not. As supply lines and customer relationships with foreign partners were broken, similar effects rippled through the domestic economy. Trade with Bulgaria, Hungary, and Romania virtually disappeared in the early 1990s. Although eastern Germany maintained only 20 to 30 percent of its previous trade levels with the countries of the former Soviet Union, Poland, and the former Czechoslovakia, in 1993, 50 percent of the region's exports continued to go to eastern Europe. Western markets that had been available were lost because products that had been heavily subsidized in the interest of attracting much needed hard currency could no longer compete. While a strong domestic/regional market might have helped, consumers in the eastern states wanted western commodities that had long been unavailable to them even when the products were more expensive and no better than locally produced goods. Therefore, the internal domestic/regional market for much of the eastern economy was lost.[3]

Between 1989 and 1991 demand in eastern Germany increased modestly by 22 percent, but imports increased by 270 percent to meet over half of total demand. At the same time, the transfer of funds from west to east continued to increase. By 1993, Germans in the western states were subsidizing the eastern states to the tune of roughly DM 3,000 per (western) capita, increasing disposable income for easterners by DM 11,700 per (eastern) capita, and leaving the country with a deficit of about DM 18 billion.[4] Eastern Germany became basically a "transfer economy" in which people and public bodies spent western money (western taxes, social security payments, and borrowed funds) on western goods.

The loss of markets accelerated a sharp drop in production. By the spring of 1991, net production in manufacturing was cut by 70 percent and by mid-1993 it still hovered under 35 percent. The drop in production pulled the united Germany from second place in terms of per capita GDP in Europe to seventh place. Employment declined by about 40 percent in the first two years after unification. Much of this decline occurred in the mining and manufacturing industries, which accounted for no more than a third of total employment. Employment in these industries was still declining in late 1993.[5]

The solution to these problems lay in investment in the economy of the eastern states. One of the key tasks facing Germany today is the recreation of a *Mittelstand,* a community of small and medium-sized enterprises in the eastern states. (The Mittelstand played a key role in the growth and strength of the economy of West Germany, but it had been entirely wiped out in East Germany.) West German sources began to subsidize eastern business starts at the time of unification. In the first two and a half years after unification the German Settlement Bank financed over 200,000 new companies with a credit volume of about DM 20 billion. About half of these companies are in manufacturing or craft industries.[6] According to the bank, these firms account for over a million jobs.

However, a variety of obstacles have resulted in significantly lower levels of investment than initially projected. In 1992, two years after unification, investment per capita in the new states was still lower than in the western states (60 percent versus 75 percent), and the capital stock gap was still widening. Barriers to investment are numerous. The infrastructure of the eastern region (particularly traffic and telecommunications) remains extremely underdeveloped despite impressive gains. In 1994, for example, it was still easier to place a call from Berlin to New York than to eastern towns a few kilometers away. Moreover, public investment in the infrastructure has been delayed—even when funding is available—by the lack of adequate public administration.[7] Other important inhibitors of investments in the new states include the disastrous state of the environment, a new-firm failure rate that is higher in the eastern states than in the western states, and unresolved questions about property rights. The government of East Germany had been more effective than other east bloc governments in discouraging any form of private enterprise. By 1972, virtually the entire economy had been socialized.[b] Thus in the first nineteen months after unification, more than 50,000 applications were filed for the restitution of property.

Privatizing the Economy

Public policies intended to ease the transition of the eastern German economy were concentrated in the *Treuhandanstalt* (literally, "true

---

[b]Only 2 percent of the population was self-employed. Private enterprises could employ no more than ten people and were required to pay a 90 percent tax on profits.

[faithful] hand institution"; hereinafter, the *Treuhand*) and in a variety of passive and active labor market policies, most financed and/or administered by the Federal Labor Ministry (*Bundesanstalt für Arbeit*).

The Treuhand.   The Treuhand is a semipublic body that was created to take over and privatize the economy of the former East Germany.[8] In July 1990, it controlled just over 13,000 enterprises and about one-third of the total eastern German labor force.[c] By March 1993, all but 2,173 of these had been broken up and/or privatized or liquidated. Of the enterprises that were still operating under the auspices of the Treuhand in late 1993, the majority were distributed fairly equally (about 100 to 200 firms per subsector) among services, retail and wholesale trade, agriculture, machine tools, textiles and apparel, and transportation (see Exhibit 6-1). Roughly half of the enterprises were privatized, 20 percent were liquidated, and 10 percent were reprivatized (turned back over to initial owners).[9] Of the companies that were privatized, about 2,000 were bought by consortia of easterners as management buy outs (MBOs), and 612 were bought by foreign investors.[d] More than half of these investors came from Great Britain, Switzerland, Austria, and France (see Exhibit 6-2 and Table 6-1). The enterprises privatized first were those that appeared most attractive to investors and thus those with the best chances of surviving in a free market environment. The Treuhand policy is that investments should only be made by the eventual owner of the company.

In mid-1993, losses for firms not yet privatized equalled about eight times their earnings.[10] About 45 percent of the people em-

---

[c] The Treuhand started with about 10,000 enterprises, some of which were broken up in order to make their parts more saleable, resulting in the 13,000 figure.

[d] Many firms continue to be disadvantaged by old debt, which has made it difficult or impossible to invest sufficiently in the modernization of capital stock. In some cases, the government has waived such financial burdens in order to attract investments by western entrepreneurs. See Bundes Ministerium für Wirtschaft, *Die Politik zum Aufbau Ostdeutschlands: Fortentwicklung des Gemeinschaftswerks Aufschwung Ost* (Policies to rebuild Eastern Germany: Developments of the joint project on eastern revitalization), Bundesministerium für Wirtschaft, Dokumentation 321 (Bonn, July 1992).

Exhibit 6-1
Treuhand Enterprises by Industry
(March 31, 1993)

Industry	Number of Enterprises
Services	303
Trade	205
Pastoral/Forestry	357
Machine Tools	255
Textile and Apparels	110
Transportation/Warehousing	124
Construction	72
Chemicals	53
Iron, Steel	68
Electronics	57
Auto/Truck	56
Stoneware/Earthenware/Ceramics/Glassware	65
Wood Products	72
Foodstuffs	88
Other misc.	288
TOTAL	2,173

Source: Based on *Treuhandanstalt Monatsinformation* (Monthly information), Internal Treuhand memorandum (Berlin, 1993): 8.

Exhibit 6-2
Management Buy Outs by State
(March 31, 1993)

Brandenburg	333
Berlin	122
Mecklenburg-Pommerania	355
Thüringia	353
Saxony-Anhalt	343
Saxony	502
MBO TOTAL	2,009

Source: Based on *Treuhandanstalt Monatsinformation* (Monthly information), Internal Treuhand memorandum (Berlin, 1993): 15.

ployed by these firms work in companies with over 1,500 workers and about 75 percent worked in organizations with more than 250 employees (see Table 6-2). As these firms have lower revenue growth than those already privatized, economic dislocation is likely to continue.[11] In 1993, almost 20 percent of the 419,000 employees at Treuhand-owned companies worked in firms that were in the process of being liquidated. Industrial subsectors hardest hit by liquidation included electrical equipment, machine tools, textiles, services, and retail and wholesale trade, with the greatest loss of jobs in the first two industries (see Table 6-3).

The Treuhand is the institution Germans love to hate. Its efficiency has been hampered by the slapdash nature of its creation, the high level of turnover among its staff, and widely suspected corruption within the institution itself.[12] When the Treuhand was founded in 1990, its assets were estimated at 1.5 trillion DM. This figure was adjusted downward to 600 billion DM just after monetary union. It has been estimated that the Treuhand will have racked up over 250

Table 6-1
Foreign Investors in Treuhand Enterprises
(March 31, 1993)

Country	Number of Enterprises	Investment (Mil. DM)	Employment Guarantees
France	61	4,800	21,039
Great Britain	81	1,628	15,998
Switzerland	111	946	14,172
USA	54	2,715	11,844
Austria	86	678	13,617
Netherlands	56	937	7,837
Canada	8	1,848	16,708
Italy	27	644	4,827
Denmark	26	429	2,805
Sweden	27	117	2,800
Other	75	2,713	14,800
TOTAL	612	17,455	126,447

Source: Based on *Treuhandanstalt Monatsinformation* (Monthly information), Internal Treuhand memorandum (Berlin, 1993): 16.

billion DM in debt by 1995.[13] Furthermore, the policies of the
Treuhand have not been tied to any comprehensive idea of industrial
transformation. Its credo has been to privatize as soon as possible
under whatever circumstances are necessary to get the job done. As
Mahnkopf puts it:

Table 6-2
Employment Levels in Treuhand Enterprises
(March 31, 1993)

Co. Size by Employment	# of Co's.	# of Employees
Over 1,500 employees	33	161,366
1,000–1,500	17	21,130
501–1,100	65	44,634
251–500	139	47,429
101–250	295	46,039
51–100	272	19,714
21–50	372	12,552
less than 20	980	4,598
TOTAL	2,173	357,462

Source: Based on *Treuhandanstalt Monatsinformation* (Monthly information), Internal Treuhand memorandum (Berlin, 1993): 9–10.

Since the Treuhand pursues a short-term cost reduction approach, the decomposition of the former [combines] took place as an abrupt separation of the individual plants and a radical down-scaling or shutdown of those departments whose future returns can hardly be calculated. However, departments such as R&D and training facilities are crucial for long-term adaptability. In paralyzing all economic and social linkages within the preexisting production system western investors destroyed irreplaceably many of the networks [that] used to exist between

Table 6-3
Treuhand Enterprises in Liquidation by Industry

Industry	Number of Enterprises	Number of Jobs Affected	Percent of Jobs Saved*
Electronics	176	48,342	29
Textiles	229	37,647	14
Machine Tools	238	28,819	32
Services	333	21,745	31
Auto/Truck	65	20,322	33
Trade	336	19,569	18
Transport	30	19,479	21
TOTAL (Above)	1,407	195,923	25
TOTAL (including other industries)	2,538	301,115	27

*Through active labor market policies

Source: Based on *Treuhandanstalt Monatsinformation* (Monthly information), Internal Treuhand memorandum (Berlin, 1993): 21.

firms, research and development facilities and academic institutions.[14]

Usually, West German government bodies created to ease economic transitions have been responsible for actively managing enterprises, not necessarily selling them as quickly as possible. Thus, the Treuhand's laissez-faire approach to the privatization of the eastern economy represents a departure from the more interventionist industrial and economic policies of postwar Germany. Events at the local and state/regional levels represent more coordinated patterns of industrial change.

Active labor market policies.   Not surprisingly, layoffs have been a common managerial response to poor economic performance and the loss of markets. Between the first half of 1991 and the second half of 1992, employment dropped from about 1 million to 300,000 in agriculture and forestry, and from 3.5 million to 1.5 million in manufacturing (see Table 6-4). By March 1993, the number of unemployed had reached 1.1 million (16 percent in a population of 16 million, and still rising). These numbers understate the extent of unemployment because they do not include the roughly 650,000 people accounted for by various active labor policy measures. Unofficial employment rates are more likely to be between 25 and 40 percent.[15]

The extremely high levels of unemployment and underemployment have led the government and various private and semiprivate organizations to build on standard labor market policy measures in a variety of ways. In fact, labor market policies, financed by western German taxes and unemployment insurance contributions, now cover about as many people as the number of people who became formally unemployed as a result of unification.

The primary active labor market instruments of the western states were introduced at the time of monetary union and include training and job creation for the unemployed, wage subsidies to encourage hiring of the unemployed, and allowances for "short-time" work.[e] An early retirement program was added to this arsenal of policy measures. Taken in combination, these efforts kept official unemployment at far lower levels than actual job losses.[16] However, as the western part of the country began to feel the squeeze of recession in the early 1990s, distributive struggles over the financing of these measures began to intensify.

Training measures are problematic in the new states in a variety of ways. Certainly one key problem is the dearth of skills appropriate to modern technology and equipment. However, the level of existing

---

[e] Short-time work has been used in the western part of the country to prevent layoffs. Such work entails employees' working and being paid for less than full time, with the government subsidizing some or all of their lost income.

Table 6-4

Economic and Labor Market Statistics for Eastern Germany

	1st half 1989	1st half 1991	2nd half 1992	3/93
Real GDP (DM bil.)	6 161.4	87.4	105.3	—
Real Expenditures on real GNP	—	—	—	—
private consumption	84.4	88.0	103.5	—
government consumption	39.5	39.0	48.0	—
fixed capital formation	28.5	37.6	56.0	—
exports minus imports	−3.1	−75.8	−94.1	—
Total employment (thousands)	9,766	7,212	6,117	—
agriculture/forestry	985	382	318	—
manufacturing	3,571	2,612	1,522	—
construction	846	569	659	—
trade/transport	1,652	1,331	1,194	—
services	962	765	988	—
government (including ETCs)	1,750	1,553	1,436	—

Table 6-4 (continued)

	1st half 1989	1st half 1991	2nd half 1992	3/93
Total unemployment (thousands)	0*	843	1,101	1,141
female	0*	482	704	708
rate (%)	0*	9.5	13.9	15.7
early retirees (thousands)	0*	521	835	890

*Under the old regime, there was no official unemployment.

Source: Adapted from Commission of the European Communities, Directorate-General, Employment, Industrial Relations and Social Affairs, Employment Observatory East Germany, *Labour Market Developments in the New German Länder*, no. 7 (Brussels, May 1993).

skills is hard to estimate in part because about one-quarter of the East Germans who received vocational training certificates in the 1980s were awarded the certificates on the basis of experience rather than training. Moreover, vocational training traditionally forced eastern employees to specialize fairly narrowly, which diminishes the flexibility with which they can be deployed. Case studies have found that eastern managers tend to overestimate their own business expertise.[17] As a result, they have trouble identifying what sorts of training are required for both management and labor. Furthermore, while almost a quarter of those employed in eastern firms received some sort of further training in 1992, many companies lack the finances or the internal expertise to carry out necessary training. Thus, private sector training initiatives are not adequately addressing the lack of skills among members of the eastern German workforce, and public sector initiatives are not sufficient to fill the gap.[18]

Job creation measures, designed to minimize social conflict over massive redundancy, have spawned an innovative new institution: the Employment and Training Company (ETC). A July 1991 agreement between business, labor, the government, and the Treuhand stipulated that ETCs were to aid structural development, economic reorientation, and the founding of new enterprises. The unions, especially the IG Metall, worked with eastern works councils to develop ETCs that would act as employers while engaging in socially and economically useful activities that might not be undertaken by private sector actors. As a result, ETCs have been active in laboratory and databank services aimed at clarifying and solving environmental problems, construction and repair activities to accommodate projected tourism, and databank services for investors and regional economic development efforts.

Funding for the ETCs comes from the Treuhand, local and state governments, the Federal Employment Agency, and sometimes employee contributions in the amount of the severance pay they would receive if they were simply laid off. Only in cases in which a union is not strongly represented have other bodies—usually local and state governments—stepped in to create ETCs. These companies reflect a negotiated compromise over how to develop job creation measures that are more than temporary manpower parking places.

In the spring of 1993, about 400 ETCs existed in eastern Germany, accounting for about 13 percent of the total number of jobs created. Much of the success of some of the ETCs can be attributed to the fact that their employees represent a wide spectrum of former Treuhand company employees, including engineers, R&D staff, and others with much needed skills. The ETCs are quite unlike other job creation measures in that they must compete for funds, for acceptance in local politics, and for access to public works projects. Thus, they help to reconstruct the sorts of networks of local cooperative relations that underpin any economy, which, to date, no other actor in the eastern economic arena has done systematically. Moreover, ETCs can teach employees how a private sector company functions as an organization.[19]

The Kohl Government's Role

Since unification and the worldwide recession of the early 1990s, industrial policy has emerged as a major national issue throughout the country.[f] During this time, the CDU has been the major partner

---

[f]I use the term "industrial policy" in the loosest sense here to mean the coordination of public and private sector activities in the interest of promoting certain core industries and subsectors that are believed to have significant positive spillover

and the FDP the minor partner in Germany's coalition government. On most major domestic policy issues, the politics of the CDU resemble the left-liberal end of the spectrum of American politics. Traditionally the opposition party, the SPD, has been more closely allied with the labor movement than the CDU. However, both major parties in Germany are naturally predisposed toward a strong role for organized labor. The differences between them have to do with how strong that role should be and in what areas it should be concentrated. On distributive matters that affect organized labor and employment relations, the Kohl government has tended to be more sympathetic than the SPD to employer interests.[g] Since the costs of unification have so dramatically exceeded early estimates, distributive issues are the chief issues of the day in contemporary German domestic politics.

Clearly, the citizens of western Germany are paying more for unification than they expected to or were led to believe they would. The cost of labor market policies in eastern Germany alone places a considerable burden on the welfare state. This financial burden is directly reflected in domestic politics. Among other things, it was expressed in an increase in support for right radical parties and groups in the early 1990s (though these groups were virtually marginalized in national elections in October 1994). For the first several years after unification, the Social Democrats were unable to win much public support for their vision of an alternative way of organizing and allocating the costs of unification. Union leaders active in the SPD believe their members are paying an unfair share of these costs and industry is paying too little.

On the face of it, the Kohl government's decisions to proceed with unification as quickly as possible, to introduce monetary union early, and to allow the Treuhand a free hand in privatizing the eastern economy tend to support western industry and burden eastern labor. Slower unification, incremental monetary union, and a more concerted privatization strategy might have reduced economic dislocation. Still, the government's actions seem to have reflected

---

effects into other parts of the economy (that is, for subcontractors, ancillary services, and so on).

[g] As earlier in the book, I use the term "distributive" here to mean relating to more or less zero-sum issues. Integrative matters allow for mutual gains; with regard to distributive issues, however, by definition one party's gain is the other's loss.

a fairly parochial political agenda rather than any conscious strategy designed to favor business over labor, as it seemed distinctly possible that the CDU-FDP coalition would lose the 1990 fall election. Unification preceded the election by just enough time to garner the votes of the majority of eastern Germans, and ensure reelection.[h]

By American standards, the unification policies of the federal government to date reflect anything but a rough-and-tumble free market agenda. On the contrary, the implementation of unification has rested on a solidarity pact, a negotiated agreement in principle among government, business, and labor on the major priorities and ground rules that are to guide the parties' strategies and policies. The pact is essential to the process of integrating and reviving the eastern German economy and would not have been possible without the active support of the labor movement. The pact lays out the basic parameters within which the main political economic actors have pledged to operate, including relative wage restraint in the west on the part of the unions and certain investment guarantees in the east on the part of business, provided the other actors also stick to the rules. It is bolstered by widespread agreement in the business community that industrial policy is not only necessary but desirable in the east. The heads of the four major employer and industry federations (the federations of employer and industry associations, the chambers of commerce and industry, and the metalworking employer association) are all on record as supporting an industrial policy of saving core economic sectors (union strongholds) in Eastern Germany.

---

[h] Had the SPD been in power at the time, one might have expected a more explicit industrial policy for the integration of the eastern economy. Prominent members of the social democratic and labor communities favor (and have developed) policies designed to expand current labor market measures; secure and rescue core industrial sectors in the east (and west); increase public and private sector investment in the east; find new markets for eastern products and services; modernize companies still owned by the Treuhand; and raise taxes on industry and higher income citizens to help pay for unification. See Arbeitsgruppe Alternative Wirtschaftspolitik, *"Memorandum '93: Beschäftigungspolitik Statt Sozialabbau—industrielle Kerne sichern"* (Employment policy instead of social decay—securing industrial core sectors) (Köln: Pappy Rosa Verlag, 1993).

Employment Relations in the New States since Unification

Contradictory Developments

As the preceding section has made clear, in the new states organizations as well as the nature of the actors, the problems they face, and their interrelations are highly heterogeneous. Jürgens, Klinzing, and Turner, for example, have distinguished among firms on the basis of their chances for success: those taken over by a major western multinational company and integrated into a European or worldwide corporate strategy (for example, automobile production operations bought by VW, General Motors, and Mercedes-Benz); those directly linked to western investments through ownership and joint ventures, and thus integrated into the Western German market (for instance, a brake parts producer taken over by a West German automaker); those spun off from the combines, seeking western partners or trying to survive on their own (such as a small Treuhand-owned steel company discussed below); and those that are going under (for instance, an eastern management buy-out shoe company that was unable to retain eastern European markets when the currency union occurred).[20] (A slightly different categorization is offered by a representative of the federation of employer associations in Berlin: successful companies bought and/or established and run by western companies; less successful companies bought by western interests but substantially managed by easterners; companies bought and run by easterners, which in general are doing poorly; and reprivatized companies, which are almost all failing or near failing.)

Given this diversity, it is not surprising that one can find evidence among these cases in favor of almost any proposition. Indeed, it is difficult to extract any trends from the mass of incomplete and contradictory facts, situations, and events presently existing in the eastern part of the country. It is clear, however, that in most cases neither labor nor management (nor, for that matter, the government) is in a position to achieve much of anything through the pursuit of unilateral strategies. The lack of social or economic networks—all of which were inextricably tied to the old system and thus shattered on October 3, 1990—leaves virtually every actor, organization, and institution relying on external resources for know-how, infrastructure, capital resources, and business connections.[21] Even managers in western-owned and run sites, such as BASF's operations in Schwarzheide, understand that the key challenge facing them is the creation, out of whole cloth, of formal and informal internal networks (i.e., a transparent and dynamic internal labor market and regular and open communications between eastern and western managers and between managers and workers).

Local and regional competition over development funds and the desperate need for expertise of all kinds, combined with the manifold and visible inequities between the eastern and western parts of the country, seem to have spawned a realignment of alliances and strategies at various levels and in various segments of the public and private sectors. Experimentation with new ways of structuring labor-management relations can be found at most of the greenfield production sites of western companies. At Opel's Eisenach plant, for instance, the works council and management have developed a work system that in many ways resembles NUMMI, the joint GM-Toyota venture in Fremont, California.

There have been, however, two developments in particular that might suggest a potential weakening of the negotiated model of adjustment: the failure of some eastern employers to join the employer associations and the decline in the levels of eastern unionization. As it turns out, these developments, reflecting the structural contortions of an almost hollow economy, are spawning a variety of different sorts of negotiated adjustment.

Weakening Employer Associations?

Just after unification, the BDA, explicitly rejecting a more company-based strategy, strongly argued for extending the collective institutions of employment relations to the new states. While the numbers are rarely publicized and constantly changing, it appears that membership in the employer associations is not as high in eastern states as it is in the western states. In the west, especially in heavily unionized industries (like metalworking, mining, or chemicals), roughly 80 to 90 percent of the workforce is employed at companies that belong to industry employer associations. Employer associations in the eastern states and Treuhand estimate membership levels between 60 and 75 percent.[22] Indeed, several highly visible operations, such as Opel's Eisenach plant, do not belong to their regional associations.[23]

A firm's decision not to join the employer association entails both benefits and costs. On the one hand, not belonging to an association allows a company to pay wages that are below the level stipulated in the collective bargaining contract. On the other hand, in the event of a conflict with labor, the company does not have the financial resources of the association to help support lockouts or weather strikes. Moreover, companies that do belong to the association tend to be hostile to firms that try to pursue a unilateral strategy that could lead to head-to-head competition among employers in the same region and industry. In fact, employers can be ostracized from their associations for failing to toe the official line and pursuing unilateral strategies with labor. Sometimes unions have imposed particularly costly "house" (employer-specific) collective bargaining contracts on companies that have not joined an association and therefore are not bound by a regional agreement. Several American multinationals (including Ford and DEC) have faced these situations. Thus, both the power of the union and works council and the power of the employer association can create pressures for membership. The fairly sparse association membership in some eastern regions has increased the leverage of the western headquarters of the associations, which are dominated by larger western firms and therefore strongly discourage any unilateralism in the eastern "periphery."[24]

Labor's willingness and ability to inflict damage through industrial action are greater in larger companies than smaller companies. Smaller companies are often in a weaker financial position than large ones to resist pressures from their customers to reduce costs. Hence, small firms are more likely to try to avoid coverage by a collective bargaining contract than large ones. Thus it is noteworthy that in 1994, for the first time in decades, a representative of the Mittelstand was elected to the position of president of the metalworking employer association. Undoubtedly this will increase the influence of smaller companies, which tend to be less friendly toward labor.

The increasingly vocal positions of groups representing the Mittelstand reflect their growing dissatisfaction with present-day institutions. The Federation of Independent Entrepreneurs, preferring contracts to establish a range of wages rather than a minimum and pushing for fewer restrictions on contract reopening, began to lobby for the deregulation of collective bargaining in the 1980s. Publications of the BDA's think tank have floated similar ideas of reform. The contract reopener idea was briefly advocated by the Kohl government but was dropped in order to ensure union acceptance of the solidarity pact in the spring of 1993. (Many larger companies are also opposed to broadening the applicability of contract reopeners, arguing that it is the association, not the individual company, that should be responsible for controlling contracts.)[25]

These developments can be read in at least two different ways. On the one hand, they do suggest the increasing willingness of German employers to challenge the unions. On the other hand, they reflect the government's continued reliance on the good will of the labor movement and the employer associations' interest in retaining control over employer behavior and over the centralized model of labor-management negotiations. Thus, the picture is mixed. While membership in the associations, at least for the time being, is lower in the eastern than in the western part of the country, it is not clear that this is in the interest of most employers or that eastern employers who have adopted this position in economically dire times may not decide to join associations under better circumstances, particularly if it looks as if a union may target them for a "house" contract. Given the surprising level of eastern worker militance in the metal-working strikes in the spring of 1993 (discussed below), such a possibility does not seem particularly far-fetched.

Weakening Unions?

The potential success of a unilateral employer strategy hinges in part on the power of organized labor, which in turn rests substantially on union membership. At the time of unification, most eastern workers joined western unions, and unionization levels remained higher in the eastern part of the country than in the west.[26] However, a combination of factors, including massive layoffs and continued economic hardship, have since lowered eastern membership levels. It is estimated that between 35 and 40 percent of the eastern workers belong to unions affiliated with the DGB, which suggests that overall unionization, which would include non-DGB unions, is slightly higher. Thus, unionization levels are still higher in the eastern states than in the former West Germany (see Table 6-5).[27]

Of course, the strength of the labor movement depends also on a variety of factors other than membership. An IG Chemie official pointed out that in the eastern states the works councils in the companies he services are often too insecure to try to influence management decision making, even when they could succeed. Because union officials are not on the spot unless they are called in to solve a particular problem, they are powerless to do much for the councils when the councils are having trouble identifying their needs and problems.[28] Furthermore, because unions are called in on a sporadic ba-

Table 6-5
Union Membership in Eastern and Western Germany
(1992)

Union	% Increase Via Members in New States	% Members in New States
Construction	56	36
Mining	51	34
Chemicals	24	19
Railroad	57	36
Education	103	51
Agriculture/Forestry	189	65
Service	63	39
Woodworking	28	22
Leather	26	21
Media	31	24
Metal	31	24
Foodstuffs	47	32
Public Sector	69	41
Police	33	25
Post	32	24

Table 6-5 (continued)

Union	% Increase Via Members in New States	% Members in New States
Textiles/Clothing	26	21
DGB TOTAL	45	31

Source: Adapted from Michael Fichter, "Where do Unions Stand in Eastern Germany? Some Reflections on Organizational Problems and Membership Concerns" (Paper prepared for the German Studies Association annual conference, Washington D.C., October 7–9, 1993), 11.

sis, employees have trouble understanding the unions' important contributions.[i]

If the level of unionization were to continue to decline, the possibilities for unilateralism would be enhanced, but there are no reasons to expect further membership losses. Some substantial portion of the membership drop in the first several years after unification can be attributed to the high percentage of people who lost their jobs. The unemployment rate is unlikely to climb much higher if only for political reasons. Indeed, the rate is more likely to drop (albeit slowly) throughout the 1990s. Furthermore, union membership may be bolstered by increased mobilization around political and economic issues.

Finally, the unions have been redefining their agenda from quantitative to qualitative demands. Rather than focusing exclusively on wages, they have expanded the range of bargaining issues to include reductions in working time, the reorganization of work and worker skills, and the structure of internal labor markets. Given the pressures

---

[i] The unions are at least as interested as the employers in maintaining central control over bargaining, as illustrated by their opposition to independent eastern works council initiatives to establish specifically eastern enterprise-level strategies. See, for example, Martin Jander and Stefan Lutz, " 'Ostdeutsche Betriebsräteinitiative' vor dem Ende?" ('East German works council initiative' going under?) (working paper, Freie Universität, Berlin, 1993).

on employers to keep wages down in the east, the unions may find employer associations relatively amenable to negotiation over these issues.

Mitigating Trends? Negotiating the Distribution of Losses

Mahnkopf argues that the combination of union losses and the crisis of the labor market in eastern Germany "may well be used as justification for an attack on one of social democracy's greatest achievements: free collective bargaining without state interference between employers' federations and trade unions . . . [which could] lead the German system of industrial relations into a serious crisis."[29] Clearly Mahnkopf anticipates the emergence of a measure of employer unilateralism hitherto unknown in Germany, but much of the evidence marshalled here supports a rather different conclusion—namely, that the crisis is breeding new political-economic accommodations that have been effective in addressing the problems of employment relations as well as other issues.

In the spring of 1993, claiming that employers could not afford to increase eastern wages at the rate agreed to in the 1991 four-year contract, Gesamtmetall, the metalworking employer association, reopened its eastern collective bargaining contracts with the IG Metall. Contract reopening is virtually unheard of in Germany, and the union viewed this move with alarm. A spectacular set of strikes—spectacular in part because union leaders themselves were surprised at the militance and constancy of members—occurred all over eastern Germany.[30] The conflict was resolved by the expansion of the time schedule that dictated when eastern wages would rise to meet western wages and by the introduction of a "hardship clause" that would allow companies facing particularly difficult economic circumstances to slow the pace of wage adjustment even further. The benefits of this clause to employers are dubious, since it can only be invoked if the union agrees with the employer's assessment of the situation.

While at first glance the expansion of the time schedule and the inclusion of the hardship clause could be interpreted as an instance of successful employer unilateralism, events as they played themselves out indicated a rather different conclusion. On the whole, the strike and its resolution are regarded as a significant victory for the union. As a representative of the BDA put it in an interview, "The union struck to preserve its image, and its image was enhanced." Of key concern to the union was the principle that wages in the east and west be brought into line as quickly as possible, and in this regard the contract remained substantially similar to its original incarnation. The union also extracted a written agreement from the employer association to the effect that the reopening of the contract had been an extraordinary step that would not be taken as a precedent. Finally, the IG Metall succeeded in derailing efforts to permit individual companies and works councils to evaluate the need for invoking the hardship clause, thus preserving this privilege for the social partners.[31] Indeed, some have argued that the employers' intention in reopening the contract was precisely to preserve a system whose costs to employers were threatening to undermine it.

There are still other signs of the employers' and the unions' continued interest in the pattern of negotiated adjustment. Despite the recession, employers promised to increase eastern investment by 20 percent in 1993 and to hire all trained apprentices. Furthermore, since 1994, the unions have exercised significant wage restraint in the west and even (in comparison to earlier demands) in the east. The two most prominent unions—the IG Metall and the IG Chemie—have worked with their respective employer associations to develop industrial policy guidelines for the former East Germany.[32]

Negotiating Adjustment in Light of the East/West Cleavage

In interviews conducted in eastern Germany, it became clear that representatives of both labor and management displayed a common disdain for the Treuhand. A Treuhand representative put it this way: "There's no clear division between labor and business in the eastern part of the country—there's no conflict of interest in many cases. The Treuhand is seen as the employer, and labor and management get together and often try to fight us. . . . In some cases they are clearly working together against us." An employer association researcher noted, "More often than not, these days, the Treuhand can't make the [privatization] deals work." Labor representatives of the IG Metall and the IG Chemie, as well as a representative on the supervisory board of a Treuhand-owned steel company, agreed with the common social democratic complaint that the Treuhand's systematic refusal to invest in its companies had allowed salvageable enterprises to deteriorate beyond the point of no return.[33]

Given the grim confluence of interests between labor and management in the failing eastern economy, the emergence of this east/west fault line is hardly surprising.[34] After all, what is at stake for both parties is basic survival, while the Treuhand seems to be more interested in getting rid of enterprises than in helping them to become profitable. To the extent that investment in the new states fails to become embedded in the local and regional economies, these cleavages are likely to be strengthened.[35] The confluence of interests is perhaps best illustrated by the fact that the supervisory board representative of the Treuhand-owned steel company mentioned above was first appointed by the union and then appointed to a second term by management. A midlevel union functionary for the IG Chemie, who is responsible for Berlin and surrounding areas, claims that eastern managers often call him for advice on personnel and even non-personnel matters simply because of the tremendous dearth of expertise. He noted, "Before the banks came in and before the Treuhand was fully established, when the markets collapsed for eastern German products, the unions were the first, and often the only, consultants on the spot." Over time, he claims, the unions have continued to play a positive role in the eyes of many managers, in part because they can sometimes moderate the works councils' economically unfeasible demands. Representatives of the BDA, the Treuhand, and managers from several western-owned companies operating in the new states have confirmed his comments.

While some works councils have made economically unviable demands because of their failure to understand the economic crises confronting management, research has found that the tenuous economic circumstances of many eastern German companies can lead to a highly cooperative labor-management relationship at the enterprise level. Stöhr's study of small engineering companies in and around Berlin has found that the works councils were much more cooperative than confrontational in four out of five in-depth case studies and that management in these companies was more participative than exclusive or restrictive.[36] According to Stöhr, "The survival pacts [between labor and management], conceived as crisis cults . . . are the most important corporate cultural dimension of the transformation process."[37] Other studies have also found that labor-management cooperation at the enterprise level is based on the fact that neither party has any viable alternatives.[38] Indeed, eastern managers are as willing to agree to social compromises as works councils, given the common struggle for survival.[39]

Unlike some of its neighbors to the east, where some of the socioeconomic networks and connections that form the interstices of a market economy were in place and in some cases actively supported by public policy, before the end of communism in eastern Europe eastern Germany had a virtual void of basic capitalist know-how. It is this void that makes the widespread nature of these alliances, which may appear odd in a western setting, understandable. One of the supervisory board representatives interviewed insisted that anyone at all from the west could run a company better than many of the eastern managers who are trying to do so. The following comments (from my interviews except where noted) speak to this issue from a variety of perspectives:

> The self-confidence of easterners was lacking at the beginning. We heard only that we were dumber, slower, more constrained, and so on, and these prejudices create obstacles . . . .
>
> *(Eastern worker)*[40]

> Since unemployment was a nonissue in the GDR, people here haven't a clue how to deal with it. They have no idea of how to look for a job or even that this is what they are supposed to do. . . . Many of our members are quite disappointed with the union because they fail to see what we accomplish for them. They are used to the unions as all-powerful pullers of all behind-the-scenes strings—the full service operation the unions were under the old system.
>
> *(IG Chemie representative)*

> Many of the works council representatives at this point would make better managers than some of the managers running our [Treuhand] companies, because at least they have received some systematic union training in employment relations law and the basics of running a productive enterprise.
>
> *(Treuhand Analyst)*

> My impression of the works council here is that it's ambivalent about everything. Sometimes they seem to identify themselves as more powerful advocates for workers' rights than the [western] union; sometimes you can see how heavily their feelings of inferiority weigh on them; and sometimes they revert into a mode of pure adoration of all things west, including the unions. . . . When I got here the maintenance and repair operation was larger than production operations. How can we expect them to think like us?
>
> *(Acting CEO, Treuhand-owned steel company)*

The following comment by a former eastern union functionary who now works for the IG Metall illustrates the difficulty eastern Germans have had in coming to terms with the western system: "Many of our eastern works councils are stronger than the western ones because they are run by people who know how to block management decisions at the workplace. The eastern councils really know how to protect the workers." This definition of works council strength—the ability to block change—is what western German employers characterize as weakness. By western standards, a strong labor movement should influence workplace outcomes, not merely block management initiatives. The mismatch between the western system and eastern orientations toward it is also revealed by a review of research on eastern German industrial relations, which has found that enterprise-level worker representation is considerably more passive than in the west; workers are relatively unwilling to run for works council office; long-time labor representatives under the East German system are frequently reelected to these new positions; works council projects are undertaken mainly at the initiative of individuals; workers are relatively uninterested in participation in works council matters; and unions tend to be suspicious of the works councils.[41] At the same time, at least some eastern works councils are equally suspicious of the unions. A gathering of works councilors from some former combines denounced the IG Metall for what it perceived to be the union's early and easy capitulation to Gesamtmetall in the 1993 strikes.[42] In the former East Germany, workers could sometimes exercise considerable power on the shop floor because of extreme labor shortages—conditions that no longer pertain.

The task of eastern managers and employee representatives is complicated by the fact that the techniques they are learning from their western counterparts were honed over time in a highly developed modern economy. Thus, they face the dual challenge of learning those techniques and then adapting them to a situation that in some ways has very little in common with the west. Given the difficulties inherent in these challenges, it is not surprising that all the parties to employment relations in the east are trying to capitalize on as many information connections and networks as possible. The disorientation that is necessarily associated with the task of giving meaning to western institutions in eastern circumstances has often led to what amounts to a pattern of negotiated adjustment. To quote Röbenack and Hartung:

In view of the economic circumstances of many companies . . . works councils are in large measure open to economically based arguments of managers. . . . In the process of assessing the situation and prospects of the firm [this results in the two sides' positions] weaving back and forth between mutual understanding and willingness to compromise, and thus the creation of a "community of fate." . . . Social partnership and cooperative strategies thus appear to the parties as appropriate solutions for enterprise level industrial adjustment.[43]

In the new state of Saxony, experiments with the development of an industrial policy for those Treuhand companies that might still be restructured profitably represent an impressive example of an eastern German version of negotiated adjustment.[44] This collective policy experiment, known as the *ATLAS* project and inspired and to a significant extent guided by the strategies of the regional IG Metall, is based both on familiar western strategies of cooperation and compromise and on the unprecedented eastern pressures for economic structuring and restructuring.

As early as the fall of 1991, the regional IG Metall began to articulate widespread dissatisfaction with the Treuhand's policy of refusing to take active measures to restructure its companies. The union called for the creation of a holding company in which firms that could be saved would be separated from the remainder of the Treuhand's holdings and given the necessary resources to turn them around. The union held an industrial policy conference that was attended by unionists, local political and industrial leaders, and members of the press and issued a memorandum arguing for their vision of industrial policy in the state of Saxony. Soon after, the union began a series of discussions with the state government, in an effort to gain the political support needed to proceed with its plans. The joint CDU-SPD government was favorably inclined toward the union's approach and became even more so as the economic situation in the state continued to deteriorate.

In March 1992, the state concluded an agreement in principle with the Treuhand. Under the terms of the agreement, the state agreed to fund and the Treuhand promised to help make possible an industrial policy modelled after the union's ideas. In April, the agreement was formalized by the president of the Treuhand, Birgit Breuel, and the state economic and labor minister, Kajo Schommer.

This agreement prepared the way for the creation of a council charged with developing the policy. The council was to include union, employer, financial, and state representation and was to be run jointly by a union and an employer representative on a consensus principle. Together with the managers and works councils at individual Treuhand companies, the council was to explore possible restructuring avenues as well as the development of new organizational, product, and market strategies.

In the fall of 1992, the political struggle over the metalworking collective bargaining contracts in eastern Germany began to take shape, and the union was temporarily diverted from its industrial policy activities. After the conclusion of the strikes and the new metalworking agreement in the spring of 1993, the union held a second industrial policy conference, calling for a more substantial set of policy measures than those agreed to by the Treuhand and the state government in the previous year. Knowing that its initiative would be taken more seriously and would therefore be more likely to succeed if it offered concrete proposals, the IG Metall formulated a plan that included the following: restructuring of the companies in the core industry collection; local content agreements favoring suppliers within the state; maquilladora-style cooperative agreements with local producers; involvement of the states' ETCs with the restructuring efforts; and establishment of a network that would link state institutions and programs of economic development and focus them on the preservation of core industrial capacities.

One of the particularly impressive aspects of this effort has been the ability of the union to articulate and bring about explicit linkages across policy areas that would not otherwise have been connected, including not only labor market, regional, and economic policies but also strategies of organizational restructuring. In the fall of 1993, Kurt Biedenkopf, the governor of Saxony, and the regional union head, Hasso Düvel, agreed to proceed with the implementation of a state industrial policy, thus setting a precedent that could provide a model for similar efforts in some of the other new states.[45]

Conclusion: New Kinds of Negotiation

Jürgens, Klinzing, and Turner conclude that while the future of industrial relations in the new states is open, the institutions that are being transferred from the west and adapted to the east are likely to allow for new forms of joint labor-management decision making (or codetermination) as well as new kinds of labor participation and influence in the emerging eastern German economy.[46] My argument goes a step further. Certainly the institutions of codetermination have made important inroads in developing the framework for extensive labor participation in management in the eastern states, but there is more going on. The IG Metall-inspired ETCs, for instance, represent an entirely new and creative institution that rests on the institutional foundation of organized labor in the western states, but also goes beyond the institutional forms developed there. The ETCs represent a unique response to a particular aspect of the eastern economic crisis. They emerged as a result of the unions' negotiating with the Treuhand, federal labor market institutions, and local government bodies and represent an alternative to more costly and short-term labor market policy measures and/or politically intolerable levels of unemployment.

The agreements between employers and unions in the metalworking and chemical industries—trading off wage restraint against investment and employment guarantees—represent another instance of a new way of negotiating the particular adjustment problems of the east. Case studies suggest that new strategies can involve more than just employers and unions. Even some eastern works councils are creative and energetic in their approaches to industrial adjustment. Indeed, sticking to the letter of the law or the contract could not possibly aid industrial adjustment in the east. The 1993 agreements between the IG Metall and Gesamtmetall in the new states can be regarded as the fine-tuning of western institutions to accommodate eastern problems. The establishment of new regional training institutions that allow companies to pool resources and structure the skills of local and regional labor forces in ways that go beyond the specific interests and needs of individual employers has created another important forum for employer (and union) collaboration and negotiation at the mesolevel. The *ATLAS* industrial policy project in Saxony embodies the creative extension of the sorts of negotiated adjustment processes on which the western German model of economic success is based.

Specific ER outcomes and the content of negotiations in the new states differ from conventional western German industrial relations. But the processes of negotiation and the commitment to negotiation appear to have weathered the severe dislocation of the immediate postunification period and to be taking on new forms. In the words of a representative of the Berlin office of the BDA/BDI during a private interview: "No one wants to take anything away from the unions or the workers. The relationships between labor and business are usually very good and flexible, especially in the east where the need for flexibility is greater. . . . We need strong unions. . . . Strong unions are ready to compromise. It's weak unions that typically oppose all change—and this is what we can't afford."

Notes

1. Silke Röbenack and Gabriele Hartung, "Strukturwandel industrieller Beziehungen in ostdeutschen Industriebetrieben: Herausbildung neuer Beziehungen zwischen Arbeitgebern und Betriebsräten sowie Wandel in der Austragung von Interessenkonflikten." (Structural shifts in industrial relations in East German enterprises: Development of new relationships between employers and works councils and change in the manifestation of interest conflicts), monograph AG 3/3 (Leipzig: Kommission für die Erforschung des sozialen und politischen Wandels in den neuen Bundesländern e.V., 1992); Ulrich Jürgens, Larissa Klinzing, and Lowell Turner, "The Transformation of Industrial Relations in Eastern Germany," *Industrial and Labor Relations Review* 46, no. 2 (1993): 229–44; and Andreas Stöhr, "Interessenwahrnehmung und Interessenvertretung in Ingenieurbetrieben" (Interest formulation and interest representation in engineering firms) (Commission for Research in Social and Political Transformation in the New States, Berlin, 1992).

2. See Charles Sabel, John Griffin, and Richard Deeg, "Making Money Talk: Toward a New Debtor-Creditor Relationship in German Banking" (paper presented at the Conference on Relational Investing, Columbia University, New York, N.Y., May 1993).

3. See *IW Dienst* (Cologne), 1 July 1993; Matthias Knuth, "Employment and Training Companies: Bridging Unemployment in the East German Crash" (paper presented at the Conference of the Society for the Advancement of Socio-Economics, New York, N.Y., March 1993).

4. *IW Dienst* (Cologne), 1 April 1993 and 13 August 1993.

5. See Knuth, "Employment and Training Companies."

6. Dietmar Harhoff and Konrad Stahl, "Firm Dynamics in East Germany—First Empirical Results," ZEW discussion paper no. 92-05 (Zentrum für Europäische Wirtschaftsforschung, Mannheim, 1993).

7. See also Michael Brandkamp, "Erfolgsaussichten von Unternehmensgründungen in den fünf neuen Bundesländern," *Zeitschrift für Betriebswirtschaft*, special issue 1 (1993): 109–44.

8. This discussion of the role of the Treuhand has been strongly informed by Knuth, "Employment and Training Companies" and by discussions with Christopher S. Allen.

9. Treuhandaustalt, "Monatsinformation" (Monthly information), internal Treuhand memorandum (Berlin, 1993).

10. *IW Dienst* (Cologne), 8 July 1993.

11. Harhoff and Stahl, "Firm Dynamics in East Germany."

12. See, for example, Röbenack and Hartung, "Strukturwandel industrieller Beziehungen in ostdeutschen Industriebetrieben."

13. Knuth, "Employment and Training Companies"; see also Horst Kern and Charles Sabel, "Zwischen Baum und Borke: zur Unsicherheit der Treuhand, was sie als nächstes sagen sollte" (Between a rock and a hard place: On the insecurity of the Treuhand, and what it should say next) (paper presented at the Conference on the Treuhandanstalt, Center for European Studies, Harvard University, Cambridge, Mass., November 1991).

14. Birgit Mahnkopf, "Ex Orient Risk: The Impact of Unification on the German System of Industrial Relations," working paper, Wissenschaftszentrum, Berlin, 1993, p. 4.

15. See Harhoff and Stahl, "Firm Dynamics in East Germany"; and Brandkamp, "Erfolgsaussichten von Unternehmensgründungen in den fünf neun Bundesländern." Part of this unemployment is accounted for by the people laid off from operations that serviced the huge combines, including hospitals, kindergartens, travel agencies, etc.

16. Knuth estimates this figure at 50 percent. See Knuth, "Employment and Training Companies," 13.

17. See, for instance, Dieter Wagner, "Personalvorstände in mitbestimmten Unternehmen," *Die Betriebswirtschaft* 5 (1993): 647–61.

18. See also Commission of the European Communities Directorate-General for Employment, Industrial Relations and Social Affairs, "Employment Observatory: East Germany; Labour Market Developments and Policies in the New German Länder," no. 6, February 1993, and no. 7, May 1993, Brussels. Treuhand companies are also having trouble finding apprentices, since everyone is skeptical of the futures of these companies. See Knuth, "Employment and Training Companies."

19. Knuth, "Employment and Training Companies," offers a detailed discussion and analysis of the ETCs, based on extensive ongoing research.

20. Jürgens, Klinzing, and Turner, "The Transformation of Industrial Relations in Eastern Germany"; and Otfried Mickler, "Modernization of East German Industry and the Development of New Structures of Industrial Relations in Enterprises—The Case of the Auto Industry," working paper, Institut für Soziologie, University of Hannover, Hannover, 1992.

21. See Gernot Grabher, "Rediscovering the Social in the Economics of Interfirm Relations," in *The Embedded Firm: On the Socioeconomics of Industrial Networks,* ed. Gernot Grabher (London: Routledge, 1993).

22. In personal conversations with the author in July 1994, both Lowell Turner and Steve Silvia estimated that these figures may still be high.

23. Reinhard Bispinck, "Collective Bargaining in East Germany: Between Economic Constraints and Political Regulations," *Cambridge Journal of Economics* 17 (1993): 309–31; and Steve Silvia, "Holding the Shop Together: Old and New Challenges to the German System of Industrial Relations in the mid-1990s," *Berliner Arbeitshefte und Berichte zur sozialwissenchaftlichen Forschung,* no. 83, Berlin, July 1993.

24. Silvia, "Holding the Shop Together," 19.

25. *IW Dienst* (Cologne), 26 August 1993; and ibid., 18–19.

26. Michael Fichter, "A House Divided: A View of German Unification as It Has Affected Organized Labor" (paper presented at the annual meeting of the Industrial Relations Research Association, Anaheim, Calif., January 1993); see also Larissa Klinzing, "Zwischen Anpassung und Öffnung—Gewerkschaftsstrukturen im beigetretenen Teil Deutschlands," study 7/1 (Commission for Research in Social and Political Transformation in the New States, Berlin, 1992); and Bispinck, "Collective Bargaining in East Germany."

27. Steve Silvia, "Holding the Shop Together."

28. See also Michael Fichter, "Where Do Unions Stand in Eastern Germany? Some Reflections on Organizational Problems and Membership Concerns" (paper presented at the annual conference of the German Studies Association, Washington D.C., October 1993).

29. Birgit Mahnkopf, "Ex Orient Risk."

30. Turner offers a compelling and exciting account of this strike. See Lowell Turner, "From Partnership to Open Conflict: Popular Mobilization in Eastern Germany in the Great Strike of 1993," in "Social Partnership in the Global Economy: Crisis and Reform in Unified Germany" (unpublished manuscript, New

York State School of Industrial and Labor Relations, Cornell University, Ithaca, N.Y., 1994).

31. Bispinck, "Collective Bargaining in East Germany."

32. Silvia, "Holding the Shop Together."

33. See also Arbeitsgruppe Alternative Wirtschaftspolitik, *Memorandum '93: Beschäftigungspolitik statt Sozialabbau—industrielle Kerne sichern* (Cologne: Papy Rossa Verlag, 1993).

34. See, for example, Fichter, "Where Do Unions Stand in East Germany?"

35. This argument is developed in Gernot Grabher, "The Dis-embedded Economy: Western Investment in Eastern German Regions," working paper, Wissenschaftszentrum, Berlin, 1993.

36. Stöhr, "Interessenwahrnehmung und Interessenvertretung in Ingenieurbetrieben," 42.

37. Ibid., 27.

38. Röbenack and Hartung, "Strukturwandel industrieller Beziehungen in ostdeutschen Industriebetrieben"; K. Lohr, "Partizipation und neue Technik. Ansätze, Erfahrungen und Ausblicke soziologischer Forschung in der ehemaligen DDR," in *DDR—Gesellschaft von innen: Arbeit und Technik im Transformationsprozeß,* ed. E. Senghaas-Knoblock and H. Lange (Bonn: Forum für Humane Technikgestaltung, 1992); and Helmut Martens, "Gewerkschaftlicher organisationsaufbau und Mitbestimmung in ostdeutschland" (Union organization and codetermination in Eastern Germany) *Arbeit: Zeitschift für Arbeitsforschung, Arbeitsgestaltung und Arbeitspolitik,* no. 4 (1992): 368–86.

39. See, for example, Mickler, "Modernization of East German Industry and the Development of New Structures of Industrial Relations in Enterprises."

40. Quoted in Stöhr, "Interessenwahrnehmung und Interessenvertretung in Ingenieurbetrieben," 27.

41. Röbenack and Hartung, "Strukturwandel industrieller Beziehungen in ostdeutschen Industriebetrieben."

42. Martin Jander and Stefan Lutz, " 'Ostdeutsche Betriebsräteinitiative' vor dem Ende?" working paper, Free University, Berlin, 1993. See also Winand Gellner, "The Integration of East Germany into the West German Interest Group System: Problems and Possibilities" (paper presented at the annual meeting of the American Political Science Association, Chicago, Ill., September 1992).

43. Röbenack and Hartung, "Strukturwandel industrieller Beziehungen in ostdeutschen Industriebetrieben," 6.

44. Much of this discussion is based on Horst Kern, "Gewerkschaftliche Industriepolitik: Beiträge der Gewerkschaften Ost und West zur Erneuerung des deutschen Produktionsmodells," working paper, Soziologiches Forschungsinstitut, Göttingen, 1993; and on interviews with the head of the Berlin office of the employer association think tank, the IW, and a representative of the BDA and Gesamtmetall in Berlin.

45. See Kern, "Gewerkschaftliche Industriepolitik."

46. Jürgens, Klinzing, and Turner, "The Transformation of Industrial Relations in Eastern Germany."

chapter seven

Decline of the Negotiated Model?

what's wrong and what's right with the german model

Even before unification and the completion of the single market, the German economy was coming under increasing internal and external pressures. The export edge was deteriorating. German companies were conspicuously absent from international high technology markets. Traditionally high labor costs and low working time, by cross-national standards, became more and more difficult to justify in the face of slow productivity growth. The enormous economic consequences of unification have thrown these weaknesses into relief. While everyone agrees that something has to change, the questions of what, how, and when remain controversial. Formulations that emphasize high labor costs and excessive government regulation account for only part of the problem. Emphasizing these factors can obscure other, more subtle, pervasive and fundamental problems. In particular, it would appear that the productivity and effectiveness of German firms can be significantly and quickly improved by changes in the nature of relationships and the substance of interactions and negotiations *within* enterprises.

Reassessing the Negotiated Model

The Main Actors

As detailed in the first five chapters, government, labor, and business have all upheld critical aspects of the negotiated model. Government has provided a strong and stable institutional infrastructure, or *Rahmenbedingungen*, within which both business and labor have found ample incentives to engage in a collaborative relationship from the micro- to the macrolevel. The reelection of the Kohl-led CDU-FDP coalition in October 1994 signals the continued stability of German politics and the likelihood that the government's basic role will remain unchanged for the time being. The business community has taken full advantage of the stability offered by a relatively quiescent labor movement and the supportive framework offered by the social market economy, including a highly skilled workforce. Steady management practices have harnessed extensive worker and managerial skills based on functional specialties, and favoring concrete technical qualifications. Unlike worker representatives in many other countries, the unions (led by the IG Metall) in a sort of tacit pact with the business community, have actively tried to influence technological change. In fact, they have been prepared to modify their wage demands when the overall economic good has called for it.

The basic positions of the main actors—the government's willingness to provide the stable outer boundaries, the private sector's interest in involving labor in determining the terms of organizational change, and labor's willingness to trade steady gain for stability—have remained more or less unchanged in the 1990s. However, both domestic and international circumstances have changed, fundamentally and irreversibly. International economic dynamics have become increasingly discontinuous; competition has not only intensified but also become more differentiated, demanding more frequent, subtle adjustments to products, services, and processes than were required in the first several postwar decades. The late 1980s brought German industry face to face with the hard economic lessons that American companies were exposed to by Japanese competition in the 1970s and early 1980s. The economic strains of unification have intensified the need for rapid adjustment. Under the circumstances, the negotiated model cannot continue to perform effectively in the tried and true ways.

The Main Problems

In recent years, three features of the German model have been cited as problems that must be solved if Germany is to maintain its standing in the world economy. The first frequently cited problem concerns the amount of regulation in the private sector.[1] In some areas, regulations representing the social part of the social market economy are seen as onerous and as restricting economic activity. Perhaps the most famous of these regulations is the *Ladenschlußgesetz,* which strictly regulates shopkeepers' hours.[a] Other laws curtail business activities in ways that baffle American observers. For example, government regulations prohibit retailers from holding sales on most merchandise except at specified times of the year. These same regulations allow only small reductions in prices. Other regulations make it illegal for merchants to offer rebates if competitors offer the same product for less. Domestic production standards, Deutsche Industrienormen, or DIN, have made it difficult for foreign producers to compete in certain markets.

The second frequently cited problem concerns the country's system of financial regulation.[2] The restricted availability of finance capital makes it harder to start a business (particularly a public stock company) in Germany than in the United States. This helps to account for a comparatively low rate of firm start-ups. The lack of access to equity capital is attributed to the nature of the conservative financial system and to government tax policies, which makes equity financing more expensive than debt, since firms can write off the interest they pay on debt. This, of course, dampens the incentive to increase equity, which may partly explain the small proportion of German companies in the high technology sectors in which Japan and the United States excel.

The third, and most commonly cited, problem involves Germany's high labor costs. Even before unification, employers had begun to raise concerns about the impact of labor costs on Germany as a site for investments, Standort Deutschland, especially in light of the continued integration of the European single market.[3] The costs of codetermination, particularly at the workplace level, have always been considered high (though not always prohibitively high). German managers lament the time it takes to make decisions about issues on which the works council must be consulted. These delays may appear all the more costly when viewed in conjunction with widespread managerial dissatisfaction over the level of bureaucracy entailed in running a German organization.

---

[a] Many of these regulations remain sacred to various powerful groups in German society. Certain large retailers have been adamant in their resistance to relaxing the Ladenschlußgesetz. See *New York Times*, 31 October 1993. Small and medium-sized companies have been critical of efforts to loosen production standards in certain industries (beer and paper goods, for example) for fear of competition from abroad. The problem of overregulation, then, is not a simple problem of adjusting government policy to match contemporary needs. Those needs remain contested.

In response to these managerial complaints, German unions argue that Germany's competitiveness problems have more to do with outdated production strategies than with labor costs.[4] They point out that labor costs have been high since the 1970s. At the same time, labor productivity, especially in the manufacturing sectors, has always been high in comparison to many other advanced industrial countries (especially France and Britain, though not the United States). In fact, between 1981 and 1992, labor productivity growth increased more than 50 percent faster in Germany than in the United States,[5] and in the new states, where investors have built new facilities or totally modernized older ones, productivity growth can be expected to be especially rapid. Still, given the costs of unification, high labor costs are no longer as evenly balanced by labor productivity as they were throughout the 1970s and into the 1980s. Moreover, in real terms, the cost of labor was raised significantly by the increased valuation of the German mark in relation to the dollar in the early 1990s. While there are problems that can be traced to employer strategies, there is also merit to the claim that high labor costs hurt German firms in international markets.

Some relaxation of business regulations, a loosening of the private sector's access to equity capital, and a lowering of labor costs could enhance the competitiveness of the German economy. It would be misleading, however, to focus on these macroeconomic problems at the expense of closer consideration of a different set of factors that are just as important.

Learning from the United States

Functional Specialization and the Division of Managerial Labor

While the negotiated model ensures that organizational changes are well planned, consensually accepted, and thoroughly implemented, recall that a number of the managers at German-owned chemicals companies felt constrained by the bureaucracy and hierarchy in their organizations, especially in comparison with the levels of bureaucracy and hierarchy they believed existed in American companies.[6] Many of them believed that their counterparts in U.S. companies were granted broader scope for decision making at lower levels of the organization. Germans employed in the American-owned firms also spoke positively about what they perceived to be their latitude for making decisions that would be reserved for higher levels in typical German organizations. Lower-level managers in the U.S. firms, for example, felt they had more budgetary discretion than their counterparts in the German firms. These perceptions suggest that the division of labor between different managerial jobs is relatively great in German companies, especially in contrast to U.S. firms. Certainly, as discussed in chapter 5, the jobs of HR managers in the American-owned companies are more loosely defined and carried out than those of HR managers in the German-owned companies. The recognition of a sharp division of managerial labor is consistent with the findings of André Laurent, who surveyed managers from nine OECD countries and found that Germans were particularly likely to view organizations as systems of hierarchical relationships.[7] According to Laurent's findings, American managers were significantly more likely than Germans to agree that efficient work relationships often require "bypass[ing] the hierarchical line," and German respondents were significantly more resistant to the notion of having more than one direct boss.[8]

Indeed, German managers appear to see themselves as fitting into fairly sharply defined, functionally specialized roles. The top executives at the German-owned chemical companies discussed in chapter 5 were overwhelmingly chemists by training. These managers characterized their organizations as placing a premium on functional specialization. This bias was also reflected in the recruitment and selection patterns of the German-owned companies. These firms sought out employees with particular formal skills, while managers at the American-owned companies looked for people at the managerial level and below with general skills and backgrounds. The perception of high levels of functional specialization is consistent with the fact that German-owned companies channel the relationship between the employer and the works council through the HR function. This elevates the status of HR within the organization but may increase the distance between worker representatives and managers in other areas. In contrast, HR management in U.S. companies was widely seen as a matter of daily concern to all managers, not just those in the personnel or HR department.

Other research confirms the central role played by functional specialization in German organizations. Lane argues that there is virtually no system of general management education in Germany because Germans do not see management as being a legitimate, unified profession.[9] Rather, they view management as the judicious deployment of functional specialists. Thus, promotion tends to occur within functions, and training across functions is rare. Maurice, Sellier, and Silvestre, who carefully compare the German and French systems of training and education, conclude that the ways in which managers are deployed in organizations closely reflect how they are trained to begin with. In France, where the system of management training is general, firms define jobs. In Germany, where management training is more functionally specialized (emphasizing above all engineering skills), jobs tend to be defined by skills.[10]

Laurent's cross-national research points to similar conclusions. In his study, German managers were particularly likely to see organizations as systems of role formalization, which would be consistent with a high degree of functional specialization. Almost all the German managers surveyed agreed with the statement, "The more complex a department's activities, the more important it is for each individual's functions to be well-defined." Americans, by contrast, were more likely to feel that managers "would achieve better results if their roles were less precisely defined."[11] Glover also found that British managers tend to see themselves as generalists, while German managers understand themselves more as specialists.[12]

Walgenbach confirms the bias toward functional specialists. His research finds that German managers tend to see themselves as functional specialists, repositories of knowledge and information that their subordinates do not possess, while British managers view themselves more as generalists, capable of leading human resources.[13] His extensive study found that functional specialization is reinforced in Germany by the systems in which managers are trained and the paths their careers follow. German managers have less cross-functional experience, more detailed training, and longer stays in any given job within their organizations than British managers. These findings are consistent with the fact that promotions in German companies tend to be slow and based strongly on internal labor markets.[14]

Rommel, Brück, Diederichs, Kempis, and Kluge also find ample evidence of functional specialization. Writing about the need for shorter decision-making processes, they note, "The key obstacle—which should be taken very seriously indeed—is a deep-rooted departmental and functional parochialism and a tendency to cling to incrementalism, with little inclination to make radical changes."[15] They go on to argue that one of the most striking differences between the highly competitive companies in their sample and those that were not doing as well was that most of the former employed extensive job rotation, organized operations by product or product group, and favored financial organization by profit center, while the latter tended not to have job rotation, were organized by function, and were controlled through set budgets. The successful companies also granted higher levels of financial authority to lower-level managers.[16]

Indirect Worker Participation

This combination of organizational features has direct implications not only for how effectively managers do their jobs but also for how employment relations are conducted at the point of production, the office or shop floor. One might think of a generic organization as a sort of hierarchical entity in which strategic decisions are derived from its "top," functional specialties from its "middle," and shop floor (or office) activities from its "bottom." One effect of the bias toward functional specialization is a sharp division of labor between the HR/personnel department and the rest of the organization. To push decision making about resource allocation down to the shop floor or office level can interfere significantly with the coordination of human resource deployment between the personnel or HR department and the works council. If shop floor production managers and workers are empowered to negotiate over the shape and movement of internal labor markets, one of the chief negotiation issues between the works council and HR department is captured at a lower level within the organization. The channeling of the labor-management relationship into contacts between the council and the personnel/HR department is inconsistent with the development of shop floor or workplace resource allocation flexibility. To the extent that enterprise-level negotiated adjustment revolves around the HR/works council axis, the processes of enterprise-level negotiated adjustment may be dysfunctional or counterproductive. In today's economic environment, the ability to respond quickly at every level of the organization to rapid and discontinuous market changes is more valuable than the capacity to adapt slowly and continuously to steady market changes.

The local maneuverability that is required to make constant small product and process adjustments calls for a more direct and less formal mechanism for labor-management negotiation and labor participation in management. The case of GM's Saturn Corporation illustrates the point. Saturn features a great deal of "bottom-up" (as opposed to "top-down") participation. Individual workers make decisions that have traditionally fallen within the purview of managerial discretion. Managers at every level of the organization are partnered with labor representatives who share fully in all decision making and its consequences. In a way, Saturn represents the extreme opposite of the functional differentiation and specialization that are the hallmark of many German organizations. At Saturn, every manager is necessarily an HR manager (necessarily has close and constant contact with the workforce and its representatives), and every labor representative is, in the most fundamental sense, a manager. Informal, on-going negotiations and direct participation and problem solving—breaking down conventional barriers between labor and management and across management functions—are central to the Saturn experiment. Yet these kinds of interactions are extremely difficult to codify, regulate, or institutionalize. They are, by their nature, informal and dynamic. Most of the key comanagement provisions that guide day-to-day practice at Saturn are not laid out in the original UAW-GM blueprints but have been developed over time through trial and error.[b]

This fluid form of labor participation in management can be traced in part to factors that are missing in the highly institutionalized German system of employment relations. Participation hinges on the ability of the parties to put aside all the familiar rules of the game and effectively reengineer the processes of management and worker representation.[17] In Germany, it would be difficult for either the employer or the works council to do this, because they are not only supported but also bound by the institutions that centralize and collectivize employment relations. Neither management nor the council, for example, could simply put aside the terms of a collective bargaining contract to develop a new form of relating at the enterprise level because both parties are accountable to their central organizations, the employer association and the union.

---

[b] As noted in chapter 4, the Saturn experiment is far from unproblematic. Powerful voices on both sides remain skeptical about the ER model that Saturn represents. These sorts of tensions do not usually arise in Germany, where the organizations of labor representation are more secure as institutions and operate in an environment in which negotiation and participation lead to tangible payoffs and firms have more latitude to make investments with only long-term, uncertain, human capital–based returns.

Implications for the Negotiated Approach

Macropolicies

To the extent that the competitive pressures on German companies do require a loose, flexible, and localized approach to adjustment, it would seem that the negotiated model with its extreme functional specialization, highly developed and relatively strict division of labor, and indirect forms of worker participation in management decision making can be of limited use. Indications in the engineering and chemicals sectors are that a more flexible mode of decision making and implementation is becoming increasingly important to firm competitiveness in the FRG. Many of the production operations of western German firms in the new states and in other countries, including the United States, feature just this kind of localized flexibility.

At the level of the political economy as a whole, then, significant policy reforms—many of which are already under way—will be required as the economy and society of the new states are built up and integrated into those of the former West Germany. The infrastructure of labor market institutions, designed for a world in which long-term, full-time employment with a single employer was the norm, needs to be adjusted to take into account the increasingly flexible career needs of the German workforce and employers' increasing need for work time flexibility. Reforms in the training system must take into account that initial vocational education is not the only training employees need. Greater efforts are needed in the private and public sectors to provide ongoing or further training on the model of "life-long learning." The systems of social and unemployment insurance and worker training and retraining need to be geared more pointedly toward active measures that shorten the amount of time people are unemployed and provide these people with skills they can use for new, stable employment. While historically German labor market and social institutional structures and policies have been comparatively effective in this regard, especially in comparison to the United States, chronically high unemployment makes this extremely difficult.

In Germany, more than in any other advanced industrial country, the manufacturing sectors still dominate over the services. Government industrial policies and private sector investment strategies need to be coordinated to expand the service industries and especially to create good service jobs with high levels of skills, pay, and labor-value-added. These kinds of service jobs can take advantage of the high skills of the labor force. Every effort should be made to avoid what might be termed the "American problem" in this regard—the creation of unstable, low-skilled, low-wage jobs that ultimately place increasing pressures on the welfare and unemployment systems. Changes in the system of financial regulation, intermittently under way since the 1970s, require mechanisms to link capital markets more closely with profitability and to ease access to equity. If German companies are to continue to make the most of their capacity for long-term planning, however, the "American" problem of subjecting firms to too many short-term performance pressures must be avoided. The literature is replete with specific policy recommendations in each of these areas.[18]

Mesopolicies

At the regional and industry level, Germany's unification has engendered renewed calls for changes in the system of centralized wage bargaining. While the metalworking strike of 1993 centered around the very principle of centralized bargaining, even representatives of the Treuhand and employers operating in eastern Germany state categorically that the system itself is not at stake. The BDA and the employer associations, which retain significant leverage in Bonn and Berlin, are on record as emphatically supporting the continuation of the centralized system of wage bargaining.[19] In the end, even the most vociferous critics of the centralized industrial relations system—for instance, The Economist—tend to agree that what is called for is change within the system, rather than changes of the system itself.[20]

It appears that the German labor and business communities are coming to terms with the need to tailor collective bargaining agreements to the increasingly varied needs of employers. The resolution of the 1993 metalworking strike in the new states serves as a relevant example. What distinguishes this contract from others in the metalworking sectors is the fact that its "hardship clause" amounts to an explicit acknowledgment on the part of the union that there are circumstances under which particular firms may not be able to meet the minimum standards set by the regional agreement. At the same time, the clause is defined so as to preserve for the parties to collective bargaining the power to accept or reject a petition for exception. The clause cannot be implemented without the approval of the employer association and the union. By opening the possibility for a more thorough exchange of information about the particular circumstances of a firm, the clause actually extends the negotiated model. While it retains the institutional integrity of regional and industrywide collective bargaining, it renders microeconomic contingencies subject to negotiation.

If this plan (called the "step plan" because it increases eastern workers' wages in steps) represents an extension of the negotiated approach, collective bargaining contracts arrived at less dramatically suggest tendencies in the same direction. At about the same time the metalworkers were struggling over their contract, the IG Chemie, representing workers in the ceramics and glass industries, among others, agreed to contract revisions that lengthened the period of time over which eastern wages are due to be raised to western levels. Because economic circumstances were less favorable in 1993 than had been projected in the previous year or two, other unions also agreed to contract revisions.[21] Recent collective bargaining agreements in the printing, clothing and textile, construction, and transport industries, among others, have contained opening clauses that allow for a deferral of wage increases or a time-bound lowering of agreed wage minima.[22] A 1993 enterprise-specific collective bargaining agreement between the IG Metall and VW—both of which are known for their innovations at the negotiating table—entails a temporary reduction of the work week to four days in order to allow the company to reorganize, to make up for losses (attributable primarily to the precarious state of VW's Spanish subsidiary, SEAT), and to take better advantage of the skilled German workforce. Another contract innovation that has gained popularity in the 1990s allows workers to choose their preferred combination of shorter hours and lower pay, with the amount of pay per hour decreasing marginally in reverse proportion to the number of hours worked.

Thus, while the wage bargaining system is still centralized by international standards, there are signs of increasing flexibility. For example, the number of sectoral/regional agreements increased by forty (from 230 to 270 between 1991 and late 1992) in the early 1990s, and the number of firm-specific agreements (house contracts) increased by 350 (to 1,200) nationally in the same time period.[23] Pay differentiation across regions and sectors is at least as high in the western part of Germany as in the former East Germany.[24] The western metalworking agreement of 1994, which accounts for 12 percent of the western workforce and 50 percent of German exports, also exhibits a striking new measure of flexibility on both sides. Aspects of this agreement were patterned after the VW agreement and reflect a growing unwillingness on the part of smaller companies to accept the dominance of larger firms in the bargaining process. The IG Metall's paramount concern during negotiation was to stem job losses, which meant that the union was open to a variety of measures that would accomplish this, including work sharing and flexible forms of employment. The March 1994 agreement includes a pay increase of about 1.2 percent over the life of the contract (with inflation at over 3 percent), which is a clear reflection of the union's willingness to restrain its economic demands. Innovations in the contract allow employers to cut workers' hours from thirty-six to thirty hours per week for a period of up to two years in exchange for secure employment levels. Within a specific time period, individual employers and their works councils are permitted to reach local agreements on weekly hour cuts involving some loss of pay. Still, while allowing for new levels of local flexibility, the agreement preserves the centralized bargaining structure. The public service contract, which was negotiated shortly thereafter, is patterned on this agreement.[25]

These adjustments to the wage bargaining system reflect an increase in the sharing of information and joint consultation about the scope of collective agreements and, at the same time, a safeguarding of the institutional integrity and security of the centralized approach. In no single case can it be said that the unions or the employers have sacrificed any of their key principles; in every case the collective bargaining partners, as opposed to the firms and their works councils, retain the final word.

Finally, the emergence of numerous regional initiatives (some of which are described in chapter 6) illustrates the ability of labor and management to devise new mechanisms at the mesolevel for coping with the unfamiliar challenges of the day. The ATLAS experiment in Saxony is one prominent example. Joint training programs (run, as ever, in tripartite fashion) in some of the new states also fall into this category. Certainly the ETCs illustrate the capacity of the unions and local social and political groupings for innovation. In short, the principal actors in the German political economy appear to be making steady progress in changing strategies and structures at the macro- and mesolevels through the negotiated adjustment approach, which is, after all, best suited to accomplishing precisely these kinds of changes.

Microchallenges

It is at the microlevel, the level of the individual enterprise or work-place, that reforms may be the most difficult to achieve. Before discussing the changes that may be needed, we need to review one last example of ER innovations in the United States.

The case of BellSouth illustrates how a highly bureaucratic, centralized company that faces a suddenly different set of environmental circumstances can undertake many of the kinds of changes that are needed in Germany today.[26] BellSouth Corporation, part of the former telecommunications giant AT&T, which was broken up when the industry was deregulated in the 1980s, is a regional Bell operating company. In the 1980s, the company and the union, District 3 of the Communication Workers of America, became leaders in developing innovative labor-management relations and workplace practices as a competitive strategy. Because the changes were introduced in the context of large bureaucracies with deeply ingrained labor-management institutions, the case is parallel to many German firms.

To manage its elaborate network organization, AT&T had developed a highly centralized system of decision making. Operational decisions were made at the top and disseminated through "standard operating procedures." Over time, the system became increasingly hierarchical and bureaucratic. The nature of the industry—involving heavy capital investment, fixed costs in infrastructure, and a reliance on technological innovation to drive down unit costs continually—resembles the conditions of mass production more than other service activities. (The same can be said of the much criticized public sector telecommunications company, the Deutsche Bundespost, the largest employer in the telecommunications industry in Germany.[27]) Prior to deregulation, the Bell telephone companies had adopted the principles of scientific management developed in mass production manufacturing. As in manufacturing, engineers designed the work process (in this case, continually improving the network infrastructure). The companies were "engineering-driven" rather than market-driven. Typically, new technologies shaped the demand for labor and the organization of work along the lines of increased functional specialization. Overall, this created organizations that were in theory "efficiency-minded," but in reality highly inefficient and ineffective in meeting customer needs.

The competitive pressures ushered in by deregulation led Bell-South to pursue organizational change in two ways. First, at the top of the organization, it attempted to shift from a functional, or "engineering-driven," focus to becoming a customer-, or "market-driven," organization. These changes involved creating a market-oriented structure that reduced management layers, shifted decision-making responsibility down the hierarchy, and reengineered work flows to provide more timely service. Second, lower down in the organizational hierarchy, the company introduced training in quality, problem solving, and team building and experimented with a number of employee participation and cooperative team approaches to improve employee morale, commitment, and customer service.

Employment security and union security have been the *quid pro quo* for labor's participation, which has been wholehearted, in these changes.[c] The "Quality of Working Life" (QWL) program at Bell-South, started in the early 1980s, provides the basis for current joint labor-management efforts to build a competitive strategy based on quality. As a result of the QWL program, many lower-level managers and workers have gained experience in working together to solve on-the-job problems. In 1989 and again 1992, the company and union put their bargaining teams through joint training programs in team building and problem solving in order to improve integrative, or "mutual gains," bargaining. Furthermore, the company and union use memoranda of agreement extensively between contracts to increase the flexibility of their agreements. In other words, they have institutionalized the conditions for continuous negotiations that Germany's dual system of worker representation creates.

In 1992, labor and management established a four-tiered "Excellence Through Quality" (ETQ) program that pairs management and union representatives to promote quality at various levels of the company. This multitiered structure creates a forum not only for union involvement in quality issues but also for consultation and information-sharing over broader issues. Union leaders have begun

---

[c] As Lowell Turner notes in *Democracy at Work? Changing World Markets and the Future of Labor Unions* (Ithaca, N.Y.: Cornell University Press, 1991), the German Postalworkers union, which represents employees in Germany's telecommunications industry, has been less visionary with regard to the shape of new work organization in this rapidly changing industry, perhaps in part because it has been able to forestall full-fledged deregulation. However, it has been more successful than the CWA at protecting workers against layoffs as a result of technological and organizational change.

to attend the full business meetings of district and state-level operating councils.[d] Through the ETQ program, the company and
union have set up joint quality training teams made up of trainers
selected in equal numbers by the union from among rank and file
members and by management from among the midlevel managerial
ranks. These teams have developed the curriculum and provided
training in quality for all management and nonmanagement employees throughout the BellSouth system.

Formal, self-directed teams take on responsibilities for both internal management and external coordination with other departments,
thus increasing workers' responsibilities by absorbing the responsibilities of supervisors. The most significant change is in workers dealing
with managerial and professional staff in outside departments and
companies, including engineering, installation and repair, the facility
assignment center, Cable TV, and the power company and customers. While supervisors used to communicate with outside departments and customers to order supplies, bring in jobs, negotiate over
"turf" responsibilities, answer customer complaints, and work with
engineers in presurvey stages, craft workers now assume these responsibilities. In the shift to self-directed teams, the supervisory span of
control has increased from a ratio of 1:5 to 1:10. In the future, it is
expected to increase to between 1:15 and 1:30. These new forms of
worker participation in management decision making at the point of
production provide perhaps the clearest contrast to the sorts of labor
involvement in industrial adjustment processes that are typically
found in Germany.

Because BellSouth illustrates a fundamental shift from a centralized, functionally specialized, Tayloristic, engineering-driven company to a much more decentralized, cross-functionally organized,
locally negotiated and market-driven organization, it may be particularly instructive to Germans. These are the kinds of challenges facing
many German firms and councils in the 1990s. There are two areas
in particular in which the strategies and policies of the parties at the
enterprise level need to be altered fundamentally.

---

[d]In a recent example, when the company decided that it needed to introduce a
round-the-clock schedule to improve service in customer service offices, it used the
joint structure to consult with local union presidents. The parties agreed on the
locations that would be affected and that senior employees would have first choice
of which tours to staff.

The framework of codetermination at the workplace. In order to take advantage of the sorts of ad hoc brainstorming and informal problem solving that characterize many U.S. ER innovations, the rules governing labor participation at the workplace must be relaxed. The Works Constitution Act, *Betriebsverfassungsgesetz*, which lays out the terms and conditions of local labor-management relations, envisions an extensive, but entirely indirect, form of worker participation. To improve competitiveness, both managerial and lower-level employees need to be able to make more decisions more autonomously than is possible under the current law. Labor and management must be able to work together at the workplace to develop appropriate forms of work and production organization and to change those forms when necessary. For this to happen, the works councils will need to cede some of their rights to information, consultation, and codetermination to smaller subgroups of workers and, possibly in some cases, to individual employees. At the same time, managers on the line will have to take over some of the negotiation functions currently reserved for the HR or personnel department. A joint training structure like that at BellSouth could provide a model for these kinds of changes.

Clearly this shift of responsibility will not be easy for either side. The institutions that historically have been charged with the negotiation of enterprise-level adjustment will have to give up much of their current influence in exchange for uncertain roles as consultants to the workers and managers on the line. It is these workers and managers who are in a position to recognize the need for, plan, and execute the kinds of organizational changes that are increasingly at stake in matters of enterprise-level adjustment. On the other hand, neither of these groups has the legal and organizational resources and knowledge that are available to the HR/personnel department and/or council. In order to make sure the changes instituted fall within the requirements of the law, workers and managers will need to consult extensively with their representatives. The challenge is to maintain the institutional integrity and security of the parties and their systems of interaction while allowing for more autonomy, initiative, and elbow room at the point of production. The BellSouth case illustrates that this challenge can be met successfully.

At least some members of the employer and labor communities are aware of the benefits of such a new approach. On the labor side, there is precedent for this shift in strategic orientation and decision making. In the 1970s, as it became increasingly important for individual employers to tailor the terms of regional and industrywide collective bargaining contracts to the specific needs of their companies and workplaces, the union movement ceded power to the works councils. The unions then turned this to their advantage by developing their own expertise in the requirements of enterprise-specific changes and making their consulting services indispensable to effective works councils.[28] The position of the unions, especially the IG Metall, in the first half of the 1990s suggests that they would be open to changes along these lines as long as the fundamental structures of the negotiated adjustment model are reaffirmed.

In fact, the IG Metall has published a strategic document that offers concrete plans for an increase in direct worker participation in management decision making, entitled *Tarifreform 2,000: Ein Gestaltungsrahmen für die Industriearbeit der Zukunft* (Collective bargaining reform 2,000: A framework for the future of industrial work). The document states in no uncertain terms that,

> It is one of the union's fundamental goals . . . to broaden the codetermination rights of . . . the directly affected workers with respect to the organization of work and technology. . . . [One] reason why . . . more democratic participation rights for individual workers is necessary is that some companies are introducing participation strategies . . . that are being accepted to some extent by the workers themselves. A rejection of this principle would not be sensible. Real alternatives [to these strategies] are posed by concepts like "codetermination at the workplace," where the direct participation possibilities for workers complement the rights of the works council.[29]

The union acknowledges that such an action will encounter resistance from works councils because it will "place into question past conceptualizations of worker interest representation."[30] Even so, the IG Metall calls for discussions on how individual workers can be given greater participation rights and recognizes that this method will vary from one organization to the next. Two things are noteworthy about the IG Metall's position. First, it recognizes that direct worker participation is increasingly necessary for the effective management of the workplace. Second, it attempts to define the terms of participation in order to provide an alternative to more unilateral management efforts in this direction.

Obviously, the willingness of individual works councils to move toward direct worker participation will vary. The councils will need to keep in mind—and the unions will need to impress upon them—that the changes will mean not so much a ceding of power as a shift in roles. Rather than spending most of their time negotiating with the HR/personnel department over the legal provisions attached to broad organizational changes, councils will have to expend more energy in predicting and helping to plan for smaller, more rapid, more frequent, and less encompassing changes in the organization of work and production. At the same time, the councils will still need to keep track of the effects of these changes on workers' skills, compensation, performance appraisals, recruitment, training, and positions on the internal labor market. Indeed, to the extent that work hours and contracts become more flexible over time, these functions will become more important.

How easy would it be for managers to make this transition? As noted in previous chapters, many German managers are well aware of the limitations of their organizational structures and managerial styles and of the way in which worker participation is codified at the workplace. As constituents of the works councils, individual mid- and lower-level managers could benefit from the councils' adoption of a more consultative role that is oriented toward career management. However, the shift will be more difficult for managers as a group. HR and personnel managers will have to take on some of the same consultative functions that the works councils will have to develop, particularly in the areas of predicting and helping to plan for numerous small, rapid, less encompassing changes in the organization of work and production. Top-level management will need to impress upon line managers the importance of calling on the expertise of their HR/personnel colleagues in order to avoid breaking the law or antagonizing a more directly empowered and involved workforce. The commitment of top-level management to these changes will go a long way toward making them possible.

Organizational structures and managerial training. Simple attitude adjustments on the part of management will not be enough. Management consultants, industrial sociologists, organizational development theorists, and others have all pointed to the need to reduce sharply the boundaries separating functionally specialized departments as well as the vertical division of labor. Such a reduction will have decisive effects on a wide variety of policies. Training will need to emphasize general skills as well as functional specialization.

Managerial career paths will need to include more horizontal shifts within the organization. Managers who hone general skills will need to be rewarded just as those who excel in specialized areas are rewarded. Multiskilling and job rotation will need to be implemented higher up in the organization as well as at the workplace level for nonmanagerial employees. Compensation and performance appraisal mechanisms will need to encourage cross-functional cooperation and movement. All these changes in the ways in which human resources (including managers) are developed and deployed will require extensive management education at all levels of the organization and across all functions, departments, divisions, and so forth.

The type of structural and strategic reorientation I envision capitalizes on the principles that underlie some of the successes of Japanese and American organizations. Aoki, for example, argues that the rapid transfer of intrafirm communications in Japanese companies helps to coordinate adjustment to external shocks and aids in the decentralized absorption of local shocks.[31] German managers can learn from Aoki's "J-firm" the need for information exchange and coordination across functions and levels within the organization.[e]

Finally, these changes will entail substantial revisions to the curricula of management training and education and employee development. To use Lane's terminology, it is time that the public and private sectors in Germany formally recognize management as a unified field.[32] In a world in which specialized technologies and skills are widely available, it is no longer sufficient for chemical companies to be run only by chemists and engineering firms only by engineers. It may be time for the German business community to consider joining other European countries by establishing more of its own broad management education programs.

Can the German managerial community take on this set of tasks successfully? On the one hand, as the axiom taught in American business schools states, organizational change is the hardest thing in the world to effect. Certainly what is called for here is organizational change of the most fundamental order. On the other hand, there is a large and growing body of literature on the need for changes in managerial education and training, much of which emanates from

---

[e] Aoki points out that the success of this endeavor hinges on workers' intellectual skills rather than firm- and/or technology-specific skills. In this regard, Germany surely has a head start over most other advanced industrial countries.

the employers' own think tanks and research institutions close to the business community.

According to the current literature, German management education does not produce adequate creativity and communication skills, and the public institutions that dominate the German educational system lack incentives to meet the changing needs of students and employers.[33] In light of the increasing internationalization of many business activities, which has been sped up by the integration of the single European market, managers are receiving insufficient general (as opposed to functionally specialized) skills. Employers, on the whole, favor a partial privatization of the colleges and universities and a shortening of the period of study.[34] Other calls for changes in how German managers manage have to do with the need for a "life-long" model of learning (reflecting the limitations of a one-time apprenticeship or formal educational training), individually geared compensation plans, more direct employee participation, and improvements in the management of innovation.

While German employers and managers are well aware of these problems, the German business community as a whole has not developed a framework that views management *not* as the efficient application of high quality skills and resources, but as the constant recalibration of high quality skills and resources that requires drawing on the strengths of different parts of the organization in different ways at different times. This type of framework would certainly entail a fundamental overhaul of the system of management education as well as the form of labor participation in management and the structure of HR policies.

Thorough changes in the nature of management education and organization may also have beneficial side-effects at the meso- and macrolevels. The narrow and specialized nature of management training must have a dampening effect on new firm creation, particularly in high-technology growth industries, because it does not encourage entrepreneurialism. This dampening effect is strengthened by the difficulty of gaining access to equity financing and reinforced by the banking system, the stock market, and the tax structure. Together these factors protect the stability of large, established players in the private sector, who have an interest in sustaining the current system. The employer associations, which are typically dominated by these players, do not take sufficient account of the needs of small and medium-sized firms, and it is these firms that could benefit even more than larger organizations from a loosening of financial regulations and a broadening of managerial skills and competencies.[f] The Germans have long understood how macro- and mesolevel policies can create incentives for microlevel behaviors that are in the overall interest of the economy and society. The point here is that changes at the microlevel could well effect beneficial developments throughout the political economy.[g] It is this possibility that has been overlooked in Germany.

Conclusion: Refining the Negotiated Approach

Any ambitious set of policy recommendations necessarily suffers from two deep flaws. First, it can only suggest the roughest outlines of a new approach, in this case, a new approach to managing employment relations. Second, the recommendations are usually so sweeping that they appear hopelessly optimistic. As to the first problem, the only possible response is to note that breathing life into such recommendations is best undertaken by those who are directly affected. The details must be hammered out by the parties themselves and implemented in accordance with a heterogeneous set of circumstances. This may be the most fundamental lesson German labor and management can learn from the United States.

The second problem—that of undue optimism—can be answered more directly. What I recommend in this chapter is not a deviation from the negotiated approach to industrial adjustment, but rather a refinement of that approach. Rather than increasing managerial unilateralism, these recommendations call for a more nuanced and differentiated mechanism for negotiating adjustment at the level of the enterprise not only between labor and management but also among different parts of the organization. Such a mechanism would be looser, more spontaneous, and more informal than the one presently in existence. While many German managers and labor repre-

---

[f] It can be argued that large firms will also benefit from these kinds of changes, especially to the degree that it makes sense for some of them to restructure into smaller units—a fairly common event in the United States but still relatively rare in Germany. See Günter Rommel et al., *Simplicity Wins: How Germany's Mid-sized Industrial Companies Succeed* (Boston: Harvard Business School Press, 1995).
[g] I am indebted to Dietmar Harhoff for helping me to clarify this argument.

sentatives may recognize the problems revealed in this chapter, they lack the conceptual tools and practical resources to tackle them. This is what top policymakers and practitioners must provide.

Notes

1. See Otto Vogel, ed., *Deregulierung und Privatisierung* (Deregulation and privatization) (Cologne: Deutscher Institutsverlag, 1988).

2. See *Manager Magazin,* 9 September 1993, 180–205; Daniel Goudevert, *Die Zukunft Ruft: Management, Märkte, Motoren* (The future beckons: Management, markets, and motors) (Bielefeld: Busse Seewald, 1990); Charles Sabel, John Griffin, and Richard Deeg, "Making Money Talk: Towards a New Debtor-Creditor Relationship in German Banking" (paper presented at the Conference on Relational Investing, Columbia University, New York, N.Y., May 1993).

3. The problem of *Standort Deutschland* is discussed by Berndt Meier, *Wettbewerb als Chance: Antworten auf die japanische Herausforderung* (Competition and opportunity: Answers to the Japanese challenge), Institut der Deutschen Wirtschaft Beiträge zur Wirtschafts- und Sozialpolitik no. 200 (Cologne: Deutscher Institutsverlag, 1992). The employers' view of the works councils is presented in Horst-Udo Niedenhoff, ed., *Die Zusammenarbeit mit dem Betriebsrat: Erfahrungen und Anregungen für den partnerschaftlichen Umgang* (Working with the works councils: Experiences and impeti for a partnership approach) (Cologne: Deutscher Institutsverlag, 1990).

4. See Reinhard Bispinck, "Der Tarifkonflikt um den Stufenplan in der ostdeutschen Metallindustrie" (The collective bargaining conflict over the step wage increase plan of the eastern metalworking industry), *WSI Mitteilungen* 8 (1993): 469–81; and Reinhard Bispinck, "Collective Bargaining in East Germany: Between Economic Constraints and Political Regulations," *Cambridge Journal of Economics* 17 (1993): 309–31.

5. *The Economist,* 13 February 1993.

6. The research suggests that German companies do not have especially many hierarchical levels. See Christel Lane, *Management and Labour in Europe* (Aldershot: Edward Elger, 1989); Marc Maurice, François Sellier, and Jean-Jacques Silvestre, *The Social Foundations of Industrial Power: A Comparison of France and Germany* (Cambridge: MIT Press, 1986). Geert Hofstede also finds that the "power distance" between superiors and subordinates tended to be relatively low in Germany (though he concludes that it is fairly similar to that in British companies). (See "Hierarchical Power Distance in Forty Countries," in *Organizations Alike and Unlike: International and Interinstitutional Studies in the Sociology of Or-*

ganizations [London: Routledge and Kegan Paul, 1991]). My argument concerns qualitative relationships among people at different levels of the firm.

7. André Laurent, "The Cultural Diversity of Western Conceptions of Management," *International Studies of Management and Organization* 13, no. 1–2 (1983): 75–96.

8. Ibid., 86.

9. Lane, *Management and Labour in Europe.*

10. Maurice, Sellier, and Silvestre, *The Social Foundations of Industrial Power.* See also Peter Walgenbach, "Führungsverhalten mittlerer Manager in Deutschland und Großbritannien" (Leadership approaches of middle managers in Germany and Great Britain), in *ZEW Newsletter,* no. 2 (1993): 16–19.

11. Laurent, "The Cultural Diversity of Western Conceptions of Management," 84.

12. Ian Glover, "Executive Career Patterns: Britain, France, Germany and Sweden," in *Manufacturing and Management,* ed. Michael Fores and Ian Glover (London: HMSO, 1978). See also Alistair Mant, "Authority and Task in Manufacturing Operations of Multinational Firms," in *Manufacturing and Management,* ed. Michael Fores and Ian Glover (London: HMSO, 1978).

13. Walgenbach, "Führungsverhalten mittlerer Manager in Deutschland und Großbritannien."

14. *Capital,* July 1987.

15. Günter Rommel et al., *Simplicity Wins.*

16. Ibid.

17. See also Saul Rubinstein, "Rethinking Labor and Management: Saturn and the UAW; The Governance and Supervision of High Performance Team Based Work Systems" (Ph.D. diss., Massachusetts Institute of Technology, forthcoming); and Saul Rubinstein, Michael Bennett, and Thomas Kochan, "The Saturn Partnership: Co-Management and the Reinvention of the Local Union," in *Employee Representation: Alternatives and Future Directions,* ed. Bruce Kaufman and Morris Kleiner (Madison, Wis.: Industrial Relations Research Association, 1993).

18. Some examples of these policy recommendations include: Arbeitsgruppe Alternative Wirtschaftspolitik, *Memorandum '93: Beschäftigungspolitik statt Sozialabbau—industrielle Kerne sichern* (Memorandum '93: Employment policy instead of social deregulation—safeguarding industrial core sectors) (Cologne: Papy Rossa Verlag, 1993); *Manager Magazin,* 9 September 1993, 10 October 1993, 12 December 1993; Franz Josef Link, *Lohnpolitik in Ostdeutschland aus ökonomischer uns*

sozialer Perspektive (Wage policy in eastern Germany from an economic and social perspective), Institut der Deutschen Wirtschaft Beiträge zure Wirtschafts- und Sozialpolitik no. 207 (Cologne: Deutscher Institutsverlag, 1993); Winfried Fuest and Rolf Kroker, *Die Finanzpolitik nach der Wiedervereinigung* (Financial policy after reunification), Institut der Deutschen Wirtschaft Beiträge zur Wirtschafts- und Sozialpolitik no. 213 (Cologne: Deutscher Institutsverlag, 1993); Meier, *Wettbewerb als Chance;* Karl Lichtblau, *Privatisierungs- und Sanierungsarbeit der Treuhandanstalt* (The privatization and redevelopment work of the Treuhandanstalt), Institut der Deutschen Wirtschaft Beiträge zur Wirtschafts- und Sozialpolitik no. 209 (Cologne: Deutscher Institutsverlag, 1993); Berthold Busch, *Die EG nach 1992: Die Gemeinschaft vor neuen Herausforderungen* (After 1992: The community faces new challenges), Institut der Deutschen Wirtschaft Beiträge zur Wirtschafts- und Sozialpolitik no. 203 (Cologne: Deutscher Institutsverlag, 1992); and Berthold Busch, *Sonderwirtschaftszonen als Instrument der Systemtransformation* (Special economic zones as an instrument of systems transformation), Institut der Deutschen Wirtschaft Beiträge zur Wirtschafts- und Sozialpolitik no. 198 (Cologne: Deutscher Institutsverlag, 1992).

19. Bundesvereinigung der deutschen Arbeitgeberverbände, "Tarifpolitik in den neuen Bundesländern—eine kritische Zwischenbilanz" (Collective bargaining policy in the new states—A critical midterm assessment), *Der Arbeitgeber* (1991): 417–19.

20. *Economist,* 23 January 1993.

21. Bispinck, "Collective Bargaining in East Germany."

22. Wirtschafts- und Sozialwissenschaftsinstitut des DGB, *Tarifpolitisches Taschenbuch 1993—Zahlen, Daten, Fakten* (Collective bargaining policy handbook 1993—numbers, data, and facts) (Cologne: Bund Verlag, 1993).

23. Bispinck, "Der Tarifkonflikt um den Stufenplan in der ostdeutschen Metallindustrie."

24. Bundesvereinigung der deutschen Arbeitgeberverbände, *Jahresbericht* (Cologne, 1992).

25. See *Industrial Relations Europe* (March 1994): 5; *IDS European Report,* no. 388 (April 1994): 18–19.

26. This discussion is based on research conducted by Rosemary Batt and reported in Kirsten Wever, Rosemary Batt, and Saul Rubinstein, "Worker's Participation in Work Organization in the United States" (Report for the International Labour Organization, Geneva, 1993).

27. Lowell Turner, *Democracy at Work? Changing World Markets and the Future of Labor Unions* (Ithaca: Cornell University Press, 1991).

28. Kathleen Thelen, *Union of Parts: Labor Politics in Postwar Germany* (Ithaca: Cornell University Press, 1991).

29. IG Metall, *Tarifreform 2,000: Ein Gestaltungsrahmen für die Industriearbeit der Zukunft* (Collective bargaining reform 2,000: A framework for the future of industrial work) (Frankfurt: IG Metall, 1991), 62–63.

30. Ibid., 63.

31. Masahiko Aoki, *Information, Incentives and Bargaining in the Japanese Economy* (Cambridge: Cambridge University Press, 1988), 49.

32. Christel Lane, *Management and Labour in Europe* (Aldershot: Edward Elgar, 1989).

33. Christiane Konegen-Grenier and Juliane List, *Die Anforderung der Wirtschaft an das BWL Studium* (The economy's challenge to the study of enterprise management), Institut der Deutschen Wirtschaft Beiträge zur Gesellschafts- und Bildungspolitik no. 188 (Cologne: Deutscher Institutsverlag, 1993).

34. Winfried Schlaffge and Christiane Konegen-Grenier, eds., *Streitsache: Wettbewerbsstrategien für die Hochschulen* (Point of contention: competitiveness strategies for the polytechnic institutes) (Cologne: Deutscher Institutsverlag, 1991).

Negotiating Competitiveness in the United States

building on the strengths of american
employment relations

Most of the major problems of employment relations and industrial adjustment in the United States do not reside at the level of the organization. In contrast to many of their German counterparts, American managers have been able to develop a wide range of effective, innovative organizational structures, policies, and practices, sometimes with the participation of workers and unions and sometimes without. Many American innovations in employment relations have become models of international "best practice."

If the United States is producing international "best practice" cases, why look for lessons from Germany? After all, the U.S. economy has been improving since the early 1990s, and Germany is struggling to cope with a recession that was sharpened by unification and a host of new social and political problems. There are two main reasons to look to the German model. First, the Germans have succeeded in an area in which U.S. companies usually fail. For a variety of reasons, American managers tend not to base their strategic decisions systematically on the long-term interests of multiple stakeholders, including employees, suppliers, and society as a whole. This is one reason why impressive employment relations and HR innovations have not diffused throughout the economy.[1] The most visible consequence of this failure is the problem of workers' skills, which has become an area of deep concern to private and public sector policymakers. Possible solutions to this problem can certainly be illuminated through the comparison with Germany. This, however, will require a shift in focus from the arena of organizational change to the ways in which dynamics at the micro-, meso- and macrolevels influence and are influenced by each other.

Second, the German economy has begun to recover and promises significant new growth during the second half of the 1990s. The strength of the economy will be augmented by rapid improvements in parts of the eastern economy and by continuing European economic integration. While U.S. firms will probably maintain a strong competitive edge in certain sectors—such as high technology industries—these successes will be balanced by significant failures in the low-trust, low-skill, low-wage sectors of the economy. Since economic success stories in the United States do not usually diffuse broadly or pull other parts of the economy along, the comparison with Germany can suggest ways to improve the U.S. economy as a whole.

The linkages between the different parts of the German ER system have helped to diffuse innovations like the HdA experiments. The relative security of both labor and management and the extensive, but not intensive, role of the government in supporting negotiations among labor and management (and other interested parties) encourage negotiated adjustment processes. The institutions governing workplace labor-management relations in Germany create incentives for labor and management to define and implement organizational strategies that take advantage of highly skilled labor. The two-channel structure of employee representation (works councils and unions) makes it possible for labor to represent those employee interests that may conflict with employers' short-term preferences and still keep in mind the long-term welfare of the company. Labor's ability to play these sometimes contradictory roles is strengthened by the institutional security and embeddedness of the works councils and unions. Having been presented with the social market economy by political fait accompli, German employers have come to accept, and even to prefer, it over a more free market–oriented approach.

In eastern Germany, labor, management, and other local and regional groups appear to be developing new forms of negotiated adjustment to make up for the inadequacies of the model imported from the western states and to accommodate new interests and cleavages, and adjustment challenges. Thus, it is not so much the institutional particulars of the German model itself as it is how the parties adapt them at any given time in any given setting that is most interesting.

I do not envision an importation of German practices or institutions. Even if this were desirable—and I do not think it is—the vast differences between the two economies and societies would rule it out. Rather, I follow the lead of others in the field who advocate a process of "adaptive learning," to translate the mechanisms that seem to work well in one setting into functional equivalents in another.[2] The adaptive learning approach is quite different from the "best practice" approach. While champions of best practice agree that all practices need to be adapted to local circumstances, they do not explicitly acknowledge the important roles that macro- and mesolevel institutions and contingencies play in the definition and implementation of business practices. There is no such thing as a practice that would be best in any setting. The quality of a given practice or set of practices cannot be assessed without a thorough understanding of how it is embedded within the context in which it developed. Knowledge of how a practice emerged in the first place makes it possible to understand how the various pieces of the puzzle of adjustment—from the workplace to national policy making—interrelate. With this understanding, it is possible to identify which features of a given set of practices are central to success, what roles these features play, and finally, which actors, institutions, regulations, and so on can be drawn on to capture the benefits of a particular practice in an alien setting.[3]

The discussion that follows is based on two premises. First, the critical dimension of contrast between the United States and Germany resides in the way in which the institutional structures of their political economies and ER systems motivate the main actors to behave in particular ways. To some extent, the configuration of power, culture, history, and institutions that characterizes any given set of employment relations is unique. Thus, no single set of institutions will have the same effect across local settings or over time. Just as there is no such thing as a universal "best practice," there is no such thing as a "best institution." The German institutional landscape has changed significantly over the postwar period, and the ways in which the actors have made use of those institutions have also changed. What is important about the German case is that institutions have consistently created incentives for the actors to negotiate adjustment processes and thus to collaborate in the maintenance of a competitive economy.[4]

This being the case, institutions themselves must be seen as fairly blunt instruments for intervening in the employment relationship. Institutional initiatives must allow the maximum possible scope for local adaptation, yet, at the same time, avoid the problem of being excessively vague. That is, public policy must use institutions to develop incentives for the parties to hammer out agreements among themselves, trusting that they have the necessary expertise for fine-tuning these structures, while trying to ensure that local resource and power imbalances do not render them meaningless.

The second premise follows from this point. To capitalize on the benefits of this sort of sensitive, incentive-based intervention, a form of macrolevel regulation that is quite foreign to American policymakers is required. While government regulation in the United States is usually avoided entirely for as long as possible, once it is accepted as necessary, it is generally intensive and detailed. The complex regulation of the banking and airline industries are prominent examples. It is not surprising that this sort of government intervention in the economy is distasteful to all but the few actors immediately benefitting from it and that it is extremely insensitive to differences in local configurations of resources and interests. What I recommend in the area of employment relations is a looser, framework-setting form of regulation that minimizes the intensity of the government's day-to-day involvement in the private sector and makes the most of local resources and capacities.

Missing Linkages

Employers

German institutions require frequent, regular contact and negotiations horizontally and vertically across levels of activity within the economy.[a] The American political economic landscape contains few structural incentives to negotiate adjustment at any level. In Germany, the union and works councils at DEC were able to gain a company-specific collective bargaining agreement that brought the company into line with the rest of the industry even though it had attempted to bypass the institutions of negotiation. Such an outcome is unlikely in the United States, however, where there are few mechanisms to encourage the standardization of ER practices across com-

---

[a] Horizontal negotiations occur among employers, between employers and employee representatives, and between both of the parties and governmental or quasi-public sector actors involved in the administration of these institutions. Vertical negotiations take place from the level of the workplace and enterprise to the level of the region/industry and finally to the level of the economy and society as a whole.

panies. In the United States, the factors that determine whether or not a given organization integrates HR considerations into its long-term strategic planning are specific to the firm.

This is not to say that all U.S. companies like the unilateral approach. Recall that Rogers and Streeck have found that managers at some Wisconsin metalworking companies would have preferred to pursue a high skill competitive strategy but felt the environment made it unfeasible for them to do so.[5] Thus, the cost of labor is a competitive factor in spite of employers' perceived interests. This has the perverse effects of lowering the overall skill level of the American workforce.

Public Policy and the Union Movement

The structure of American labor law reinforces the fragmentation of employers' interests. The Wagner Act more or less defines labor-management relations as the processes and products of collective bargaining over wages, hours, and working conditions. In this regard the law has not been changed since the 1930s. The term "labor-management relations" is usually taken to mean the relationship between a union and a company (collective bargaining, grievance management, and strikes/lockouts) rather than the relationship between employers and employees more generally. Collective business interests have no place in this scheme, and the interests of employees in general are considered to coincide with those of the unions representing groups of workers at isolated workplaces. Given that over 85 percent of American workers have no union to represent their interests, they are excluded by definition from labor-management relations. The field of human resource management has arisen in large measure to fill that gap. However, the HRM literature does not address the relationship of HR, IR, and ER policies to the broader political economy, and the HRM field has little status in the United States. This both reflects and reinforces the fact that American companies have no systematic understanding of their collective interests as employers. Indeed, most employers have no forum in which these interests can be articulated or debated.[6]

The Wagner Act also exempts all employees with supervisory or managerial functions from collective representation. Thus, by definition, many employees who would be represented by unions or councils in Germany cannot be represented in the United States. While this may have made sense when work and production organization reflected fairly clear distinctions between workers and managers, these distinctions have faded significantly, even in the manufacturing sectors. This is especially the case where there is teamwork of any kind. In any case, these distinctions may never have been appropriate in many service industries. Thus, this provision of the Wagner Act merely perpetuates the adversarial, zero-sum aspect of American labor-management relations.

Moreover, under the terms of the act, layoffs and recalls, sick leave, incentive pay, paid holidays, vacation schedules, hours of work, and certain fringe benefits are mandatory bargaining subjects. Other topics are labeled nonmandatory on explicitly illegal subjects of bargaining. This was done to prevent the union or management from raising so many issues that serious negotiation became impossible, and to prevent either party from using economic pressure to influence outcomes regarding nonmandatory issues. The effect today, however, is to make it difficult and, in some cases, illegal for the parties to bargain over important issues of mutual concern, such as employment security, which is of increasing importance to employees and unions. Because this is a nonmandatory subject, unions cannot compel companies to negotiate over it.[7]

Should the parties involved in collective bargaining agree that the collective bargaining forum is inappropriate for the discussion of some issues and want to create a separate venue for negotiations, they must be sure the new forum does not conflict with Section 8(a)(2) of the Wagner Act, which prevents "employer dominated" employee representative bodies.[b] While in practice many cases of labor-management innovation probably do infringe on this provision of the law, the parties usually have a strong interest in continuing such negotiations and therefore do not press the matter. However, this is not always the case, and there is growing concern on the part of employers that the creation of various kinds of participative labor-management committees may leave them open to legal action on the part of unions wishing to undermine these efforts.[8] In fact, this problem may prevent nonunion employers from developing employee participation mechanisms that could benefit all concerned.

Under the terms of the Wagner Act, there can be only one union

---

[b] For instance, they might want to establish continual negotiations, or to conclude agreements that by their nature must be amended every few months, or at least more frequently than the typical period during which a collective bargaining contract is in force (usually two to three years).

representing a given unit of workers. In theory, if more than 50 percent of the employees vote to unionize, the union becomes the bargaining agent for all employees and must represent the interests of nonmembers as well as members. This was thought to strengthen workers' strike leverage, which would be greater if a majority of the workers were union members.[c] If, however, the union loses the vote, there is no union representation. From the standpoint of the unions, there are two significant problems with this "exclusive" model. To begin with, while many unions probably can secure the votes of some significant proportion of the workforce when organizing, they may not be able to get 51 percent of the votes. Surveys commonly show that about 30 percent of the nonunion workforce would prefer to be represented by a union if given the opportunity.[9] Since the mid-1980s, the AFL-CIO and various unions have argued for the development of a "minority representation" provision that would allow unions that can sign up one-quarter or one-third of the work-force some legal standing short of full-fledged exclusive collective bargaining status.[10] Second, under the terms of the Wagner Act, what is at stake is not marginal changes in the percentage of employees represented by a given union at a given workplace but the entire "unit" (as defined by the NLRB), that is, 100 percent of the "non-exempt"[d] workers at that workplace. This all-or-nothing procedure can result in bitter conflict among unions. Since the mid-1980s, the AFL-CIO has engineered a number of mergers between unions representing similar kinds of workers and readmitted several unions that had not been affiliated for several decades, including the teamsters and the mine workers. However, the AFL-CIO has only been able to make limited progress in tackling the "raiding" problem.

Some labor leaders have long recognized the limiting aspects of the Wagner Act. Concerned over the labor movement's precipitous decline, the AFL-CIO's CEW began meeting in the early 1980s to

---

[c] The opposite of this scenario is the French case, where it is not uncommon for three or four unions to represent small percentages of the workforce at a single workplace. In some cases, notably Britain during the 1980s, companies have tried to play different unions off against each other, making a deal with the one that offers the least costly contract. Other advanced industrial countries (except Canada) also have nonexclusive systems of representation.

[d] "Non-exempt" workers are those who are not exempted by law from coverage under the Wagner Act.

NEGOTIATING COMPETITIVENESS

consider new forms of labor-management relations and worker representation. The CEW has issued three reports laying out the problems it perceives and policies that could address them. The first two reports focus primarily on the ways in which the Wagner Act no longer yields the results originally intended. Although the committee's chair, AFL-CIO Secretary-Treasurer Thomas Donahue, has long favored significant change, political divisions within the union movement have tended to rule out such an approach. The combination of a hostile political climate and continuing internecine battles for power between various factions within the union led to the de facto disbanding of the CEW in the late 1980s after a failed effort to issue a report recommending sweeping changes in the American ER scene. Reestablished in 1993 after the election of a Democratic administration, the committee issued a report in 1994 that explicitly recognized the need for new forms of labor-management relations and labor participation in management. Nevertheless, the unions continue to be divided over how to pursue new modes of interest representation and labor-management relations.[11]

Finally, the fragmented nature of employment relations in the United States is both reflected in and perpetuated by the training strategies of business, labor, and the government. Chapter 4 has already noted the ways in which U.S. employers and unions are constrained to pursue training that is unlikely to support ER innovations that will help companies adjust to changing market pressures. The U.S. government's role in training does little to alleviate these problems since training is treated as an extension of welfare policy rather than as a part of an economic or industrial policy. Almost all national training initiatives are structured to meet the needs of individual workers, not the companies for which they do, or might, work. Such programs fail to provide employers with incentives to make the most of human resources. In this regard, the contrast to Germany is again striking. Over the last decade, one of the central goals of German labor, management, and government initiatives in the area of apprenticeship training, for instance, has been to restructure employee development to conform to the demands of changing technologies and methods of organizing production and work.[12]

Clearly U.S. employment relations are characterized by significant problems. Employers lack incentives to coordinate employment relations or to invest adequately in human resources. Unions are constrained to behave in ways that limit both their membership and the ways in which they are able to represent members' interests. A vast majority of American workers have no collective representation at the workplace, even though 90 percent of U.S. employees would like to be able to discuss workplace concerns with employers through some sort of collective body.[13] Finally, perhaps the most dispiriting consequence of these problems is the widely acknowledged skills deficit in the U.S. workforce as a whole.

Over the past decade, researchers focusing on a broad array of socioeconomic dynamics, from the microlevel to the meso- and macrolevels, have illustrated the benefits of linked and coordinated strategy.[14] The task for American employers, employees, and policymakers is to establish incentive structures that have effects similar to the German model but without requiring those features that would be out of place, dysfunctional, or politically unfeasible in the U.S. context. The proposal presented here has three components that together attempt to capitalize on the proven capacity of American workers and managers for innovation. The first is designed to take some of the costs of labor—specifically, training—out of competition through federal tax incentives. The second is meant to encourage the coordination and collectivization of joint employer interests in raising the overall skills of the workforces in their industries and regions (the mesolevel)—especially the interests of small and medium-sized companies. Finally, at the level of the individual organization (the microlevel), I propose the establishment of an enterprise-specific mechanism for ongoing collaboration and information exchange between employers and employees over the nature of HR training and development. As will become apparent, for any of these initiatives to be effective, they must be interrelated.

American Framework Regulation

Training Incentives

Recognizing the close relationship between the low skill level of the U.S. workforce and the competitiveness problems of the U.S. economy, since the early 1990s academics from a variety of disciplines have advocated a tax-related mechanism that would increase overall employer investments in employees.[15] Such a policy would take some of the costs of human resources out of competition among employers, thus making it easier for companies to pursue high-performance strategies. There is a strong case to be made for a training tax similar to the French model in which employers are encouraged to spend 1 to 1.5 percent of their payroll on employee training and are taxed in whatever amount short of that they actually spend on training. This kind of policy would create the strongest possible incentives for companies to invest in their human resources, but as the debate over health-care reform in the mid-1990s has illustrated, it would undoubtedly meet with powerful resistance from the employer community. Thus, should it be possible to implement a tax, it would be a negative incentive and not particularly helpful in getting employers to think creatively about their own long-term interests in HR investments. Therefore, I and several of my colleagues support a tax incentive for companies that undertake more training than is average in the United States. Tax credits for training would function like credits for investing in physical capital. Employers spending more than a certain percentage of payroll on employee training would fall into a lower tax bracket than those who do not.[16]

Employer Consortia

While an increase in the level of employer spending on training would help to raise the overall skill level, a training tax incentive by itself would not be enough. For one thing, employers might simply spend more on management training, which is the one kind of training in which American companies do adequately invest. What is needed is a mechanism for ensuring that any training companies undertake in response to the tax incentive is designed to deliver broad problem-solving skills to front-line employees—the sorts of skills needed to introduce flexible, high-performance forms of work and production organization. However, to provide these skills, companies need to know exactly what kind of training is required. Many companies, especially small ones, lack the information to make this determination by themselves. Therefore, it is necessary to create training consortia at the region/industry level. Interested parties, including managers from competing companies, could join together to pool information and determine the kinds of skills they would like to have available in their regional and local labor markets.

These consortia would allow employers, training institutions such as community colleges and technical schools, and unions, where they play a role, to develop training plans that meet their specific needs. Thus, training would be geared to the collective needs of local economies rather than the individual needs of specific companies or groups of employees. This might encourage companies to take advantage of the training tax incentive, which in turn would create incentives to participate in the joint definition and coordination of their collective interests. Finally, the consortia would provide forums in which employers could develop joint training facilities and programs, thus pooling the costs of training, from which they will benefit more or less equally. This would help many smaller companies that lack the resources to engage in long-term planning concerning their HR investments and ease what is perhaps the most significant obstacle to general skills training, the free-rider problem.

Enterprise Skills Boards

At this point, any student of regulation theory will raise the issue of enforcement. It is one thing to establish standards and create mechanisms for meeting them; it is quite another to monitor and enforce those standards in a fair, timely, and encompassing fashion. U.S. labor laws are notoriously bad at this.[17] The NLRB has not been able to enforce the laws protecting the right to join unions. OSHA has not been able to enforce its standards either widely or adequately. While relatively low penalties on employers account for part of the problem of enforcement, another significant obstacle is the sheer size of the U.S. economy. The most effective remedy for this problem is to delegate the enforcement of training standards to those who have the greatest interest in meeting those standards—the employees themselves.

Therefore, I recommend the creation of an enterprise-level joint labor-management skills board at all companies with more than twenty full-time employees.[18] The board would be charged with the task of sharing information and discussing the current and future skills profile of the workforce at the organization. Thus, the substantive concerns of each board would vary from company to company. Each board would be elected by all employees except top-level management, and white-collar and blue-collar workers would be represented proportionately. If a union is present, it would appoint board members representing its membership, but an election would be held for supervisory, managerial, and any other employees who are not represented by the union. Employers would meet with their boards every few months to make available information pertaining to possible work or production organization changes and the nature and extent of the training associated with these changes. Hence, each company would be required to develop an internal labor market plan if one does not already exist, to share that plan with the joint skills board, and to consult with the board on any changes anticipated.

The board's powers would be limited to (1) the right to receive information early enough to develop alternatives to the company's training plans if it chooses to do so, (2) the right to consult with the employer about such alternatives, and (3) the right to participate in the drafting of regular reports on the current state of the internal labor market and any anticipated changes. While the board's consultative and information-sharing activities could occur parallel to the collective bargaining process, it would not interfere with or undermine any training-related issues then being negotiated.

By introducing the long-term career interests of employees into the equation, joint labor-management skills boards could provide critical institutional support for the training tax incentive and the mesolevel consortia. The training tax incentive would be granted only if a company's board certified that it had delivered the sorts of broad skills (involving problem solving, teamwork, and cross-utilization) that are associated with new, flexible forms of work and production organization. This would prevent companies from cashing in on training they would have done anyway or training that does not address the broad skills needs of the community and/or region in question.

The effectiveness of the boards would hinge on the intellectual and strategic resources available to them. It is probable that in many cases a board would lack the expertise to develop an effective internal labor market strategy. In these situations, unions, particularly national unions, could play the role of consultants and draw on their research staffs and the experiences of their locals. In some areas, the boards and unions would probably strike up natural alliances. In other areas, other local organizations and institutions (vocational schools or community colleges, for instance) might be better able to provide the sort of expertise the boards require. In the case of smaller companies, local public and private sector resources, as well as the training consortia, could play important roles.

In some ways, the joint skills boards would resemble works councils, but in other ways, they would look like Japanese company unions, Canadian Health and Safety Committees, or any number of other enterprise-specific employee organs. The substantive concerns of the skills boards would vary from case to case, leaving ample room for variation across companies. The boards would depart significantly from the usual American approach to employment relations in that they would not apply detailed rules and regulations to a few companies, but rather would provide a loose framework for discussion, negotiation, and problem solving for all companies of a given size. This builds on a crucial feature of the German model: that by broadening its reach, public policy minimizes the depth of its intervention in the market. However, because the board would be both a mechanism for employee interest representation and a joint forum for labor-management collaboration, it would be fundamentally different from a German works council. (One of the problems with the German works councils, as indicated in the previous chapter, is that they do not encourage direct, informal, on-the-spot problem solving.)

Coordinating the National Interest in a Skilled Workforce

Together, these three components could begin to address five pressing problems. First, because it would be necessary for companies to keep records of and think strategically about their internal labor markets, the consortia and joint labor-management skills boards would force companies to be conscious of their training strategies and to develop rationalized HR planning mechanisms. Thus, HR considerations would be elevated to a considerably higher level of priority than they currently occupy in most U.S. companies. If the skills boards' employee representatives are capable of thinking strategically, alternatives to management's training plans could be introduced onto the agenda. An adroit skills board could articulate the longer term training interests of employees at every level of the organization, even if it could not force its will on the employer. If the German experience is any guide, managers think and act more carefully and more strategically when they must explain their decisions in a joint forum. This would probably help stabilize employment in some cases, especially if employee representatives on the board were able to show that the long-term costs of turnover exceed those of investing in a regularized internal labor market.

Second, through the consortia, small companies that cannot afford to invest as much in their workers as large firms could engage in concerted, coordinated long-term strategy development to facilitate the adoption of high-performance production strategies. Because the consortia would involve local public bodies as well as any unions or other organizations that could contribute to the attainment of their goals, they would reflect the interests of the many stakeholders involved in employment relations.

Third, by standardizing the conditions of employment relations, these components would remove formidable obstacles to the adoption of productive labor-management innovations throughout companies, industries, and regions.

Fourth, these components would promote the direct involvement of parties at the meso- and microlevels in substantive decisions about employees' skills, thus reducing the overall level of government involvement. Indeed, should this model work well, the skills boards' purview might be broadened to cover other issues of concern to employers, employees, and their communities, such as health and safety.[19] Moreover, to the extent that mesolevel coordination succeeded in helping employers meet their common goals and introducing the collective long-term interests of employees into ER decision-making processes, these consortia could broaden their mandate to include the design of those apprenticeship and remedial training initiatives that are currently run by a variety of disconnected federal, state, and local government bodies and public-private sector initiatives.[20]

Fifth, the skills boards would accomplish what no amount of adaptation of the Wagner Act has accomplished: the establishment of collective representation for the majority of American employees, including managerial employees. The direct political and indirect economic advantages of closing the gap between the percentage of workers who want collective representation and the percentage of those who actually have it would be formidable.[21] It is the micropolitical and microeconomic considerations of individual actors in the free market that present the largest obstacle to the attainment of this public good.

Conclusion: Reconceptualizing Employment Relations

To extract appropriate lessons for the United States from this comparison of ER systems in the United States and Germany, we need to develop a perspective that allows us to think about American employment relations in much broader terms than current conceptual models make possible. Both the HRM literature and the IR school of thought capture only limited portions of what goes on in American employment relations. Among other shortcomings, the HRM conceptualization limits its scope to the level of the enterprise and thus offers few if any insights into important higher level phenomena. The IR school of thought has little to say about that huge segment of the workforce that is not unionized. What is needed, then, is a perspective that encompasses events and dynamics occurring at different levels of the economy and society. These events and dynamics are not only economic but also social and political and thus not subject to the dictates of the market. The field of comparative political economy can provide the perspective that is needed.[22] Consider the following issues, which fall squarely within the domain of employment relations but are inadequately (or not at all) explained by available models.

One of the critical problems of U.S. employment relations is the way in which market pressures on individual firms create disincentives for investment in human resources, especially investments in the broad skills needed for high-performance competitive strategies. The net result is an undertrained workforce. While these dynamics clearly have major implications for the HR policies of individual firms, for public policies, for unions and unionization, and so on, neither the HR nor IR approach deals with them satisfactorily.

An important and continuing trend in the U.S. workforce is the increase in contingent workers. These workers are either subcontractors who are employed by companies other than those where they actually work, or temporary, or both. Thus, the employment relationship for these people does not reside primarily in their connection to the company at which they are geographically located at any given point in time. Again, the IR and HR approaches have little to say about how this phenomenon should be understood or what it means. The fragmented and conflicting interests found in the petrochemicals sector clearly indicates that the individual firm is not the appropriate unit of analysis for explaining employment relations in this sector. Since aspects of the union and nonunion models apply, the IR model is also unable to provide a satisfactory explanation of these problems. Understanding the problems in this industry and developing policies for solving them requires a conceptual schema that includes much more than just HR and IR considerations.

A hallmark of successful U.S. labor-management innovations is the capacity of the parties involved to recognize and negotiate simultaneously over both conflicting and overlapping interests. With its assumption that employees and employers basically share the same interests (in the success of the firm), the HRM approach cannot explain such experiments. Although the IR literature since the mid-1980s has begun to come to terms with the limits of the conflictual and economistic side of the traditional model of industrial relations, the environmental constraints on unions and companies trying to juggle these conflicting demands require a broader theoretical framework. (The market and political pressures leading to the continuing ambivalence of both GM and the UAW about the Saturn experiment illustrate this point.)

The German conceptualization of employment relations is broader and, for the most part, takes into account these dynamics. The Germans understand the ways in which their system of employment relations and their political (social market) economy are designed to allow the main actors to navigate these dynamics through the processes of negotiation. The German framework acknowledges the overlapping and conflicting interests of the multiple stakeholders and understands the linkages and interconnections among the organizations and institutions involved.

In the absence of a broader American perspective, it will be difficult, if not impossible, for public and private sector actors to develop appropriate policies and strategies for addressing the problems they face. Because of the labor movement's narrow conception of employment relations, it continues to focus on labor law changes that do little more than strengthen its rights within the existing Wagner Act framework. This strategy fails to address two big problems. First, the majority of American workers are not organized and will not be organized even with the most favorable changes in current labor law. Second, many workers' primary interests, such as employment security, long-term career management, or employers' adoption of high-performance competitive strategies are not addressed by mandatory bargaining issues. Put differently, the labor law reform strategy of the labor movement is inadequate, if not to some extent irrelevant, as a consequence of this narrow conceptualization of employment relations.[23]

It is in part because individual employers fail to recognize their collective interests that the U.S. workforce is poorly trained in comparison to those of many other advanced industrial countries. The reliance on market dynamics as the best mechanism for allocating resources also supports the short-term orientation of the U.S. financial system, which is widely acknowledged to inhibit the adoption of high-performance competitive strategies.

As a result of the predominance of the "best practice" model of management, which is based on a narrow microeconomic approach, many managers lack the conceptual tools to understand their organizations in both domestic and international contexts.[24] If managers take environmental influences and possibilities as given, they severely limit their options. When enough managers in enough microeconomic settings make choices on this basis, the negative consequences at the macrolevel can be significant.[25] Indeed, a good part of the competitiveness problem of the U.S. political economy can be traced to this dynamic. The adaptive learning approach, outlined at the beginning of this chapter, is the most concrete way for individual actors to avoid this problem. However—and here the argument comes full circle—in order to understand what to adapt and how, one must start with a theory of management that is rooted in the social science disciplines and is therefore able to capture increasingly important super- and extra-microeconomic variables at work.

Finally, what is the political feasibility of a public policy, supported by private sector strategies, that is based on a broad political economic approach and capable of addressing the competitiveness problems of the U.S. economy? The lessons of the German case have more to do with how institutions influence the actors in employment relations than with specific institutions. Loose, relatively unrestrictive kinds of regulation that allow the parties involved substantial influence over the nature and substance of their negotiations can avoid some of the negative side-effects of stringent, detailed legislation while creating incentives to negotiate in ways that will benefit the main actors collectively in the long term (even though individual actors may suffer in the short term). These lessons are all the more compelling because it is the extraordinary innovative capacities of local labor and management, in the face of powerful environmental odds against them, that represent the particular strengths of the American model. Indeed, a shift in our conceptual perspective on employment relations and how they fit into the broader political economy would permit us to develop policies that would allow employees and employers and the communities in which they work to make the most of their practical strengths.

Notes

1. See, for example, James Kotter and William Heskett, *Corporate Culture* (Boston: Harvard Business School Press, 1991); and Richard Walton, *Innovating to Compete: Lessons for Diffusing and Managing Change in the Workplace* (San Francisco: Jossey-Bass, 1987).

2. See, for instance, D. Eleanor Westney, *Imitation and Innovation: The Transfer of Western Organizational Patterns to Meiji Japan* (Cambridge: Harvard University Press, 1987); and Thomas Kochan and Michael Useem, "Creating the Learning Organization," in *Transforming Organizations,* ed. Thomas Kochan and Michael Useem (London: Oxford University Press, 1991).

3. Companies throughout the world have applied this kind of approach as they have sought to develop, refine, and adapt American management strategies, structures, and practices. In adapting quality circles (which were first fully developed in Japan) to their needs, American companies took this route at the level of the organization. See Robert E. Cole, *Strategies for Learning: Small-Group Activities in American, Japanese, and Swedish Industry* (Berkeley: University of California Press, 1989). At the mesolevel, several states, such as California, Oregon, and Hawaii, have experimented with adaptive learning as they have sought to introduce aspects of European-style apprenticeship training programs or health insurance systems. Similar experiments exist at the regional and/or industry level. See Rosemary Batt and Paul Osterman, *Workplace Training Policy: Case Studies from State and Local Experience* (Washington, D.C.: Economic Policy Institute, 1993). In each of these cases, the basic principles underlying a foreign model have been translated into terms that meet the specific needs of the local actors. The resulting organizational and institutional innovations have differed from the original model as much as they have resembled it. See also Eileen Applebaum and Rosemary Batt, *The New American Workplace: Transforming Work Systems in the United States* (Ithaca, N.Y.: ILR Press, 1994).

4. See Suzanne Berger and Michael Piore, *Dualism and Discontinuity in Industrial Societies* (Cambridge: Cambridge University Press, 1980); Richard M. Locke, "The Decline of the National Union in Italy: Lessons for Comparative Industrial Relations Theory," *Industrial and Labor Relations Review* 45, no. 2 (1992): 229–49; and Gary Herrigel, "The National Context: Two Different Patterns of Regional Economic Order in a Single Nation: 1871–1945," working paper, Department of Political Science, University of Chicago, 1992.

5. Joel Rogers and Wolfgang Streeck, *The Wisconsin Metalworking Training Consortium, Recommendations for Action* (paper presented at the Center on Wisconsin Strategy, Madison, Wis., December 1991); see also Paul Osterman, "How Common Is Workplace Transformation and Who Adopts It?" *Industrial and Labor Relations Review* 47, no. 2 (1994): 173–88; Steven Smith, "On the Economic Rationale for Codetermination Law," *Journal of Economic Behavior and Organization* 16 (1991): 26–81.

6. Not surprisingly, given the important role of German HR managers in administering the Works Constitution Act, HR professionals have more status in German organizations than American ones. See Dieter Wagner, "Personalvorstände in mitbestimmten Unternehmen" (Top personnel managers in companies with codetermination), *Die Betriebswirtschaft* 5 (1993): 647–61.

7. William B. Gould, *A Primer on American Labor Law* (Cambridge: MIT Press, 1986).

8. See Stephen Schlossberg and Miriam Reinhart, "Electromation and the Future of Labor-Management Cooperation in the U.S.," *Labor Law Journal* 43 (1992): 608–20.

9. Thomas Kochan, "How American Workers View Unions," *Monthly Labor Review* 102 (1979): 23–31; American Federation of Labor and Congress of Industrial Organizations, Committee on the Evolution of Work, "The Changing Situation of Workers and Their Unions" (Washington, D.C.: AFL-CIO, 1985).

10. A provision something like this, covering certain public sector workers, was enacted into law by executive order under President Kennedy.

11. AFL-CIO, "The Changing Situation of Workers and Their Unions"; AFL-CIO, Committee on the Evolution of Work, *The Future of Workers and Their Unions* (Washington, D.C.: AFL-CIO, 1983); AFL-CIO, Committee on the Evolution of Work, *The New American Workplace: A Labor Perspective* (Washington, D.C.: AFL-CIO, 1994).

12. Applebaum and Batt, *The New American Workplace;* and Peter Berg, "The Restructuring of Work and the Role of Training: A Comparative Analysis of the United States and German Automobile Industries" (Ph.D. diss., University of Notre Dame, 1993).

13. Rogers calls this a "representation gap." See Joel Rogers, "Reforming U.S. Labor Relations" (paper presented at the Labor Law Reform Conference, Linthicum Heights, Md., October 1993.)

14. Studies focusing on the microlevel include Masahiko Aoki, *Information, Incentives, and Bargaining in the Japanese Economy* (Cambridge: Cambridge University Press, 1988); and Richard Freeman and Edward P. Lazear, "An Economic Analysis of Works Councils" (unpublished paper, Department of Economics, Harvard University and Graduate School of Management, University of Chicago, May 1992). Events at the mesolevel are considered in Herrigel, "The National Context"; Rogers and Streeck, *The Wisconsin Metalworking Training Consortium;* and Charles Heckscher, *The New Unionism: Employee Involvement in the Changing Corporation* (New York: Basic Books, 1988). Macrolevel studies include Robert E. Cole, *Strategies for Learning;* Christopher S. Allen and Kirsten Wever, "Workplace Change and the Politics of Industrial Adjustment: The Shipping Industry in Six Northwest European Countries" (unpublished paper, Department of Political Science, University of Georgia, 1993); David Soskice, "The Institutional Infrastructure for International Competitiveness: A Comparative Analysis of the UK and Germany" (paper prepared for the International Economic Association Conference, Venice, Italy, February 1991); Arndt Sorge and Wolfgang Streeck, "Industrial Relations and Technical Change: The Case for an Extended Perspective," in

New Technology and Industrial Relations, ed. Richard Hyman and Wolfgang Streeck (London: Basil Blackwell, 1988).

15. Cuomo Commission on Trade and Competitiveness, *The Cuomo Commission Report* (New York: Simon and Schuster, 1988); Rogers and Streeck, *The Wisconsin Metalworking Training Consortium.*

16. This idea is developed more extensively in Kirsten Wever, Peter Berg, and Thomas Kochan, *Employee Development in the U.S. and Germany: Coordinating Interests in Employment Relations,"* Economic Policy Institute Monograph (Washington, D.C.: 1995).

17. Michael Smith, Thomas Kochan, and John Wells, "Managing the Safety of Contingent Workers: A Study of Contract Workers in the Petrochemical Industry" (Sloan School of Management, Massachusetts Institute of Technology, Cambridge, March 1992); Paul Osterman, *Employment Futures: Reorganization, Dislocation, and Public Policy* (New York: Oxford University Press, 1988); David Weil, "Enforcing OSHA: The Role of Labor Unions," *Industrial Relations* 30, no. 1 (1991): 20–36; Thomas Kochan and Kirsten Wever, "American Unions and the Future of Worker Representation," in *The State of the Unions,* ed. George Strauss, Daniel Gallagher, and Jack Fiorito (Madison, Wis.: Industrial Relations Research Association, 1991).

18. An enterprise-level worker representative body roughly resembling a works council has been suggested by a variety of academics in recent years. See Freeman and Lazear, "An Economic Analysis of Works Councils"; Rogers and Streeck, *The Wisconsin Metalworking Training Consortium;* Kochan and Wever, "American Unions and the Future of Worker Representation"; Thomas Kochan and Paul Osterman, "Human Resource Development and Utilization: Is There Too Little in the U.S.?" working paper, Sloan School of Management, Massachusetts Institute of Technology, Cambridge, 1990; Paul Weiler, *The Law at Work: The Past and Future of Labor and Employment Law* (Cambridge: Harvard University Press, 1990); Janice Bellace, "Mandating Employee Information and Consultation Rights," working paper, Wharton School, University of Pennsylvania, Philadelphia, 1990.

19. Joel Rogers and Barbara Wootton, "Works Councils in the United States: Could We Get There from Here?" in *Works Councils: Consultation, Representation, and Cooperation in Industrial Relations,* ed. Joel Rogers and Wolfgang Streeck (Chicago: University of Chicago Press in association with the National Bureau of Economic Research, forthcoming), recommend a health and safety committee that in some ways resembles the skills board I recommend.

20. See, for instance, Batt and Osterman, *Workplace Training Policy.*

21. As noted previously, about 90 percent of American employees want some form of independent representation at the workplace, 30 percent want to be unionized along the traditional model, and only 15 percent are collectively organized. Moreover, the majority of employers are in favor of collective employee representation in principle. See Joel Rogers, "Reforming U.S. Labor Relations."

22. Excellent examples include Richard Locke, "The Decline of the National Union in Italy"; Kathleen Thelen, *Union of Parts: Labor Politics in Postwar Germany* (Ithaca: Cornell University Press, 1991); Lowell Turner, *Democracy at Work? Changing World Markets and the Future of Labor Unions* (Ithaca: Cornell University Press, 1991); Christopher S. Allen, "Ideas, Institutions, and Capital Investment in the United States and West Germany: The Politics of Banking and Stock Market Regulation" (paper presented at the annual meetings of the American Political Science Association, Washington, D.C., August 1994).

23. Some leaders in the union movement have adopted a broader view of employment relations; my argument focuses on the formal legislative agenda of the AFL-CIO.

24. Earlier classics in the field of management emerge directly from various social science disciplines and are more dynamically and more contextually oriented. See, for example, Reinhard Bendix, *Work and Authority in Industry* (New York: John Wiley and Sons, 1956); Alfred Chandler, *Strategies and Structure: Chapters in the History of the American Industrial Enterprise* (Cambridge: MIT Press, 1962); Alfred Chandler, *The Visible Hand* (Cambridge: Harvard University Press, 1977); and Raymond Vernon, *Sovereignty at Bay: The Multinational Spread of U.S. Enterprises* (New York: Basic Books, 1971).

The 1980s also produced richer theorizing in works covering a wide range of management topics. See, for example, Ronald Dore, *Taking Japan Seriously: A Confucian Perspective on Leading Economic Issues* (Stanford: Stanford University Press, 1987); Sanford Jacoby, *Employing Bureaucracy: Managers, Unions, and the Transformation of Work in American Industry 1900–1945* (New York: Columbia University Press, 1985); Richard Walton, *Innovating to Compete;* and Robert Cole, *Strategies for Learning.* The insights of these works have not been sufficiently integrated into mainstream management literature.

25. See also Thomas Schelling, *Micromotives and Macrobehavior* (New York: Norton, 1978).

Index